3 8015 00931 2962

LE CORDON BLEU

CLASSIC FRENCH COOKBOOK

Le Cordon Bleu
Paris 1895

LE CORDON BLEU
CLASSIC FRENCH COOKBOOK

DORLING KINDERSLEY
London • New York • Stuttgart

A DORLING KINDERSLEY BOOK

Created and Produced by
CARROLL & BROWN LIMITED
5 Lonsdale Road
London NW6 6RA

Editorial Director Jeni Wright
Editor Julia Alcock

Art Editor Louisa Cameron
Designer Nicola Kirkman

Production Wendy Rogers and Amanda Mackie

First published in Great Britain in 1994
by Dorling Kindersley Limited
9 Henrietta Street, London WC2E 8PS

A CIP catalogue record for this book is available
from the British Library

ISBN 0-7513-0142-6

Reproduced by Colourscan, Singapore
Printed and bound in Italy by A. Mondadori, Verona

FOREWORD

This Classic French Cookbook is a collection of more than a hundred recipes from Le Cordon Bleu, created to celebrate our 100th anniversary. Founded in Paris in 1895, Le Cordon Bleu continues to teach the art of classical French cuisine in its classes worldwide. Each year, the Paris school, which is situated near the Eiffel Tower, welcomes students from over fifty different countries.

Starting as a small culinary institution, Le Cordon Bleu has expanded over the years, especially recently under my presidency. There are Le Cordon Bleu schools in Paris, London, Tokyo, and Ottawa, and chef-instructors also teach classes at restaurant and hotel management schools around the world.

Le Cordon Bleu, because of its origins, its experience, and its research nationally and internationally, is considered the most faithful custodian of French culinary tradition. The organization continues to evolve. It is able to take account of many different cultures, trends, and cuisines, while maintaining its status as home of classical French cooking.

We hope this cookbook will give you a solid understanding of French *haute cuisine*, as well as the trends in, and secrets of, the culinary arts.

ANDRE COINTREAU

Contents

First Courses

An appropriate first course will set the tone: a light soup should precede a hearty meal, whereas an omelette may be served before a simple main course. Traditionally, sorbets refresh the palate before the main course.

Main Courses

Every meal has a heart: the main course should be well-chosen and well-prepared in order to satisfy your guests.

Desserts

The French are very proud of their desserts. With the choice of recipes in this section your meal should reach a grand finale.

Techniques

Historically, French cookery has been based on a comprehensive set of techniques. Mastering these is half the battle of becoming a successful cook.

Introduction

Welcome to the **Classic French Cookbook**. *This book is a celebration of Le Cordon Bleu, of France, and of the history of food. Guided by our texts and illustrations describing the best French cooking techniques, you are invited to prepare an exciting range of dishes from the classical, regional, and modern repertoires of Le Cordon Bleu's schools in Paris, London, Tokyo, and Ottawa. This recipe collection is eclectic: while including French classics, it also features the innovative creations of the 26 chef-instructors currently teaching at the schools. Le Cordon Bleu builds a bridge between classical French cuisine and the latest gastronomy from around the world. The school, which has now reached its centenary year, enters its second century committed to this concept.*

For centuries, French chefs have made two important contributions to the international world of cooking. First, they mastered and standardized techniques. This gave them a vocabulary of skills that could be practised and passed on in a precise manner. Second, they acted on the need to classify cooking methods and ingredients. This codification of techniques and recipes provided a record, a standard, against which others could work. This approach to cookery has been instilled into Le Cordon Bleu's teaching method. First the students learn the basics, then they are encouraged to adapt them to local ingredients and cuisines.

One cannot write about French cooking without writing about France. It is a large nation, embraced by the Atlantic Ocean, the Mediterranean Sea, and the English Channel. As a result, French markets are filled with a rich variety of seafood. France's vast mountain ranges and sweeping agricultural regions are cleaved by three great rivers: the Seine, the Loire, and the Rhône. Our country is also blessed with an agricultural tradition that believes excellence is primary. What better place for a great cooking tradition to evolve and flourish? France is a great crossroads of international trade, and the neighbouring countries of Germany, Spain, Italy, and Switzerland, as well as the ethnic cultures alongside and within our French borders – such as the Basques – have contributed greatly to the local and regional flavours that make French cuisine so memorable.

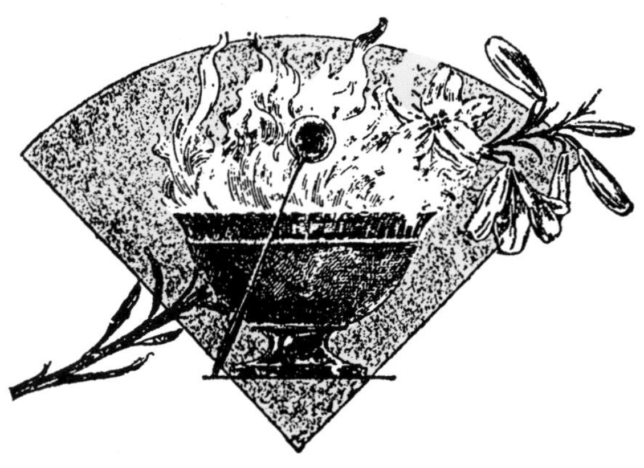

Early Civilizations

We know very little about prehistoric diet, except that it was predominantly meat based. During the course of the neolithic era, this changed to a predominantly grain diet. Archaeological evidence suggests that early Egyptians ate well. Although the basic peasant diet probably consisted mainly of bread, beer, and various forms of onions, wealthy families dined on fruits, olives, asparagus, small birds, fish, and honey. Unfortunately, few records remain explaining how specific dishes were prepared, making it difficult to recapture an important aspect of Egyptian culture.

The first cookbook is attributed to the Greek poet Archestratus, who lived in the 4th century BC. In his poem "Gastronomy", he delights readers with images such as eels cooked in beet leaves. Allegedly, he "diligently traversed all lands and seas in his desire ... of testing carefully the delights of the belly". A century later, the Greek writer Athenaeus added vastly to our knowledge of early gastronomy in his writing about the daily life of the Greeks. He recorded their eating and cooking habits, their great chefs, and the various utensils they employed in their kitchens.

The most important name in ancient gastronomy is Roman: Apicius. There were, in fact, three gastronomes with that name. The first (2nd-1st century BC) deserves notice only because of the records of his gluttony. The third (2nd century AD) is best known for creating a way to keep oysters fresh. But the second Apicius (Marcus Gavius, born c. AD 25) made major contributions to the food of his day. In his great work, *De re conquinaria libri decem* (Cuisine in Ten Books), he describes ingredients and methods needed to prepare soups, meat, and sauces. Indeed, adaptations of his recipes have been included in this book.

The second Apicius is one of the great tragic figures in the history of gastronomy. His banquets were lavish, and he dined as much on praise from his band of gluttonous followers as on the foods he created. At last, his purse diminished and he was faced with a lower standard of living. The loss was too much and he chose poison over penury.

Medieval Influences

Throughout history, royal households have influenced the development of cuisine. During the Middle Ages, for example, a commission from Charles V stimulated the great French chef Taillevent (Guillaume Tirel, 1310-1395) to systematically compile a number of recipes: sauces made with saffron, pepper, and ginger; liaisons with breadcrumbs; and sweet-and-sour dishes, are among his most notable culinary contributions. He published the recipes in a cookbook, *Le Viandier* (1375), which has been quoted, re-written, translated, and interpreted as an important historical culinary publication.

In 1533, when Henri II of France married the Italian Catherine de Medici, this mighty woman arrived in France with many artists, heralding the French Renaissance, and with her came Italian cooks and their Florentine recipes. The range of kitchen equipment and tableware that they brought was unknown to their French contemporaries – and when she introduced a fork as a culinary fashion accessory, it was rejected by the French. Catherine also encouraged the cultivation of new foods (artichokes, for example) and demanded the

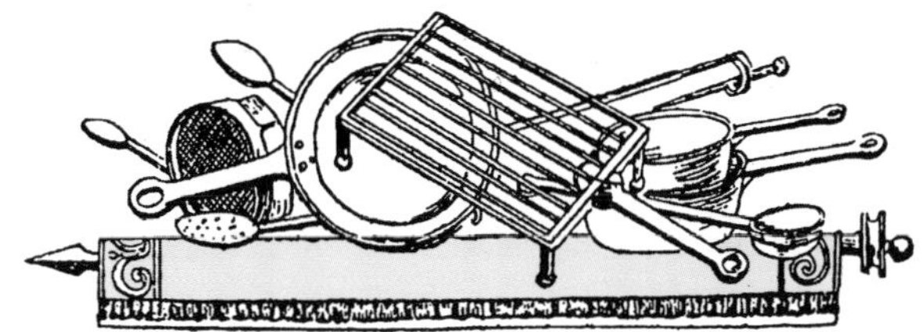

creation of new and exciting extravagances for royal guests. She gave birth to three kings and, in her role as Queen Mother, oversaw great progress in the manners and content of court behaviour. Her influence permeated all of France, stimulating an interest in food and innovation in culinary matters.

"*With the bread eaten up, up breaks the company.*"
Miguel de Cervantes (1547 - 1616)
Don Quixote 1615

The Renaissance of Cuisine

The origin of the name Le Cordon Bleu dates back to 1578, when Henri III of France established the highest and most exclusive order of knighthood: L'Ordre des Chevaliers du Saint-Esprit. The knights of this order – royalty included – were identified by wearing a gold cross on a blue sash or ribbon. This élite group set high standards for themselves and those who served them, and soon the notion of a blue ribbon became synonymous with skills of the highest calibre, especially in matters of the table. The fact that their cooks tied their aprons with blue ribbons also added to the connection of the colour blue with culinary excellence. The link between gastronomy and a blue ribbon was firmly established.

Le Cordon Bleu Silver Cross

In 1651, François Pierre La Varenne (1618-1678) published the masterwork, *Le Cuisinier Français*. In this and later books, La Varenne systematically codified and carefully explained the preparation of the full range of French cuisine. La Varenne was in charge of the kitchen of the Marquis d'Uxelles, the governor of Chalon-sur-Saône. He immortalized his employer's name with the creation of the mushroom garnish "duxelle". His work demonstrates that by the middle of the 17th century, France had established a cuisine of her own, one that would influence the world for centuries to come.

During the reign of Louis XVI, the first restaurant was established, boasting a menu of more than 200 different items, including 50 desserts. The king committed resources of agronomy as well as gastronomy to the creation of its dishes, and new vegetables were as popular as the new dances were at court. Meanwhile, the rural and less well-off city populations were enjoying better and greater quantities of meat and fresh produce.

The great families of France continued to be leaders in matters of *l'art de la table*. French doctors and cooks debated the values of new food, such as tea, chocolate, and coffee. Classical recipes were refined, presentations invented, and recipes elaborated. There was also an increase in the availability of cooking literature. Cheap reading material found its way all over France. Modern developments were all absorbed by the housewife, who had hitherto only been accustomed to local traditions.

> *"The destiny of nations depends upon the manner in which they are fed."*
>
> **Jean-Anthelme Brillat-Savarin** (1775-1826)
> Le Physiologie du Goût 1825

The French Revolution of 1789 changed everything. As heads dropped from the guillotine, the inspiration for the art of living drained away. For a time, all appeared lost; then two things happened. First, the cooks from the great houses had to find a new source of income to support themselves. This led to the establishment of eating houses, or restaurants, for the public. Second, a young chef, Antonin Carême (1738-1833), was employed by the French statesman Charles Maurice de Talleyrand-Périgord, to run his kitchens. Carême's eye for detail and mastery of technique lead him to write several important cookbooks, to re-design kitchen equipment, and to invent new dishes.

Soon the kitchens of Paris were alive again, and food history continued to be dominated by great French chefs. Dubois, Appert, Dugléré, and Pellaprat defined, redefined, and masterfully made innovations central to modern French cuisine. One of these chefs, Pellaprat, is closely associated with Le Cordon Bleu and its early days in Paris.

Pellaprat in the kitchen, 1899

Le Cordon Bleu's Beginnings

In the late 19th century, a French journalist, Marthe Distel, first commercialized the term "cordon bleu" when she started a cookery magazine *La Cuisinière Cordon Bleu*, in 1895. The great chefs of Paris wrote recipes for the magazine describing the best way to select ingredients, the exact methods of preparation, and information about the history or significance of a dish.

> *"... the ever-growing popularity of La Cuisinière Cordon Bleu makes the management feel that it has a duty to find new ways of satisfying those who have faithfully supported our enterprises; hence we have decided to offer free cooking classes to our subscribers and to publish the recipes taught in those classes in future issues of our magazines."*
>
> **Marthe Distel**
> La Cuisinière Cordon Bleu (December 1895)

In December 1895, Marthe Distel offered her subscribers an opportunity to see the great chefs at work. The first class was held in the Palais Royal in Paris, on January 14, 1896. Le Cordon Bleu, Paris, was thus established.

Le Cordon Bleu's instructors have included Chef Charles Poulain, chef des cuisines de l'Automobile-Club de France, Chef August Colombié, and perhaps the most famous, Chef Henri-Paul Pellaprat (1869-1950). Some of Pellaprat's books, such as *L'Art Culinaire Moderne*, and *La Cuisine Familiale et Pratique*, are modern classics.

Although *La Cuisinière Cordon Bleu* had a loyal readership, it was the cookery classes that became the primary focus of interest in the school. Nonetheless, the magazine continued to be published until the 1960s. Some recipes from early issues of Madame Distel's magazine have been adapted for inclusion in this book.

London's School

Word of Le Cordon Bleu's publications and classes spread, and soon students from Russia, America, and across Europe were "turning" vegetables and whisking egg whites. One of Chef Pellaprat's students during the 1920s was a slender English woman called Rosemary Hume.

After completing her course and returning to her home in England in the early 1930s, Rosemary Hume established Ecole du Petit Cordon Bleu in London. In 1947, she joined forces with Constance Spry, an expert in flower design, and together they founded a new school called Winkfield Place.

Rosemary Hume committed herself to maintaining the same high standards of culinary excellence she had practised in Paris. Courses at Ecole du Petit Cordon Bleu in London and Winkfield, and their cookbooks, had a profound influence on English-speaking cooks around the world. The school's contributions were honoured in many ways, but the greatest honour came when the school was asked to prepare a luncheon to celebrate the coronation of Her Majesty Queen Elizabeth II in 1953. For her contributions to the world of cookery, Rosemary Hume was awarded the MBE in 1970.

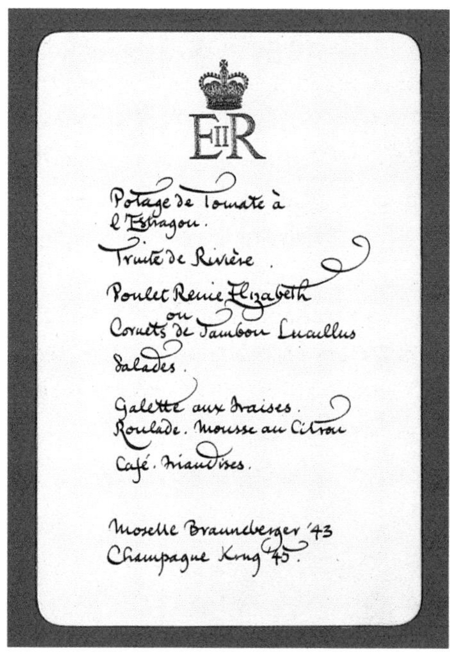

EIIR

Potage de Tomate à l'Estragon.

Truite de Rivière.

Poulet Reine Elizabeth
ou
Cornets de Jambon Lucullus

Salades.

Galette aux Fraises.
Roulade. Mousse au Citron

Café. Friandises.

Moselle Brauneberger '43
Champagne Krug '45.

The Coronation Menu

"Ladies and gentlemen, the very phrase 'minimum hygiene standards' should strike terror into the hearts of any true-born Frenchman. It certainly frightens me ... life is not worth living unless you can have a choice of all the gloriously unhygienic things which mankind – especially the French portion of it – has lovingly created out of the fruits of God's earth."

from an address by
HRH The Prince of Wales on the 75th Anniversary of the Association of France–Grande-Bretagne,
Paris, 2 March 1992

The American Connection

After Marthe Distel, Elisabeth Brassart took over the Cordon Bleu school in Paris. She revised the curriculum and supervised a special programme of cookery classes that was funded by the United States government for American GIs in Paris after World War II.

Among Elisabeth Brassart's students was a young American housewife who earned the *Grand Diplôme*. Who has watched American television and not seen Julia Child, making French cooking look so simple? Another well-known American "foodie", Dione Lucas, was also a graduate of the Paris school.

Le Cordon Bleu's popularity greatly increased when Hollywood shot Billy Wilder's film *Sabrina*, starring Audrey Hepburn and Humphrey Bogart. The film portrayed the life of a young American girl in Paris – and where else was Audrey Hepburn going to learn to whisk egg whites but at Le Cordon Bleu?

Le Cordon Bleu Today

In 1984, when Elisabeth Brassart was well into her eighties, she sold the Paris school to André J. Cointreau, a descendant of two of France's most esteemed families (Cointreau and Rémy-Martin). After opening a brand new cookery school in Tokyo in April 1991, and consolidating the London-based school fully into Le Cordon Bleu's teaching programmes in June 1991, Monsieur Cointreau and his international team begin their second century with a broad perspective.

Le Cordon Bleu now has four schools around the world and has developed academic alliances with the major leaders in the fields of hospitality and culinary training. It has also developed products related to teaching – from books and videos to CD-ROMs. It has its own gourmet food line, offering the best ingredients and flavours from around the world, and a whole range of prepared dishes, developed by the schools' teams of chefs. Le Cordon Bleu has also broadened the concept of *l'art de la table*, and has associated itself with Pierre Deux, the American leader of French country home furnishing and decorating. What arrangement could bring better opportunities for synergy in a company committed to conviviality and excellence in gastronomy?

In the future, as in the past, Le Cordon Bleu will strive to bring enjoyment to dining tables around the world. We hope the **Classic French Cookbook** helps bring great pleasure to your home.

Glossary

Aïoli Mayonnaise-like sauce made from crushed garlic, olive oil, and egg yolks.

Al dente Italian term used to describe pasta or vegetables that are just cooked.

Allumette Thick matchstick-shaped vegetable.

Aspic Clarified stock that has been set with gelatine.

Baguette French bread stick.

Bain-marie One vessel placed inside, or over, another containing water. Used for slow, gentle cooking, and for keeping food warm. A double boiler acts as a bain-marie.

Bake blind To partially or fully bake a pastry shell before adding a filling. The shell is lined with non-stick paper and filled with dried beans so that the pastry is weighted down flat and does not bubble up during baking.

Balsamic vinegar Sweet-tasting vinegar made from the slow fermentation of grapes, from Modena in northern Italy.

Bard To place pieces of fat around joints of meat or poultry to keep meat moist.

Baste To spoon cooking juices over ingredients several times throughout cooking to keep them moist.

Bâtonnet Vegetable cut into large sticks.

Beignet Savoury or sweet food dipped in batter and deep-fried.

Beurre manié Equal amounts of butter and flour mixed together to form a paste, used as a thickener at the end of cooking.

Beurre noisette Butter cooked until nut-brown.

Beurre rouge Fish and wine sauce that has been finished with butter.

Blanc Mixture of water, lemon juice, and flour used for cooking vegetables and meat.

Blanch Literally "to whiten", but used in culinary terms to describe a variety of techniques for purifying, desalting, firming up, removing bitterness, etc.

Bouillon Unclarified stock or broth made from meat and vegetables.

Bouquet garni Aromatic bundle of herbs used to flavour stocks, soups, and stews, usually consisting of parsley, thyme, and bay leaf.

Braise To cook ingredients in a closed casserole with aromatic vegetables and a liquid, such as stock or wine.

Brioche Soft, slightly sweet yeast bread, enriched with eggs and butter.

Broth - see Bouillon.

Brunoise Vegetables cut into small dice.

Candy To cook an ingredient in a sugar and water syrup until crystallized.

Caramelize To cook an ingredient in sugar and sometimes water and butter until coated in sticky brown caramel.

Caul Thin membrane veined with lacy fat that encloses an animal's stomach. Pork caul is the most common. Often used to keep stuffed meat together.

Cep Cèpe in French, and porcini in Italian. A wild mushroom with a round brown cap and a thick stem that widens at the base. When cooked, it is very rich in flavour and soft in texture.

Chanterelle Girolle in French. A wild mushroom that is deep yellow in colour. Grey chanterelles are also available. Chanterelles have an aroma of apricots, with a rich peppery taste when cooked.

Charlotte mould Deep, aluminium mould with slightly sloping sides. Usually two-handled to help with unmoulding.

Chevron Decorative technique for cutting fruit or vegetables into graduated "V" shapes.

Chiffonnade Vegetables or herbs shredded in strips similar to, but thicker than, julienne.

Chinois Conical sieve used for straining.

Clarify To clear liquids of impurities. Used in stocks for consommé or aspic, or butter for frying.

Compote Thick pulp of fresh or dried fruit cooked in a sugar syrup and reduced to thicken. May be flavoured with spices.

Concassée Roughly chopped vegetables. Most often applied to tomatoes.

Coulis Puréed and sieved fruit or vegetables, served as a sauce.

Court bouillon Also called nage in French. Aromatic stock made with water, wine or vinegar, and vegetables, used to cook fish.

Couverture Covering chocolate containing a higher percentage of cocoa butter than plain chocolate.

Crème anglaise Thin custard or dessert sauce, made with egg yolks, sugar, and milk.

Crème fraîche Thick, slightly sour cream treated with a special culture that makes it taste pleasantly acidic. An important ingredient in French cooking.

Crème pâtissière Thick pastry cream made with eggs, butter, sugar, vanilla, milk, and a thickening agent, such as flour or cornflour.

Crêpe Thin, lacy pancake, often rolled or folded.

Croquante Pastry filled with pastry cream.

Croquette Savoury or sweet mixture bound with a thick sauce and formed into small shapes. Usually coated in egg and breadcrumbs and deep-fried or oven-baked.

Croûte Bread cut into slices or other shapes, fried, toasted, or oven-baked.

Croûton Small diced piece of bread, fried, toasted, or oven-baked. Usually served with soups.

Dacquoise Almond meringue usually piped into rounds and used between layers of other ingredients to make a meringue cake.

Dariole Small cylinder-shaped mould used for sweet and savoury foods. Term also used to describe food prepared in mould.

Deep-fry To immerse food in very hot fat or oil at 140-190°C (275-375°F) until crisp and golden. The fat or oil should not turn brown or give off acrid smoke.

Deglaze To add liquid to a pan to dissolve pan juices and sediment left on the bottom after cooking.

Dégorge To soak food in water, and salt or vinegar, to expel impurities or blood.

Demi-glace - see Meat glaze.

Dice To cut ingredients into equal-sized cubes.

Dredge To sprinkle flour or icing sugar over food.

Entrecôte Thick juicy steak, taken from between ribs of beef.

Escalope Thin slice of meat, such as veal or chicken.

Farce Stuffing or forcemeat.

Fécule - see Potato starch.

Filleting knife Thin, narrow, flexible knife usually used for filleting fish.

Fines herbes Combination of finely chopped aromatic herbs, usually parsley, chervil, tarragon, and chives, although sometimes other herbs are added.

Foie gras Enlarged liver of a goose or duck.

Fricassée French term for a meat dish, usually veal or chicken, slowly cooked or sautéed in cream sauce.

Galette Flat, round shape of pastry or cake. Usually sweet, but also sometimes savoury, such as potato.

Ganache Chocolate-flavoured pastry cream.

Gaufrette Thin waffle-shaped potato, cut with a mandolin.

Génoise Genoese sponge cake, prepared with equal amounts of eggs, flour, sugar, and butter.

Goujonette Thin slice of fish, poultry, or meat, dipped in batter or egg and breadcrumbs and deep-fried.

Hard-ball stage Sugar and water syrup boiled until 120°C (248°F) on a sugar thermometer. It will form a firm, pliable ball when plunged into iced water.

Herbes de Provence Mixture of dried herbs, such as thyme, rosemary, bay leaf, and basil, from the Provence region of southern France.

Horn of plenty Trompette de la mort in French. This wild mushroom is thin and wavy at the cap, and looks greyish brown and leathery. Its earthy taste complements game.

Ice bath Bowl or pan containing ice cubes or a mixture of ice cubes and water. Used for cooling mixtures quickly.

Infusion A hot liquid for steeping herbs and flavourings, such as lemon zest, cloves, and vanilla pods.

Julienne Vegetable cut into thin matchstick strips.

Lamelle Vegetable cut into thin slices or strips.

Lard To insert small pieces of fat into meat to keep it moist while cooking.

Lardon Pork fat or bacon cut into strips and used to flavour soups and stews.

Liaison Mixture of egg yolk and cream, used to thicken sauces, stews, and soups.

Liver mousse Mousse de foie in French. A smooth, pâté-like ingredient bought commercially.

Macerate To soak an ingredient in a liquid, usually alcohol, to soften and flavour.

Madeira Wine fortified with a spirit during fermentation. From the island of Madeira.

Magret Breast fillet taken from a duck fattened especially for its liver.

Mandolin Wooden or stainless steel utensil with one or two blades for slicing or grating vegetables in varying sizes.

Marinate To flavour food with other seasonings. The food is left for varying lengths of time in a marinade so that the flavours develop. A marinade also tenderizes, softens, and preserves ingredients.

Meat glaze Demi-glace in French. A congealed concentrated stock, added to dishes by the spoonful because of its intense flavour.

Meat jus Jus de viande in French. Between a stock and a meat glaze in flavour and richness. Similar to a gravy, made from the pan juices of roasted foods. Juices are mixed with water, stock, and wine, and reduced to make a sauce.

Melon baller Also known as a Parisienne spoon. For cutting ingredients into ball shapes.

Mignon Also known as filet mignon or tournedos. A small round steak, cut from the tender beef fillet.

Mignonette pepper Coarsely ground black or white peppercorns.

Mijoté Slowly simmered dish.

Mirepoix Named after the 18th-century Duc de Lévis-Mirepoix. Rough dice of mixed vegetables containing equal amounts of carrot, onion, celery, and leek. Used in many French recipes, to enhance the flavour of other ingredients.

Mousseline Sweet or savoury mousse containing a high proportion of cream.

Muslin Loosely woven white cloth, used for straining ingredients.

Nage - see Court bouillon.

Pare To cut off the skin or zest of a fruit or vegetable using a small knife or vegetable peeler.

Parisienne Vegetable or fruit cut into balls using a melon baller or Parisienne spoon.

Paupiette Thin slice of meat or fish wrapped around a stuffing or mousseline, rolled, and secured with string or wooden cocktail sticks.

Pestle and mortar Old-fashioned utensil used for grinding or puréeing ingredients, consisting of a bowl (mortar) and a heavy utensil (pestle) for pounding.

Phyllo pastry Also spelt filo. Paper-thin pastry made with flour and water. Popular in Eastern Europe and Greece.

Pistou Sauce made with crushed garlic, basil, and olive oil or butter. Tomatoes can be added.

Potato starch Fécule in French. A type of flour used as a thickening agent.

Quatre-épices Blend of ground pepper, nutmeg, cloves, and cinnamon, often used as a seasoning for poultry or game.

Quenelle Oval-shaped garnish, traditionally made out of fish mousseline. Now refers to any food shaped into an oval when served.

Reduce To boil a liquid in an uncovered pan to evaporate and produce a more concentrated flavour.

Refresh To cool ingredients quickly by plunging them into iced water, stopping the cooking process.

Rocket Roquette in French, and rucola in Italian. Salad herb with a distinctive peppery taste.

Rouille Thick rust-coloured sauce made with red pepper, potato, and olive oil, traditionally served with bouillabaisse.

Roux Butter and flour mixture used as a thickener. Either white, blond, or brown, depending on how long butter is cooked.

Sauté To cook or brown food on a high heat in butter or oil, or a mixture of the two.

Scale To remove tough discs or scales from the skin of a fish, with a scaler or the back of a knife.

Seal To fry an ingredient over a high heat until the edges have firmed up to seal in the juices.

Season To add salt and pepper to a dish according to personal taste.

Shuck To remove shellfish from their shells. A term most often applied to oysters.

Simmer To cook food in water just below boiling point – small bubbles should break the surface.

Skim To remove impurities from the surface of a liquid using a metal spoon.

Soupçon Very small quantity of an ingredient.

Soya oil Neutral-flavoured oil useful for general purposes. Vegetable or sunflower oil can be substituted.

Springform pan Two-part cake tin that has a removable side, useful for unmoulding soft or fragile cakes and desserts.

Steam To cook food in the steam created in a closed container.

Sûpreme Skinless chicken breast that has a little of the wing bone attached.

Sweat To cook vegetables, such as leeks and onions, over a low heat until they steam themselves soft.

Sweetbread Ris in French. The thymus glands around the neck and heart. Veal sweetbreads are the most widely available.

Terrine Rectangular or round mould made out of porcelain, glass, or enamelled cast iron. Often used to shape pâtés.

Tournedos Also known as filet mignon. Round slice of beef, cut from the centre of the fillet.

Truss To sew or tie string or trussing thread around meat, especially poultry and game birds, to secure together during cooking.

Trussing needle Long stainless-steel needle with a large eye. Used for threading string or thread to truss meat and poultry.

Tureen Large bowl-like dish with a dome-shaped lid, used to serve soup.

Turn To pare vegetables into barrel shapes, traditionally with seven sides.

Vinaigrette Dressing commonly used with salad. Usually consists of oil, vinegar, and seasoning.

Wilt To cook salad or vegetable leaves until they droop or lose their firmness.

Zest Outer coloured rind of citrus fruits. Best removed with a citrus zester or vegetable peeler. Adds tangy flavour to food, especially fish dishes and desserts.

FIRST COURSES

In this chapter, Le Cordon Bleu presents a series of recipes for soups, tarts, salads, and terrines that reflect both the traditional and new in French cooking. Many of these first courses are light, or légère in French, to meet the demands of modern gastronomes. Others are hearty, and when served in larger portions would make ideal lunch time main courses.

Consomme de Volaille aux Quenelles

Chicken Consomme with Quenelles

Consommé is one of the great dishes of the French classical repertoire. This particular consommé is rich in flavour, with chicken quenelles making a delicate garnish. It is also known as Consommé Princesse when served with asparagus.

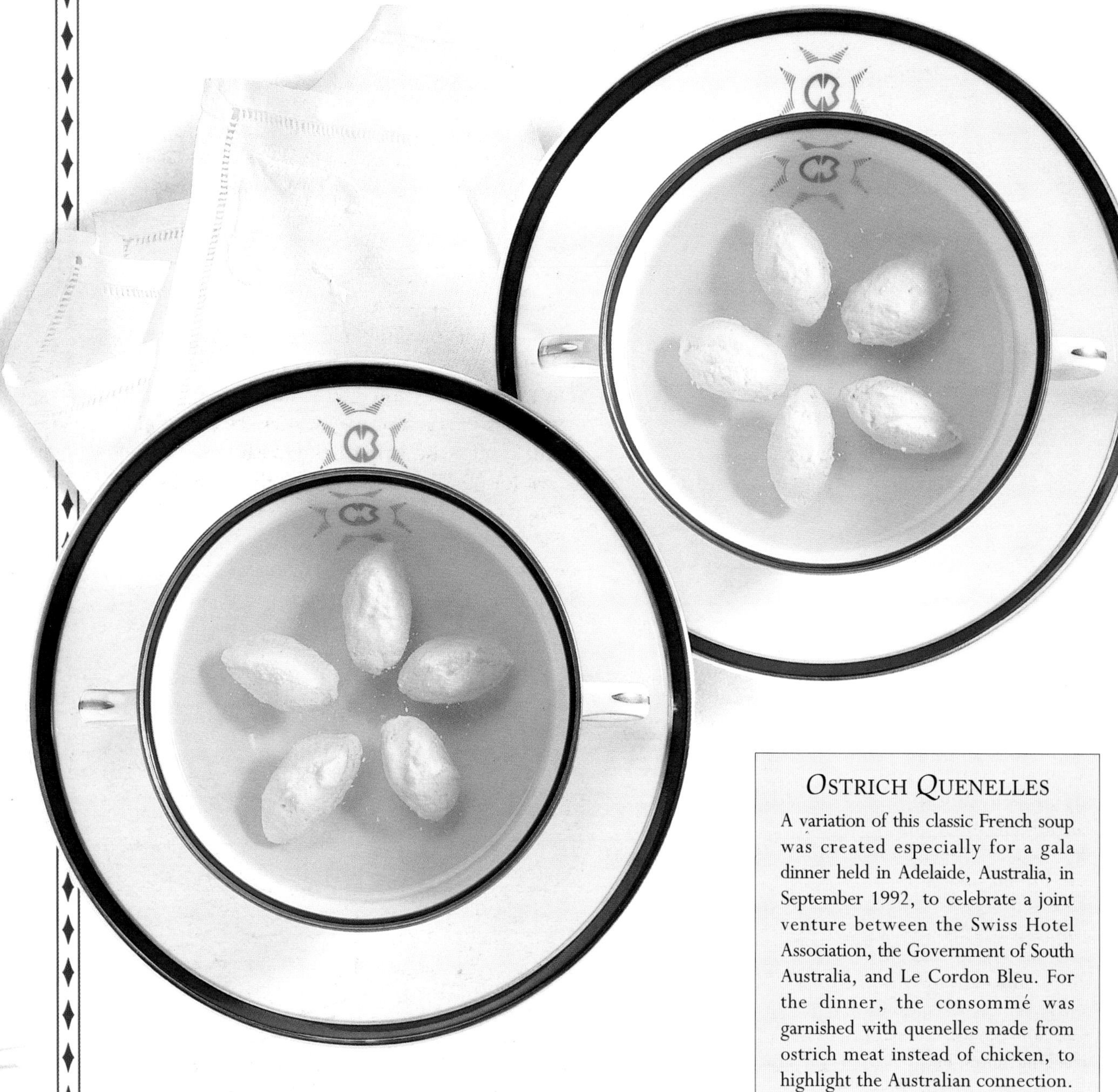

Ostrich Quenelles

A variation of this classic French soup was created especially for a gala dinner held in Adelaide, Australia, in September 1992, to celebrate a joint venture between the Swiss Hotel Association, the Government of South Australia, and Le Cordon Bleu. For the dinner, the consommé was garnished with quenelles made from ostrich meat instead of chicken, to highlight the Australian connection.

INGREDIENTS

Serves 8–10

1 chicken, weighing 2·5–3 kg (5–6 lb)
1 carrot
1 large onion, studded with 3 cloves
1 celery stalk
1 leek
a bouquet garni
3 garlic cloves, crushed
1 tomato
a few black peppercorns
5 litres (8 3/4 pints) water
salt and freshly ground pepper
Cognac, to taste

For the quenelles

150 ml (5 fl oz) double cream
1 egg white
a pinch of freshly grated nutmeg
2 tbsp Cognac

For the clarification mixture

1 small carrot, chopped
2 celery stalks, chopped
1/2 leek, chopped
3 tomatoes, chopped
4 egg whites, lightly beaten

PREPARATION

1 Remove the breast meat from the chicken and discard the skin. Set the meat aside for the quenelles. Cut the legs off the chicken and bone them; chop the leg meat and set it aside to use in the clarification mixture later.

2 Put the remaining chicken and the leg bones in a pan of cold water, and bring to a boil. Drain and rinse, then return to pan.

3 Add the carrot, onion, celery, leek, bouquet garni, garlic, tomato, peppercorns, water, and a little salt. Bring to a boil, and simmer for about 3 hours, skimming occasionally. Remove the chicken and strain the stock into a clean pan: there should be about 3 litres (5 pints).

4 Make the quenelle mixture: purée the chicken breast in a food processor. Press the purée through a sieve into a bowl. Set this bowl over a bowl of iced water and gradually beat in the cream and egg white. Season the mixture with salt, pepper, and nutmeg. Stir in the Cognac.

5 Bring the stock to a simmer. Shape and cook the quenelles (see below).

6 Prepare the clarification mixture: mix the chicken leg meat with the carrot, celery, leek, tomatoes, egg whites, and seasoning.

7 Add the clarification mixture to the stock and mix well. Bring slowly to a boil, stirring constantly. When the egg whites start to solidify into a soft crust, stop stirring. Leave over a low heat for 20–25 minutes. Carefully strain the liquid through a muslin-lined sieve. Do not press the solids left in the sieve or the impurities will go through the sieve into the consommé.

8 Reheat, season, and add Cognac. Place the quenelles in bowls and ladle over the consommé.

Shaping and Cooking Quenelles

A quenelle is traditionally made of fish or meat *mousseline* (a mousse-like preparation), shaped into an oval, and poached in stock. The term is sometimes used to describe other ingredients that are shaped into ovals, such as ice cream or sorbet. Here, teaspoons are used to make small quenelles, but dessertspoons can be used to make larger ones.

1 Scoop out a mound of quenelle mixture with one spoon. Use another to smooth it into an oval shape.

2 Slide a spoon under quenelle and lower into the simmering stock. Repeat with remaining mixture.

3 Poach the quenelles until firm, about 10 minutes. Remove them, cover, and set aside.

Consomme Celestine

Beef Consomme with a Julienne of Herb Crepes

INGREDIENTS

Serves 4-6

2 litres (3½ pints) cold beef stock
½ bunch of tarragon

For the clarification mixture

400 g (14 oz) lean minced beef
200 g (7 oz) mirepoix of vegetables (see page 133)
4 egg whites, lightly beaten
2 tsp crushed peppercorns
1 tsp salt

For the crêpe garnish

100 g (3½ oz) flour
2 eggs
1 egg yolk
about 140 ml (4½ fl oz) milk
25 g (¾ oz) butter, melted
2 tbsp finely chopped fresh herbs
salt and freshly ground pepper
clarified butter, for frying

PREPARATION

1 Make the batter for the crêpes: gradually beat together the flour, eggs, egg yolk, milk, and melted butter until smooth. Stir in the herbs and seasoning. Set aside to rest for 1 hour.

2 Meanwhile, clarify the stock: mix the minced beef, mirepoix, egg whites, crushed peppercorns, and salt. Combine this clarification mixture with the cold stock in a saucepan and slowly bring to a boil, stirring constantly. When the egg whites start to solidify into a soft crust on top of the stock, stop stirring. Leave over a low heat for 20-25 minutes. Carefully strain the liquid through a muslin-lined sieve. Do not press the solids left in the sieve or the impurities will go through the sieve into the consommé.

3 Pour the consommé into a clean pan and add the tarragon. Cover and leave to infuse.

4 If the crêpe batter has thickened too much while resting, stir in a little more milk so that the batter is the consistency of single cream. Brush a crêpe pan with clarified butter and wipe out the excess with a paper towel. Heat the pan until it is very hot, then make thin, lacy crêpes with the batter (see page 147). Roll up the crêpes, cut into thin strips, and divide them among soup plates.

5 Remove the tarragon and gently reheat the consommé. Check the seasoning, and ladle into the soup plates. Serve immediately.

Crushed Peppercorns

Known in the culinary world as mignonette pepper, crushed peppercorns add a stronger pepper flavour to food than ordinary freshly ground pepper. They are usually crushed in a pestle and mortar, but an electric spice mill can also be used. It is better to crush peppercorns just before using because they tend to lose their strong aroma if left to stand.

Bouillon de Decembre

Rich Winter Bouillon

INGREDIENTS

Serves 10-12

1 chicken
2 turkey legs
1 shin of beef, weighing about
1·75 kg (3 1/2 lb), cut into pieces
1 shin of veal, weighing about
1·25 kg (2 1/2 lb), cut into pieces
1/2 oxtail, weighing about 500 g (1 lb), trimmed of all fat and cut into pieces
1 small onion
6 ripe tomatoes, halved
4 carrots, roughly chopped
1 leek, roughly chopped
2 celery stalks, roughly chopped
2 garlic cloves, crushed
200 g (7 oz) mushrooms, chopped
a bouquet garni
1 sprig of tarragon
12 black peppercorns

For the optional garnish

mustard
gherkins
finely chopped fresh herbs

PREPARATION

1 Blanch the poultry and meat in a large pan of boiling water. Drain and rinse off any scum.
2 Halve the onion and brown the cut sides under a hot grill.
3 Return the poultry and meat to the pan and add the onion halves and all the remaining ingredients. Pour in enough cold water to cover. Bring to a boil, and simmer for about 2 hours.
4 Strain the bouillon through a fine sieve. Reserve the poultry and meat; keep warm. Cool the bouillon and remove any fat from the surface.
5 Reheat the bouillon and check the seasoning.
6 Serve the bouillon as a first course. Follow with the poultry and meat, served with mustard, gherkins, and herbs, if you like.

Consomme Japonais

Beef Consomme with Tofu

INGREDIENTS

Serves 4-6

2 litres (3 1/2 pints) cold beef stock
300 g (10 oz) firm tofu
1 stalk of lemon grass

For the clarification mixture

400 g (14 oz) lean minced beef
200 g (7 oz) mirepoix of vegetables (see page 133)
4 egg whites, lightly beaten
2 tsp crushed peppercorns

PREPARATION

1 Prepare the clarification mixture: mix together the minced beef, mirepoix, egg whites, and crushed peppercorns. Combine this mixture with the cold stock in a saucepan and slowly bring to a boil, stirring constantly. When the egg whites start to solidify into a soft crust, stop stirring. Leave over a low heat for 20-25 minutes.
2 Strain the liquid through a muslin-lined sieve. Do not press the solids left or the impurities will go through the sieve into the consommé.
3 Cut the tofu into small even-sized cubes, and place in the bottom of a soup tureen.
4 Pour the clarified consommé into a clean pan, and add the lemon grass. Check the seasoning and bring to a boil. Skim off any scum, remove the lemon grass, and slowly pour the consommé over the tofu cubes. Serve immediately.

East Meets West

In this oriental variation of a French classical recipe, rich beef consommé is flavoured with tofu, a favourite Japanese ingredient. Tofu is made commercially by soaking, puréeing, boiling, and sieving soya beans; the resulting high-protein liquid is then solidified by adding a coagulant.

This soup was created at Le Cordon Bleu, Tokyo, to commemorate the French film festival that was held in Yokohama, Japan, in August 1994.

Potage de Tomate a l'Estragon

Winkfield Soup

This tomato and tarragon soup was one of the dishes served at a luncheon in honour of the coronation of Queen Elizabeth II in 1953. It can be served hot or cold, which makes it adaptable for any menu.

INGREDIENTS

Serves 4–6

500 g (1 lb) ripe red tomatoes
30 g (1 oz) butter
1 onion, sliced
1/4 garlic clove, crushed
1/2 bay leaf
1/2 tsp salt and freshly ground pepper
900 ml (1 1/2 pints) beef stock
300 ml (1/2 pint) tomato juice
2 tsp tomato purée
2 tsp arrowroot
a little extra stock or tomato juice
a few tarragon leaves, for the garnish

"SOUP, TO THE GASTRONOME, IS THE ONLY FITTING PRELUDE TO THE MEAL. THERE IS A SOUP FOR EVERY MEAL, AS THERE IS A KEY FOR EVERY SONG."

Rosemary Hume, Au Petit Cordon Bleu

PREPARATION

1 Cut the tomatoes in half and extract the juice from the pulp and seeds (see below).
2 Melt the butter in a heavy saucepan and add the tomato halves, onion, garlic, bay leaf, and salt. Cover and cook over a very low heat for 45 minutes to 1 hour, stirring occasionally.
3 Rub the mixture through a sieve into a bowl; discard the contents of the sieve.
4 Rinse the pan well. Return the sieved mixture to the pan and add the tomato purée, tomato juice, and stock, together with the juice extracted from the pulp and seeds of the tomato halves. Stir to mix. Bring to a boil, and simmer for 20-30 minutes.
5 Mix the arrowroot with the extra stock or tomato juice, stir into the soup, and bring back to a boil, stirring constantly.
6 Taste the soup and season. Serve hot or cold, sprinkled with tarragon leaves.

Extracting Juice from Tomato Pulp and Seeds

The pulp and seeds from tomatoes need not be discarded. Sieve them to provide extra juice for soups, sauces, and stocks. This technique also removes the seeds, which can be bitter or irritating when left in a dish.

1 Set a sieve over a bowl. Squeeze the tomato halves so that the pulp and seeds fall into the sieve.

2 Press the pulp and seeds so that the tomato juice goes through into the bowl.

Regal Cuisine

Rosemary Hume was one of the best-known recipients of the prestigious advanced diploma, or *Grand Diplôme* in French, from Le Cordon Bleu, Paris. In the 1930s she established Ecole du Petit Cordon Bleu in London and in 1947, together with Constance Spry, founded another school known as Winkfield Place. Although the schools received many accolades, none was more important than a request to cater for one of the several luncheons given to celebrate the coronation of Queen Elizabeth II.

The menu started with a tomato and tarragon soup, then known as Winkfield Soup after the address of the second school.

Creme Cressoniere Frappe

Chilled Cream of Watercress Soup

INGREDIENTS

Serves 6-8

2-3 tbsp vegetable oil
200 g (7 oz) leek, white part only, sliced
200 g (7 oz) potato, sliced
2 bunches of watercress
1 garlic clove, crushed
1 litre (1¾ pints) chicken stock or water
salt and freshly ground pepper

For the garnish
150 ml (5 fl oz) single cream
juice of 1 lime
blanched zest of 1 lime

PREPARATION

1 Heat the oil in a saucepan and add the leek and potato. Cover and cook for 10 minutes, or until soft, stirring occasionally.
2 Add the watercress and garlic. Cook for 2-3 minutes, or until the watercress starts to wilt.
3 Pour in the stock, season, and bring to a boil. Simmer gently for 10-15 minutes.
4 Purée the soup until smooth in a blender or food processor, then pour into a bowl and stir in most of the cream and the lime juice. Cool, then chill.
5 Stir the soup and check the seasoning, then pour into chilled soup plates. Garnish with the remaining cream and the lime zest.

Peppery Greens

Soup flavoured with the peppery green leaves of the aquatic plant, watercress, appears among the recipes of the 14th-century French cook, Guillaume Taillevent. This recipe is dedicated to the newest of Le Cordon Bleu's cuisine and pastry schools, located in Tokyo, Japan.

Creme Cendrillon

Cream of Pumpkin Soup

INGREDIENTS

Serves 6

6 small or 3 medium pumpkins
2 leeks, sliced
150 g (5 oz) butter
1 litre (1 3/4 pints) chicken stock
salt and freshly ground pepper
a pinch of freshly grated nutmeg
300 ml (1/2 pint) double cream
50 g (1 3/4 oz) petits pois
1 bunch of sorrel, cut into julienne *strips*

For the optional finish

250 ml (8 fl oz) whipping cream
1 egg yolk

PREPARATION

1 If using small pumpkins, cut off the tops. Alternatively, cut medium pumpkins in half. Discard the seeds and fibres. Scoop out the flesh, without damaging the pumpkin shells. Chop the flesh. Set the shells aside on a baking sheet.

2 Sweat the leeks in a saucepan in 100 g (3 1/2 oz) of the butter. Add the pumpkin flesh, stock, seasoning, and grated nutmeg. Bring to a boil, and simmer, covered, for about 30 minutes, or until the vegetables are very soft.

3 Purée the soup until smooth in a blender or food processor. Return to the rinsed-out pan and stir in the double cream. Cover and keep hot.

4 Cook the petits pois in boiling salted water; drain. Sweat the sorrel in the remaining butter.

5 Divide the petits pois and sorrel among the pumpkin shells. Ladle in the soup. Place the filled shells in a preheated oven at 170°C (325°F, Gas 3) for 10 minutes.

6 For the optional finish: whip the cream with salt, pepper, and nutmeg to taste. Fold in the egg yolk. Put a large spoonful of the cream mixture on top of each serving and glaze quickly under a hot grill. Serve immediately.

"COOKERY HAS BECOME AN ART; A NOBLE SCIENCE: COOKS ARE GENTLEMEN."

Robert Burton (1577-1640)

Vichyssoise

Chilled Leek and Potato Cream Soup on Jellied Consomme

INGREDIENTS

Serves 8

4 leeks, white part only, sliced
1 onion, finely chopped
1 garlic clove, finely chopped
50 g (1 3/4 oz) butter
400 g (14 oz) potatoes, sliced
1·5 litres (2 1/3 pints) chicken stock
250 ml (8 fl oz) double cream
salt and freshly ground pepper
snipped chives, for the garnish

For the jellied consommé base

1 calf's foot, weighing about 875 g (1 3/4 lb); cut into pieces
2 litres (3 1/2 pints) beef stock
750 g (1 1/2 lb) lean minced beef
4 egg whites, lightly beaten
200 g (7 oz) mirepoix of vegetables (see page 133)
2 tsp crushed peppercorns

PREPARATION

1 Make the jellied consommé base: mix all the ingredients together in a saucepan and slowly bring to a boil, stirring constantly. When the egg whites start to solidify into a soft crust, stop stirring. Leave over a low heat for 20 minutes. Carefully strain the liquid through a muslin-lined sieve, without pressing the solids through. Let cool slightly, then pour into a glass serving bowl. Chill until firm.

2 Sweat the leeks, onion, and garlic in the butter until soft. Add the potatoes and stock and bring to a boil. Cover and simmer for 20 minutes.

3 Purée the mixture until smooth in a blender or food processor. Cool, then chill for 3-4 hours.

4 Pass the soup through a sieve. Stir in the cream and seasoning to taste.

5 Pour the soup over the jellied consommé in the serving bowl. Garnish with the snipped chives.

Parissoise

This is another name for our contemporary version of the time-honoured classic *Vichyssoise*. A rich jellied veal consommé forms the base of the soup, and the classic, velvety smooth purée of potatoes, leeks, and cream forms the top. Both the soup and the jellied base can be served separately, but when brought together they look decorative and taste delicious.

Gaspacho aux Ecrevisses

Gazpacho with Crayfish

This Spanish classic has been "Frenchified" with the addition of crayfish. Simple to make and refreshing to eat, its fresh, spicy flavour complements many classic French dishes, and is the perfect start to a meal on a hot summer's day.

INGREDIENTS

Serves 4-6

24 raw crayfish
salt and freshly ground pepper
a little vinegar
1 cucumber, halved lengthwise, and seeded
1 red pepper, cored, halved, and seeded
1 green pepper, cored, halved, and seeded
6 ripe red tomatoes, concassées (see page 136)
2 large onions, chopped
3 garlic cloves, chopped
6 slices of white bread, crusts trimmed, cut into small cubes
500 ml (16 fl oz) tomato juice
100 ml (3½ fl oz) olive oil
1 tbsp tomato purée
about 250 ml (8 fl oz) consommé or chicken stock

For the garnish

½ bunch of basil, finely chopped
½ bunch of flat-leaf parsley, finely chopped

PREPARATION

1 Prepare and cook the crayfish (see below). Peel the crayfish, leaving 4-6 of the best-looking ones unpeeled for the garnish.

2 Dice one of the cucumber halves and one-quarter each of the red and green peppers. Set aside for the garnish.

3 Roughly chop the remaining cucumber and peppers. Put into a bowl and add the tomatoes, onions, garlic, and bread cubes. Pour in the tomato juice and oil and add the tomato purée. Mix well. Leave to stand for several hours, stirring occasionally.

4 Work the mixture in a food processor until quite smooth. Turn the gazpacho into a bowl, and add enough consommé or chicken stock to thin it down to the desired consistency. Season to taste.

5 Divide the peeled crayfish among soup bowls and ladle in the gazpacho. Garnish with the cucumber and pepper dice, the unpeeled crayfish, and the finely chopped herbs.

Preparing and Cooking Crayfish

Crayfish turn from grey to red when cooked. It is easier to remove the intestinal vein from the crayfish before cooking, whereas it is easier to peel the crayfish after they have been cooked.

1 Remove the intestinal vein by twisting the central tail section and pulling the vein out.

2 Drop the crayfish into a pan of boiling salted water to which a little vinegar has been added.

3 Cook until the shells turn red-orange. Remove the crayfish with a slotted spoon, and let cool.

Foreign Influences

Good ideas do not stay long in one country: the Arabic roots for the name of this classic Spanish soup, gazpacho, mean "soaked bread". What simpler food could farmers make than an uncooked mixture of fresh tomatoes, cucumber, onion, red and green sweet peppers, garlic, tomato juice, and olive oil, all blended together with bread to absorb the flavours of the vegetables?

The French have also aquired a taste for gazpacho, spelling it "gaspacho", and adapting it slightly with the distinctive taste of freshly cooked crayfish.

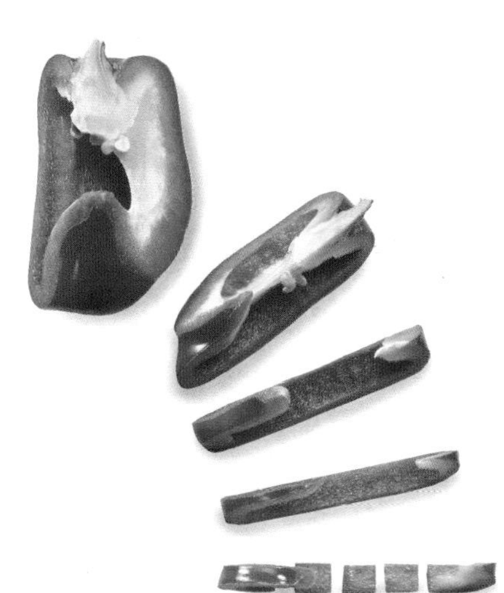

Garbure Paysanne

Country Vegetable Soup

INGREDIENTS

Serves 4–6

100 g (3½ oz) butter
1 small white cabbage, finely chopped
2 leeks, thinly sliced into rings
1 onion, finely chopped
125 g (4 oz) carrots, diced
1–2 heads of celeriac, diced
125 g (4 oz) potatoes, diced
1·5 litres (2⅓ pints) chicken stock
salt and freshly ground pepper
½ baguette, *cut into thin slices*
50 g (1¾ oz) Gruyère cheese, grated

PREPARATION

1 Melt 30 g (1 oz) of the butter in a heavy saucepan and add the cabbage, leeks, and onion. Cover and cook over a low heat until the vegetables are very soft, stirring occasionally.

2 Add the carrots, celeriac, and potatoes. Pour in the chicken stock and add the seasoning. Bring to a boil, and simmer for about 1 hour.

3 Melt 30 g (1 oz) of the remaining butter in a large frying pan and fry the slices of baguette until golden on both sides. Set these *croûtes* aside.

4 Remove 2 or 3 spoonfuls of the vegetables from the soup and mash them to a pulp. Spread the vegetable pulp over the croûtes and sprinkle the Gruyère on top. Arrange on a baking tray. Bake in a preheated oven at 220°C (425°F, Gas 7) for 5-10 minutes, or until golden brown.

5 Meanwhile, purée the soup until smooth in a blender or food processor. Return it to the pan and bring to a boil. Lower the heat and whisk in the remaining butter, cut into small pieces. Check seasoning. Serve hot, with the croûtes.

Garbure and its Variations

Béarn, near the Pyrenees in the south-west of France, was the birthplace of Henri IV, and the region most closely associated with garbure. When it is made elsewhere, this chunky soup may also contain garlic, local herbs, and cured meat – usually goose. Le Cordon Bleu's version takes its richness from butter, making it somewhat lighter in taste than versions made with goose fat. Bacon, cut into small pieces and sautéed in butter, can also be added for additional flavour if you like.

Soupe aux Haricots Beurres au Champagne

White Bean and Champagne Soup

INGREDIENTS

Serves 10-12
1 ham bone
3 litres (5¼ pints) water
3 celery stalks, with leaves
1 large carrot
1 large onion
4 medium potatoes
1 bay leaf
8 black peppercorns
8 whole cloves
500 g (1 lb) dried white beans, such as butter beans or cannellini beans, soaked in cold water overnight
salt and freshly ground pepper
1 bottle of Champagne
finely chopped parsley, for the garnish

PREPARATION

1 Put the ham bone into a large saucepan and add the water. Coarsely chop the celery, carrot, onion, and potatoes, and add to the pan with the bay leaf, peppercorns, and whole cloves. Bring to a boil, cover, and simmer for about 1 hour.

2 Strain the broth and allow to cool. Reserve the potatoes and ham; remove the meat from the bone and chop. Discard the bone and other vegetables.

3 Skim any fat from the surface of the cooled broth, then pour the broth back into the pan.

4 Drain the white beans and add to the broth. Bring to a boil, and simmer for 1-2 hours, or until the beans are very tender.

5 Add the potatoes to the beans. Lightly crush the beans and potatoes with a potato masher, until the soup is thick. Add the chopped ham to the soup, and check the seasoning.

6 Add half to three-quarters of the Champagne and stir the soup over a medium heat. Serve hot, garnished with parsley. Add a splash of Champagne to each soup bowl as it is served. This causes an immediate "fizzle" that will surprise your guests.

American Connection

After completing courses at Le Cordon Bleu in Paris, an American couple, Jimmy and Gwen Bently, returned to the United States and created this entertaining version of an American favourite: butter bean soup.

Soupe a l'Oignon

French Onion Soup

INGREDIENTS

Serves 4-6
500 g (1 lb) onions, thinly sliced
7 garlic cloves, chopped
75 g (2½ oz) butter
50 g (1¾ oz) smoked bacon
1·5 litres (2½ pints) beef or chicken stock
200 ml (7 fl oz) dry white wine
a bouquet garni

For the garnish
1 small baguette
100 g (3½ oz) Gruyère cheese, grated

For the finish
100 ml (3½ fl oz) port
100 ml (3½ fl oz) double cream
2 egg yolks

PREPARATION

1 In a large pan, gently sweat the onions and garlic in the butter for about 20 minutes, until tender.

2 Add the bacon, stock, wine, and bouquet garni. Simmer, covered, for 30 minutes. Remove bacon.

3 Purée the soup in a blender or food processor.

4 Slice the baguette and sprinkle grated Gruyère cheese on top of each slice.

5 Ladle the soup into heatproof bowls, float a cheese-topped *croûte* on top of each serving, and put under a hot grill until the cheese has melted and is golden brown.

6 Mix the port, cream, and egg yolks in a bowl. At the last minute before serving, lift each croûte up with a fork and pour some of the port mixture into each bowl. Serve immediately.

Veritable Bouillabaisse

Mediterranean Fish Soup

Purists claim it is not possible to make a real bouillabaisse without the distinctive texture and flavour of rascasse *(red fish), found only in the Mediterranean, but any oily white fish can be used. The soup is best enjoyed by serving fish and broth separately.*

INGREDIENTS

Serves 8
2 kg (4 lb) red fish
1 kg (2 lb) hog fish
1 kg (2 lb) conger eel
750 g (1 1/2 lb) monkfish
1 weever
1 wrasse
1 John Dory
a little olive oil
a few threads of saffron
a few basil leaves
freshly ground pepper
2 litres (3 1/2 pints) fish stock
finely chopped parsley, for the garnish
cheese-topped croûtes, *to serve*

For the marinade
1 leek
1 celery stalk
1 fennel bulb
1 onion, finely chopped
2 garlic cloves, crushed
200 g (7 oz) tomatoes, concassées (see page 136)
a bouquet garni
300 g (10 oz) potatoes, thinly sliced
250 ml (8 fl oz) dry white wine
2 1/2 tbsp Pernod

For the rouille
1 small red pepper
1 baked potato
1 egg yolk
1 tbsp tomato purée
200 ml (7 fl oz) olive oil
salt and freshly ground pepper

PREPARATION

1 Fillet the fish (see page 139), except the eel, reserving the heads and bones. Remove and discard the eyes and gills. Cut the fish fillets and the eel into large chunks. The skin can be removed, if you like.

2 Make the marinade: cut the leek, celery, and fennel into *julienne* strips. Mix with the remaining marinade ingredients. Add the fish fillet and eel chunks. Cover and leave overnight.

3 Make the rouille (see page 31).

4 Heat a little oil in a large pan and add the reserved fish heads and bones, the saffron, basil, and some pepper. Pour in the stock. Bring to a boil, lower the heat, and simmer for 20 minutes. Strain the fish bouillon and return it to the pan.

5 Add the fish and all the marinade ingredients. Bring to a boil, and simmer for 20 minutes.

6 Put the fish and eel, vegetable julienne, and potatoes into a tureen; keep warm. Sieve the bouillon into a clean pan and reheat.

7 Whisk half of the rouille into the bouillon to thicken it. Pour the thickened bouillon into the tureen on top of the fish and vegetables. Sprinkle with parsley, and serve with croûtes and the remaining rouille.

Coastal Treat

As its name suggests, bouillabaisse is a soup rapidly cooked to reduce, or thicken, its stock. This recipe is based on the same combination of fish and shellfish, vegetables, and herbs that has been used for centuries by fishermen along the Mediterranean coast. In the past, catch not suitable for the market soon found its way into cauldrons hung over wood fires on the beach, where the fresh essence of the sea blended with the tastes of red pepper, tomato, garlic, olive oil, fennel, Pernod, and saffron.

Making Rouille

Rouille is a thick sauce from Provence in the south of France; its name means rust, which denotes its colour. It serves as a thickener in soups as well as being delicious spread on croûtes or slices of French bread. Here, rouille is made in a food processor or blender, but it can be made by hand with a mortar and pestle.

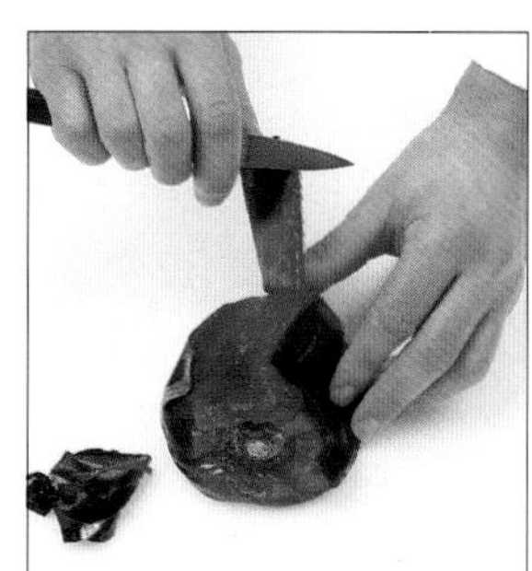

1 *Roast the pepper under a hot grill until it blackens slightly. Peel, halve, and remove the seeds.*

2 *Scoop out the potato flesh. Purée the pepper, potato, egg yolk, and tomato purée until smooth.*

3 *With the machine running, gradually add the oil. Season the rouille and set aside.*

Creme de Brocoli aux Huitres

Cream of Broccoli Soup with Oysters

INGREDIENTS

Serves 6

6 large fresh oysters, in their shells
150 g (5 oz) butter
2 shallots, finely chopped
125 g (4 oz) leeks, thinly sliced
150 g (5 oz) potatoes, thinly sliced
500 g (1 lb) broccoli, cut into florets
600 ml (1 pint) chicken stock
500 ml (16 fl oz) fish stock
200 ml (7 fl oz) double cream, more for the garnish
salt and freshly ground pepper

For the garnish

a few small broccoli florets, lightly cooked
a few sprigs of chervil

PREPARATION

1 Shuck the oysters (see page 137), retaining all the liquor from the shells. Put the oysters and liquor in a saucepan and poach gently just until the edges start to curl. Remove the oysters with a slotted spoon and set aside. Strain the oyster cooking liquid through a sieve and reserve.

2 Melt 50 g (1¾ oz) of the butter in a pan and sweat the shallots and leeks gently until softened. Add the potatoes and broccoli. Pour in the chicken and fish stocks. Bring to a boil, cover, and simmer for 15-20 minutes, until the vegetables are tender.

3 Purée the soup until smooth in a blender or food processor. Press it through a sieve and return it to the pan. Reheat, and add the cream and the reserved oyster liquid. Whisk in the remaining butter, cut into small pieces. Check the seasoning.

4 Ladle into warmed soup cups and garnish with the poached oysters, broccoli florets, and chervil sprigs. At the last moment, drizzle a thin ribbon of cream around the garnish. Serve immediately.

"Oysters are more beautiful than any religion ... there's nothing in Christianity or Buddhism that quite matches the sympathetic unselfishness of an oyster."

Saki (1870-1916)
The Match-Maker

Bourride de Lotte a la Setoise

Fish Stew Sete Style

INGREDIENTS

Serves 8

2 kg (4 lb) monkfish tails
200 ml (7 fl oz) clarified butter
3 tbsp olive oil
1 large whiting, cleaned and cut into pieces
200 g (7 oz) mirepoix of vegetables (see page 133)
a bouquet garni
3 garlic cloves, crushed
200 ml (7 fl oz) dry white wine
croûtons, *for the garnish (optional)*

For the aïoli sauce

1 baked potato
2-3 garlic cloves, crushed
2 egg yolks
150 ml (5 fl oz) olive oil
salt and cayenne pepper

PREPARATION

1 First make the aïoli sauce: scoop the flesh out of the baked potato and put it in a food processor with the garlic and egg yolks. Blend until smooth. With the machine running, gradually add the oil, a few drops at a time at first and then in a steady stream. Season the sauce and set aside.

2 Fillet the monkfish and reserve the bones. Trim the fillets and cut into chunks. Cook the chunks in hot clarified butter just until they are sealed. Drain off the excess butter and discard; set the chunks of monkfish aside.

3 Heat the oil in a saucepan and lightly brown the pieces of whiting, the mirepoix, and the monkfish bones. Add the bouquet garni, garlic, and wine. Pour in enough water to cover the ingredients. Bring to a boil, and simmer for 15-20 minutes. Strain the broth and return it to the pan. Discard the whiting, mirepoix, and bones left in the sieve.

4 Add the chunks of monkfish to the broth and simmer gently for 12 minutes. Remove the chunks with a slotted spoon. Strain the broth and return it to the pan.

5 Mix the aïoli sauce into the broth and heat gently, stirring, until thickened.

6 Return the chunks of monkfish to the soup and serve immediately, with croûtons, if you like.

Minestrone de Coques et Saint-Jacques

Cockle and Scallop Minestrone

INGREDIENTS

Serves 8
2 kg (4 lb) fresh cockles
1 kg (2 lb) fresh mussels
300 ml (1/2 pint) dry white wine
2 courgettes
2 red peppers, cored, halved, and seeded
100 g (3 1/2 oz) green beans
1 kg (2 lb) scallops, white meat only
3 large onions, finely chopped
1 fennel bulb, finely chopped
a bouquet garni
500 ml (16 fl oz) fish stock
4 tomatoes, concassées (see page 136)
1-2 tbsp olive oil
50 g (1 3/4 oz) macaroni, broken into 6 mm (1/4 inch) pieces
salt and freshly ground pepper
saffron threads, for the garnish

For the pistou
2 garlic cloves
1 bunch of basil
100 g (3 1/2 oz) butter

PREPARATION

1 Scrub the cockles and mussels under cold running water with a small stiff brush. Remove any barnacles, weeds, or "beards". Discard any cockles or mussels that do not close when tapped.
2 Steam the cockles and mussels open in the wine. Remove them from their shells, keeping all the cooking liquid.
3 Cut the courgettes, peppers, and beans into a fine dice (see page 133). Cut the scallops into thin slices or into dice.
4 Put the onions, fennel, bouquet garni, and stock in a saucepan. Strain in the cooking liquid from the cockles and mussels. Bring to a boil, and simmer for 5-10 minutes.
5 Meanwhile, make the pistou: put the garlic, basil, and butter in a blender or a food processor and purée until smooth.
6 Strain the fish broth and return it to the pan. Add the diced vegetables and simmer just until tender.
7 In a separate pan, cook the tomatoes in the olive oil until soft.
8 Add the macaroni to the fish broth and simmer until it is *al dente*.
9 Add the tomatoes to the broth, together with the cockles, mussels, and pistou. Stir well and season.
10 Put the scallops in a soup tureen or divide among soup bowls. Pour in the hot soup. Garnish with saffron and serve.

Terrine de Langoustines aux Legumes Safranes

Langoustine and Vegetable Terrine with Saffron

Lining and Layering Ingredients in a Mould

Blanched leek greens are ideal for lining a terrine mould because they keep the terrine ingredients together. Layering the ingredients produces a decorative effect and enables the ingredients to be easily identified.

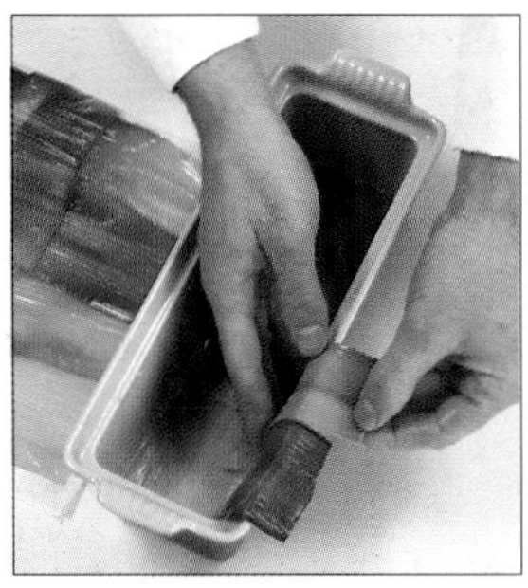

1 Line the mould with most of the blanched leek greens, overlapping them slightly.

2 Layer all the ingredients, both starting and finishing with the julienne of vegetables.

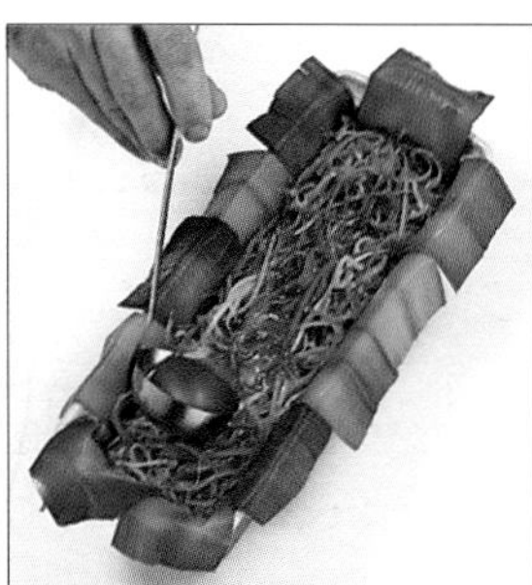

3 Slowly ladle the saffron jelly into the mould. Cover with the remaining leek greens.

INGREDIENTS

Serves 8
2 kg (4 lb) large raw langoustines
3 tbsp olive oil
150 g (5 oz) mirepoix of vegetables (see page 133)
a few saffron threads
a bouquet garni
100 ml (3 1/2 fl oz) dry white wine
4 leaves of gelatine, soaked in cold water
350 g (12 oz) mixed vegetable julienne *strips, such as carrot, leek, celery, and fennel*
a pinch of salt
2 bunches of baby leeks
10 large pieces of leek greens, to line the mould
1 tbsp hazelnut oil
radish vinaigrette (see below), to serve
a few sprigs of chervil, for the garnish

PREPARATION

1 Peel and devein the langoustines (see page 137), and put them in a saucepan with some of the claws; set aside. Reserve the remaining langoustine claws, the shells, and the heads.
2 Heat half of the olive oil in another saucepan and add the mirepoix. Cover and cook over a low heat, until the vegetables are soft. Add the reserved langoustine claws with the shells and heads, some of the saffron threads, and the bouquet garni. Moisten with the wine and bring to a boil. Pour in enough water to cover the ingredients. Bring back to a boil, and simmer for 10 minutes.
3 Strain the bouillon over the peeled langoustines. Bring to a boil and immediately remove the langoustines and claws. Leave to drain and cool.
4 Add a few more saffron threads to the bouillon and boil until reduced by two-thirds. Remove from the heat. Drain the gelatine and add it to the bouillon. Stir until the gelatine has melted. Strain this saffron jelly and set aside.
5 Cook the vegetable julienne in the remaining olive oil just until tender but still crisp. Season with salt, and set aside to cool.
6 Cook the baby leeks in a little salted water until tender. Drain well, season, and set aside to cool.
7 Blanch the leek greens just until tender; drain.
8 Use the hazelnut oil to grease a terrine mould measuring 22 x 9 x 5 cm (8 1/2 x 3 3/4 x 2 inches). Line and layer the ingredients in the mould (see page 34), keeping the langoustine claws for the garnish. Chill the terrine for at least 3 hours, or until set. (If you like, cover the terrine mixture with a small piece of wood covered with foil; this will compress the terrine, making it easier to slice.)
9 When ready to serve, dip the base of the mould into hot water, then turn out the terrine. Cut the terrine into slices about 2 cm (3/4 inch) thick, and arrange the slices on individual plates. Spoon a little radish vinaigrette on each plate, and garnish with the langoustine claws and chervil.

SAFFRON

In this recipe, the pungent, slightly bitter taste of saffron provides the culinary link between the sea taste of langoustines and the more subtle flavours of vegetables. Saffron is highly prized as an ingredient in much of Europe and Asia. It is obtained by manually removing the dried stigmas from flowers of a specific crocus bulb. Between 3,500 and 4,000 stigmas are required to produce 30 g (1 oz) of saffron.

RADISH VINAIGRETTE

Used like a relish, the colours of this radish vinaigrette complement any dish – as does the subtle tang of its flavours.

♦

♦ 1 hard-boiled egg ♦ 2 tbsp cider vinegar ♦ 2 tsp balsamic vinegar ♦ salt and freshly ground pepper ♦ 4 tbsp vegetable oil ♦ 2 tomatoes, concassées (see page 136) ♦ 1 bunch of chives, snipped ♦ 6 radishes, sliced

Cut the hard-boiled egg in half and remove the yolk – use the yolk for another purpose. Finely chop the egg white. Mix the two vinegars together in a bowl, and season with salt and plenty of freshly ground pepper. Gradually add the oil, at first whisking in a few drops at a time, then pouring in a thin, steady stream. Add the chopped egg white, the tomatoes, chives, and radishes. Stir gently to mix. Leave for 30 minutes, to allow the flavours to develop.

Petits Gateaux de Foies Blonds

Chicken Liver Creams

INGREDIENTS

Serves 8

60 g (2 oz) butter
250 g (8 oz) chicken livers, soaked in
500 ml (16 fl oz) milk
60 g (2 oz) cooked goose or duck foie gras *(optional)*
1/2 garlic clove, finely chopped
2 eggs
2 egg yolks
150 ml (5 fl oz) milk
150 ml (5 fl oz) double cream
salt and freshly ground pepper
a pinch of freshly grated nutmeg

For the Madeira sauce

90 g (3 oz) butter
50 g (1 3/4 oz) mirepoix of vegetables (see page 133)
50 g (1 3/4 oz) mushrooms, chopped
1 bay leaf
100 ml (3 1/2 fl oz) sherry vinegar
10 g (1/3 oz) peppercorns, crushed
150 ml (5 fl oz) Madeira
350 ml (12 fl oz) veal stock
350 ml (12 fl oz) chicken stock
4 tbsp single cream (optional)

For the garnish

8 baby sweetcorn, cooked
2 tomatoes, peeled and diced
a few sprigs of chervil

PREPARATION

1 Butter 8 *dariole* moulds. Chill, then butter the moulds again.

2 Drain the milk from the chicken livers and discard. Quickly fry the livers in a little melted butter just to seal them on all sides. Allow to cool.

3 Put the chicken livers in a food processor and add the foie gras (if using), garlic, eggs, egg yolks, milk, and cream. Work until smooth. Season well with salt and pepper, and the nutmeg.

4 Divide the chicken liver mixture among the buttered moulds. Cover each mould tightly with foil. Cook in a *bain marie* in a preheated oven at 180°C (350°F, Gas 4) for about 15 minutes, or just until set.

5 Meanwhile, make the Madeira sauce. Melt 30 g (1 oz) of the butter in a saucepan and add the mirepoix and mushrooms. Cook until soft.

6 Add the bay leaf, vinegar, and crushed peppercorns. Bring to a boil, and boil until almost completely reduced. Pour in one-third of the Madeira and reduce by half. Add the stocks and simmer until syrupy. Sieve the mixture and return to the pan. Add the remaining Madeira and the cream, if using. Check the seasoning. Whisk in the remaining butter, cut into pieces.

7 Turn out the chicken liver creams. Spoon the sauce around or over them. Garnish with the sweetcorn, tomato dice, and chervil.

Terrine de Foie Gras et sa Gelee au Porto

Duck Liver Terrine with Port Aspic

INGREDIENTS

Serves 6

1 fresh duck liver (foie gras), *weighing*
about 300 g (10 oz)
100 ml (3 1/2 fl oz) port
3 1/2 tbsp Cognac
salt and freshly ground pepper

For the port aspic

1 carrot, chopped
1/4 onion, chopped
1 tomato, chopped
a few parsley stalks
2 egg whites
400 ml (14 fl oz) veal stock
7 leaves of gelatine, soaked in cold water
100 ml (3 1/2 fl oz) port

PREPARATION

1 Remove and discard any green sections from the liver. Soak the liver in a bowl of iced water for 2-3 hours; this will remove any excess blood.

2 Drain the liver and pat dry with paper towels. Remove the thin membrane around the liver. Separate the lobes into two. Gently open the liver by slitting it lengthwise with a sharp knife, and remove the blood vessels without tearing the flesh.

3 Put the liver in a bowl and add the port and Cognac. Season with 1 1/2 tsp salt and 1 tsp pepper. Cover and marinate for about 6 hours.

4 Drain the liver and transfer it to a terrine mould into which it will just fit comfortably. Cook in a *bain marie* in a preheated oven at 110°C (225°F, Gas 1/4) for about 40 minutes.

5 Meanwhile, prepare the port aspic. Mix the chopped vegetables, herbs, egg whites, and seasoning. Add this clarification mixture to the stock in a large pan and mix well. Bring the mixture slowly to a boil, stirring constantly. When the egg whites start to solidify into a soft crust on top of the stock, stop stirring. Leave over a low heat for 20-25 minutes, then carefully strain through a muslin-lined sieve into a bowl. Do not press the solids left in the sieve or the impurities will go through into the stock. Drain the gelatine and add it to the stock with the port. Stir until the gelatine has melted. Set aside at a cool room temperature so that it remains liquid.

6 Pour off the duck fat from the mould and leave the liver to cool to room temperature. When cool, pour enough liquid aspic into the mould to just cover the liver. Chill overnight to set. Chill the remaining aspic in a bowl.

7 To serve, turn out the liver in aspic and cut it into slices. Present the slices on a large platter, garnished with the remaining aspic, cut into dice.

Terrine de Lapin aux Noisettes

Rabbit Terrine with Hazelnuts

INGREDIENTS

Serves 8

1 rabbit, weighing about 1·25 kg (2½ lb)
30 g (1 oz) butter
60 g (2 oz) parsley, finely chopped
3 shallots, chopped
300 g (10 oz) neck of pork, boned
50 g (1¾ oz) veal
100 g (3½ oz) liver mousse (mousse de foie)
salt and freshly ground pepper
1 egg, lightly beaten
100 ml (3½ fl oz) double cream
30 g (1 oz) hazelnuts, toasted (see page 148), and each nut cut into 4 or 6 pieces
200 g (7 oz) streaky bacon rashers
a few thyme sprigs and a bay leaf (optional)

For the stock

30 g (1 oz) butter
300 g (10 oz) mirepoix of vegetables (see page 133)
a bouquet garni
a few black peppercorns

PREPARATION

1 Bone the rabbit (see page 141). Reserve the rabbit bones and put all the rabbit meat aside.

2 Make the stock: melt the butter in a saucepan, add the rabbit bones, mirepoix, bouquet garni, and peppercorns, and sauté until lightly browned. Add enough water to cover. Bring to a boil, and simmer for 1 hour. Strain the stock, return to the pan, and skim off any scum as it rises to the surface. Boil to reduce to a glaze. Set aside.

3 Fry 2 strips of rabbit flesh in the butter to seal them. Allow to cool, then roll them in the chopped parsley to coat. Chill.

4 Sweat the shallots in the same pan and let cool. Pass the remaining rabbit meat through a mincer with the pork, veal, and liver mousse. Season and mix with the shallots, egg, cream, hazelnuts, and rabbit glaze.

5 Use the bacon rashers to line a terrine mould measuring 25 x 8 x 8 cm (10 x 3 x 3 inches), leaving the ends of the rashers hanging over the sides of the mould.

6 Spread half of the rabbit and hazelnut mixture in the mould. Lay the parsley-coated rabbit strips down the middle and cover with the remaining rabbit and hazelnut mixture. Fold the ends of the bacon rashers over the surface. Place the thyme and a bay leaf on top, if you like.

7 Cover the mould tightly with greaseproof paper and foil. Cook in a *bain marie* in a preheated oven at 180°C (350°F, Gas 4) for 1-1¼ hours. (If you like, cover the terrine mixture, while it is cooking, with a small piece of wood covered with foil; this will compress the terrine, making it easier to slice.)

8 Unmould the terrine: dip a small knife into hot water and slide it around the edges of the terrine to loosen. Invert a plate on top of the terrine and quickly reverse the two.

9 Cut the terrine into slices. Serve the terrine either warm or chilled, with toast, if you like.

SALADE DE VOLAILLE AUX SESAMES

CHICKEN SALAD WITH SESAME SEEDS

Le Cordon Bleu chefs have created a true East-meets-West dish in this beautiful salad – a Western concept – with deep flavour tones from the oriental combination of garlic, sesame, and ginger.

INGREDIENTS

Serves 6

1 chicken or guinea fowl, weighing 1·5 kg (3 lb)
3½ tbsp sesame oil
2 tbsp cider vinegar
4 tsp soy sauce
50 g (1¾ oz) root ginger, peeled and chopped
4 garlic cloves, crushed
50 g (1¾ oz) flour
salt and freshly ground pepper
1 egg, lightly beaten
50 g (1¾ oz) sesame seeds
vegetable oil, for deep frying

For the sauce

2 garlic cloves, roughly chopped
30 g (1 oz) root ginger, peeled and chopped
3½ tbsp soy sauce
2 tbsp sesame oil
a pinch of sugar

For the garnish

2 carrots, cut into small sticks
1 tbsp honey
1 lettuce
2 tbsp sesame seeds, toasted
fresh coriander
root ginger julienne, *deep-fried*

PREPARATION

1 Remove all the meat from the bird, discarding the skin. Set the breast meat aside. Cut all the remaining meat into large dice.

2 Mix together the sesame oil, vinegar, soy sauce, ginger, and garlic in a bowl. Add the diced meat and stir to mix well. Cover and marinate while preparing the remaining ingredients.

3 Put all the sauce ingredients in a blender and blend until smooth. Set aside.

4 For the garnish, put the carrots in a saucepan with enough water to cover, and add the honey. Bring to a boil, and simmer, until the water has evaporated and the carrots are just tender and lightly caramelized. Allow to cool.

5 Make goujonettes with the breast meat, seasoned flour, beaten egg, and sesame seeds (see page 39).

6 Remove the diced meat from the marinade. Spoon the oil from the top of the marinade and heat it in a frying pan. Briskly sauté the diced meat in the hot oil until cooked and golden brown. Drain and set aside.

7 Toss the lettuce with a little sauce and place in the centre of individual plates. Top with the sautéed meat, sauce, goujonettes, and carrots. Sprinkle with the toasted sesame seeds, and garnish with coriander and deep-fried ginger.

SESAME SEEDS

Sesame, an aromatic herb from the East Indies, is grown in hot climates to produce highly prized seeds. There are three varieties – white, brown, and black. The seed, although small, is quite rich, containing 50 per cent oil, which is extracted for culinary use. With a versatile nutty flavour, sesame is popular in many dishes, both sweet and savoury.

Making Goujonettes

Goujonettes are thin strips of poultry, meat, or fish that are usually coated in flour, egg, and breadcrumbs. They are an ideal garnish for salads, but they can also be served as an hors d'oeuvre. Here, they are given extra crunch by being coated in sesame seeds rather than breadcrumbs.

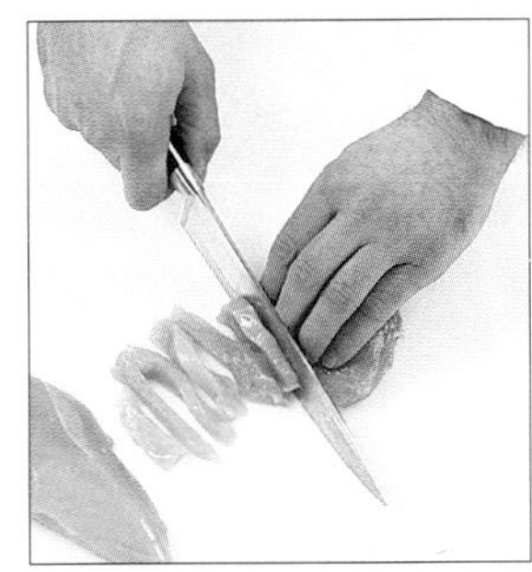

1 Cut chicken breasts into strips. Coat them in flour seasoned with salt and pepper.

2 Dip the chicken strips into beaten egg, then roll in sesame seeds to coat thoroughly.

3 Deep-fry in hot oil until golden brown. Remove with a slotted spoon and drain on paper towels.

SALADE D'ARTICHAUTS ET DE RIS DE VEAU

ARTICHOKE AND SWEETBREAD SALAD

INGREDIENTS

Serves 6

2 veal sweetbreads, each weighing about 750 g (1 1/2 lb)
salt and freshly ground pepper
6 globe artichokes
1 lemon, halved
1 litre (1 2/3 pints) water
30 g (1 oz) flour
15 g (1/2 oz) clarified butter
200 g (7 oz) lamb's lettuce
1 tomato, diced
a few vegetables, such as carrot, turnip, and courgette, cut into sticks and cooked

For the mustard vinaigrette

2 tbsp whole-grain mustard
2 tbsp white wine vinegar
90 ml (3 fl oz) soya oil
finely chopped herbs

PREPARATION

1 Place the sweetbreads in iced water and leave to *dégorge* for at least 2 hours. Drain, and blanch in lightly salted water. Drain the sweetbreads again, and allow to cool. When cold, remove the skins with the point of a sharp knife. Press the sweetbreads under a plate, put a weight on top, and refrigerate for 2-3 hours.
2 Turn the artichokes (see page 134). Rub them with lemon to prevent discolouring.
3 Cook the turned artichokes in a classic *blanc*: whisk together the water and flour, add the artichokes, and bring to a boil. Cook for 25-30 minutes, or until the artichokes are tender. Do not overcook; they should still be crunchy. Drain well. Allow to cool, then remove the chokes. Set aside.
4 Mix together the ingredients for the vinaigrette, except the herbs. Season with pepper.
5 Slice the sweetbreads and pound them out into thin escalopes. Fry them in the clarified butter in a non-stick frying pan until they are nicely coloured on both sides. Season with salt and pepper. Cut the sweetbreads into dice.
6 Cut 6 small rounds from the artichoke hearts, then cut the remainder into short, thin strips.
7 Assemble the salad ingredients in the centre of individual plates by layering the artichoke strips and sweetbread dice, dressing with vinaigrette as you go. Arrange the lamb's lettuce, tomato dice, and vegetable sticks around. Top each of the salads with an artichoke round.
8 Mix the remaining vinaigrette with the herbs and sprinkle over the salads. Serve immediately, while the sweetbreads are still slightly warm.

LE CEVICHE

LIME-MARINATED FISH WITH PEPPERS AND CHILLI

INGREDIENTS

Serves 6

1·25 kg (2 1/2 lb) very fresh white fish, such as sea bass or halibut, filleted (see page 139)
salt and freshly ground pepper
200 ml (7 fl oz) lime juice
200 ml (7 fl oz) olive oil
1 bunch of coriander, chopped
2 garlic cloves, finely chopped
1/2 red and 1/2 green pepper, cored, seeded, and finely diced
1 small fresh green chilli, seeded and finely diced
1 large white onion, thinly sliced and separated into rings
625 g (1 1/4 lb) new potatoes

PREPARATION

1 Cut the fish into slices. Put the slices in a shallow dish. Season the fish and add the lime juice, olive oil, coriander, garlic, peppers, chilli, and onion. Cover the dish and leave the fish to marinate in a cool place for at least 1 hour.
2 Meanwhile, cook the potatoes, in their skins, in boiling salted water just until tender. Drain. When cool enough to handle, peel the potatoes and cut them into slices.
3 Serve the marinated fish with the potato slices.

CORDON BLEU WORLDWIDE

Le Cordon Bleu's team of master chefs teach classical French cuisine around the globe, and its students come from more than 50 countries. Le Ceviche, a light fish dish that originated in Peru, marries well with the basic French techniques of chopping fresh herbs, dicing vegetables, and filleting fish. The fish is not conventially cooked: it is the lime juice in the marinating liquid that does the "cooking".

Salade de Chevre Chaud Marine

Warm Salad of Grilled Marinated Goat's Cheese

INGREDIENTS

Serves 8

8 small firm-textured goat's cheeses, such as chèvre du Larzac

2 litres (3½ pints) walnut oil

1 bunch of rosemary

1 bunch of basil

a few sprigs of thyme

a few bay leaves

salt and freshly ground pepper

2 frisée lettuces

2 heads of radicchio

1 bunch each of chervil, tarragon, and chives

croûtes (see page 88), cut into semicircles, for the garnish

For the vinaigrette

2 tbsp whole-grain mustard

2 tbsp Dijon mustard

1 shallot, finely chopped

1 garlic clove, finely chopped

4 tbsp red wine vinegar

PREPARATION

1 Put the cheeses in a large non-metallic jar or bowl. Add the oil, rosemary, basil, thyme, and bay leaves. Add salt and pepper to taste. Cover and leave to marinate in a cool place for several days.

2 Drain the cheeses, reserving the flavoured oil. Arrange them on a baking tray.

3 Prepare the vinaigrette: mix the mustards with the shallot, garlic, wine vinegar, and seasoning. Add 200 ml (7 fl oz) of the walnut oil used to marinate the cheeses, and mix well.

4 Wash the salad leaves, and dry well. Arrange a mixture of salad leaves on individual plates.

5 Cook the cheeses under a hot grill for several minutes, or until golden on top.

6 Set a cheese in the centre of each bed of salad leaves. Sprinkle with the vinaigrette and garnish with the chervil, tarragon, and chives. Serve warm, with the croûtes.

Oeufs en Gelee

Eggs in Aspic

This classic French recipe has remained popular to this day. The eggs can be decorated with a variety of ingredients, but traditionally they are topped with truffles. Here, the dish looks stylish and modern with its simple but effective decoration of different coloured peppers.

INGREDIENTS

Serves 8
30 g (1 oz) celery, chopped
30 g (1 oz) carrot, chopped
1 leek, chopped
10 g (1/3 oz) parsley, chopped
a few sprigs of tarragon, chopped
10 g (1/3 oz) peppercorns, crushed
4 egg whites
1·5 litres (2 1/3 pints) strong chicken or beef stock
10 leaves of gelatine, soaked in cold water
100 ml (3 1/2 fl oz) port
salt and freshly ground pepper
8 eggs
1 red, 1 yellow, and 1 green pepper, cut into diamonds
2 slices of ham, cut into strips
lamb's lettuce salad (see page 43), to serve

"Yet, who can help loving the land that has taught us six hundred and eighty-five ways to dress eggs?"

Thomas Moore (1779-1852)
The Fudge Family in Paris (1818)

PREPARATION

1 Mix together the celery, carrot, leek, herbs, peppercorns, and egg whites. Combine this clarification mixture with the stock in a pan and slowly bring to a boil, stirring constantly. When the egg whites start to solidify into a soft crust, stop stirring. Simmer over a low heat for 20-25 minutes. Strain through a muslin-lined sieve. Do not press the solids in the sieve or the impurities will go into the clarified stock.
2 Drain the gelatine and add to the stock. Stir until melted. Add the port and seasoning. Leave to cool slightly until cold but not set.
3 Meanwhile, poach the eggs (see page 146). Refresh the eggs in a bowl of iced water. Drain thoroughly on paper towels. Trim off the ragged edges with a sharp knife.
4 Decorate 8 individual moulds with the liquid aspic, peppers, and ham (see below).
5 Put an egg into the centre of each decorated mould and fill with liquid aspic. Chill the filled moulds in the refrigerator until set to a jelly.
6 To turn out, first dip each mould into hot water. Serve on a bed of lamb's lettuce salad.

Decorating Moulds

Presenting eggs or meat in aspic jelly that has been decorated looks both attractive and professional. Aspic is traditionally decorated with truffles, but ham, herbs, tomato, and peppers may also be used. Here, a simple yet effective design has been created with a mixture of different coloured peppers and ham.

1 Ladle some cold liquid aspic into the mould so that it coats the base. Chill until set to a jelly.

2 Place the pepper diamonds around the base and the ham around the sides. Chill until set.

Lamb's Lettuce Salad

Lamb's lettuce, which is also known as mâche, *makes a delicious salad. Its small leaves produce a delicate decorative effect on any plate or platter.*

- *250 g (8 oz) lamb's lettuce*
- *1 bunch of rocket*
- *1 bunch of chives*

For the vinaigrette

- *4 tbsp red wine vinegar*
- *salt and freshly ground pepper*
- *a pinch of sugar*
- *2 tsp Dijon mustard (optional)*
- *180 ml (6 fl oz) olive oil*

Prepare the salad greens: wash and dry the leaves, removing any stalks or discoloured leaves. Cut the chives into 1·25-cm (1/2-inch) lengths. If they have any flowers, reserve them for the garnish. Prepare the vinaigrette: in a small bowl, whisk the vinegar, salt and pepper, and sugar. Add the mustard (if using), and mix well. Gradually whisk in the oil, a few drops at a time initially, then in a thin, steady stream. The vinaigrette should emulsify and thicken slightly. Taste for seasoning. Mix the salad greens, chives, and vinaigrette in a large bowl. Garnish with chive flowers, if reserved.

Oeufs Frits Pastourelle

Deep-Fried Eggs with Kidneys and Mushrooms

INGREDIENTS

Serves 6

1 whole calf's kidney
300 g (10 oz) streaky bacon rashers
150 g (5 oz) horns of plenty
(wild black mushrooms), cleaned
50 g (1 3/4 oz) shallots, finely chopped
125 g (4 oz) butter
salt and freshly ground pepper
150 ml (5 fl oz) double cream
6 eggs
vegetable oil, for deep frying
100 g (3 1/2 oz) flat-leaf parsley sprigs

PREPARATION

1 Trim the kidney, keeping it whole and leaving about 1 cm (3/8 inch) of fat around it. Roast the kidney in a preheated oven at 180°C (350°F, Gas 4) for about 1 hour. Keep the kidney warm.

2 Blanch the bacon in boiling water for 1-2 minutes, drain, and pat dry. Cook under a hot grill until golden brown on both sides. Keep warm.

3 Sauté the wild mushrooms and shallots in the butter until the mushrooms have given up their liquid and the shallots are tender. Season and add the cream. Boil the mixture until most of the liquid has evaporated.

4 Deep-fry the eggs in oil (see page 146). Remove and drain briefly on paper towels.

5 Deep-fry the parsley sprigs until crisp and deep green. Remove and drain on paper towels.

6 Arrange the bacon rashers in the centre of individual plates and pile the creamed mushrooms on top. Cut the kidney into at least 12 slices. Put 2 slices of kidney and 1 fried egg on top of each serving. Garnish with the deep-fried parsley sprigs and serve immediately.

Wild Mushrooms

Cultivated wild mushrooms have an intensely concentrated flavour that is very earthy. They should not be washed, but brushed and wiped with a damp cloth. If fresh wild mushrooms are not available, they can be bought dried and reconstituted in warm water.

Omelette Indo-Chine

Omelette with Pork and Prawns

INGREDIENTS

Serves 4–8
3 tbsp vegetable oil
250 g (8 oz) lean boneless pork, cut into 1·25-cm (1/2-inch) cubes
150 g (5 oz) onion, chopped
1/4 tsp cayenne pepper
5 tbsp chicken stock
24 mussels
125 g (4 oz) mushrooms, sliced
125 g (4 oz) peeled cooked prawns, chopped
2 tsp chopped fresh mint
8 fresh basil leaves, chopped
salt and freshly ground pepper
8 eggs, lightly beaten
soy sauce, to serve

PREPARATION

1 Heat 1 tbsp of the oil in a frying pan and fry the pork with the onion and cayenne pepper until browned. Add the stock, cover, and simmer gently for about 20 minutes.

2 Meanwhile, prepare the mussels: scrape with a small knife to remove barnacles, weeds, or "beards". Scrub the mussels under cold running water. Discard any that do not close when tapped. Steam open the mussels in a little water. Remove them from their shells and set aside. Strain and reserve the cooking liquid.

3 Add the mushrooms, prawns, mint, and basil to the pork and onions and stir well. Season. Cook for a further 5 minutes.

4 Add the mussels and their reserved cooking liquid and cook for 3 minutes, stirring constantly. Remove from the heat and keep warm.

5 Season the beaten eggs, and make 4 large, thin omelettes (see page 147), using the remaining oil instead of butter. Spoon some of the filling into each omelette and roll up with the seam underneath. Serve hot, with soy sauce.

Eastern Influence

This omelette is based on flavours from Vietnam, once a French colony called Indo-Chine, hence its name. This dish combines the Vietnamese ingredients of pork, prawns, and basil, in a classic French omelette.

Souffle Chaud au Fromage et Jambon

Hot Cheese Souffle with Ham

INGREDIENTS

Serves 6
60 g (2 oz) butter, more for soufflé dish
60 g (2 oz) flour, more for soufflé dish
350 ml (12 fl oz) milk
100 g (3 1/2 oz) Gruyère cheese, grated
75 g (2 1/2 oz) cooked ham, chopped
3 egg yolks
salt and freshly ground pepper
a pinch of freshly grated nutmeg
7 egg whites

For the garnish
2 slices cooked ham, cut into diamond shapes
2 slices Gruyère cheese, cut into diamond shapes

PREPARATION

1 Generously butter and flour a 2-litre (3 1/2-pint) soufflé dish.

2 Make a white *roux* with the butter and flour (see page 155). Add the milk and cook until thick, stirring constantly.

3 Remove from the heat and stir in the grated Gruyère, chopped ham, and the egg yolks. Season with salt, pepper, and nutmeg.

4 Whisk the egg whites until stiff peaks form. Carefully fold them into the mixture.

5 Spoon the mixture into the prepared soufflé dish. Bake in a preheated oven at 200°C (400°F, Gas 6), for about 40 minutes, or until golden brown.

6 Garnish the top of the soufflé with the diamond shapes of ham and Gruyère. Serve immediately.

Feuilletee d'Oeufs Poches

Poached Eggs in Pastry Triangles with Bordelaise Sauce

INGREDIENTS

Serves 6

350 g (12 oz) puff pastry (see page 154)
1 egg, lightly beaten, for the glaze
30 baby onions
salt and freshly ground pepper
125 g (4 oz) sugar
250 g (8 oz) butter
1 small celeriac, cut into parisienne (see page 135)
juice of 1 lemon
175 g (6 oz) button mushrooms, turned (see page 134)
160 g (5 1/2 oz) bacon rashers, cut into small pieces
6 eggs
bordelaise sauce (see page 47), to serve
tarragon leaves, for the garnish

PREPARATION

1 Preheat the oven to 220°C (425°F, Gas 7). Roll out the pastry on a floured surface until about 3 mm (1/8 inch) thick and use to make 6 puff pastry triangles (see below).

2 Cook the baby onions in salted water with half of the sugar and 60 g (2 oz) of the butter for 15 minutes, or until tender and glazed.

3 Cook the balls of celeriac in salted water with the remaining sugar, 60 g (2 oz) of the butter, and the lemon juice until tender and glazed.

4 Meanwhile, sauté the turned mushrooms in 60 g (2 oz) of the butter until golden brown.

5 Blanch the pieces of bacon in cold water, removing them when the water boils. Drain and pat dry on paper towels. Sauté in 30 g (1 oz) of the butter until golden brown.

6 Combine the onions, celeriac, mushrooms, and bacon, and stir in the remaining butter. Season and keep warm for the garnish.

7 Poach the eggs (see page 146).

8 Place the bottom halves of the pastry triangles on individual plates. Divide the garnish among them and add a poached egg to each. Cover with the decorative pastry lids.

9 Spoon some bordelaise sauce around the pastry triangles, garnish with tarragon, and serve.

Making Puff Pastry Triangles

Puff pastry is a buttery flaky pastry that rises into many layers when cooked. It can be cut into decorative shapes for an attractive presentation. These triangles can be used for both savoury and sweet dishes.

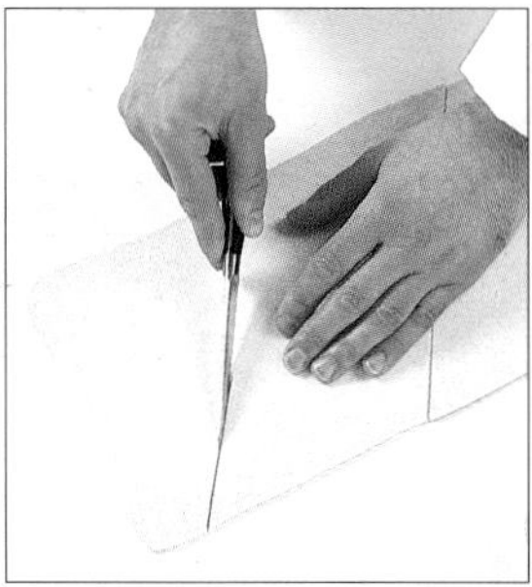

1 Cut out 6 even-sized triangles and place on a dampened baking tray. Brush with egg glaze.

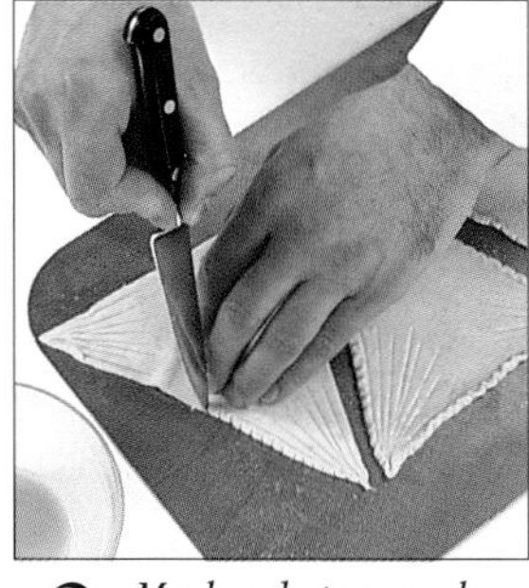

2 Mark a design on the top with the back of a knife. Scallop the sides. Bake in the oven for 20 minutes.

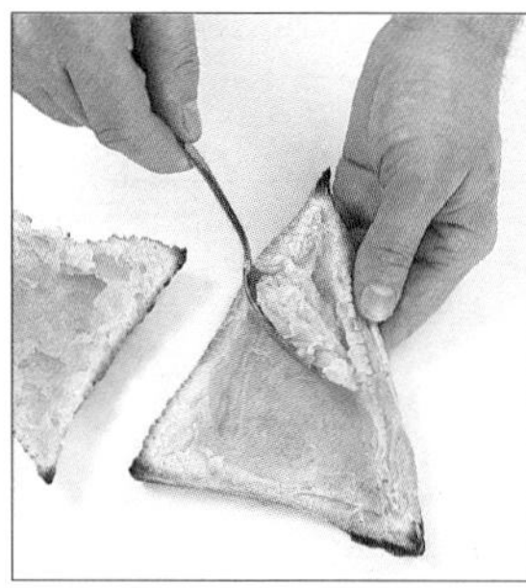

3 When baked, cut the triangles in half and remove any uncooked dough from the inside.

Bordelaise Sauce

This rich sauce is usually served with meat dishes, but Le Cordon Bleu chefs have found it to be particularly good when served with pastry. In the name of a recipe, "à la bordelaise" *denotes that it is served with a red Bordeaux wine, stock, and shallot sauce.*

♦

♦ 75 g (2 1/2 oz) shallots ♦ 60 g (2 oz) butter
♦ 500 ml (16 fl oz) red wine from Bordeaux
♦ 300 ml (1/2 pint) veal stock

Finely chop the shallots. Melt 30 g (1 oz) of the butter in a heavy-based pan, add the shallots, and sweat them until they are very soft. Pour the red wine into the pan and reduce over a medium heat until there is only one-third of the liquid left in the pan. Add the veal stock and continue to reduce until there is only half the amount of liquid left in the pan and the sauce has become syrupy. Remove the sauce from the heat and slowly whisk in the remaining butter, cut into small pieces.

Quiche au Roquefort

Roquefort, Celery, and Walnut Quiche

INGREDIENTS

Serves 6–8

175 g (6 oz) Roquefort cheese
75 ml (2 1/2 fl oz) milk
4 tsp port
2 eggs
2 egg yolks
200 ml (7 fl oz) crème fraîche
salt and freshly ground pepper
2 celery stalks, thickly sliced
20 walnut halves

For the pâte brisée

200 g (7 oz) flour
90 g (3 oz) butter
1 egg
1/4 tsp salt
1 tbsp water

PREPARATION

1 Make the pâte brisée, line a 23-cm (9-inch) flan tin, and bake the shell blind (see pages 152-53).
2 Put the Roquefort, milk, and port in a blender or food processor and blend until smooth. In a bowl, lightly whisk the eggs and yolks with the crème fraîche, add the Roquefort mixture, and season.
3 Blanch the celery in boiling salted water. Drain and pat dry with paper towels.
4 Arrange the walnut halves in the pastry shell and scatter over the blanched celery. Pour in the Roquefort mixture. Bake in a preheated oven at 180°C (350°F, Gas 4) for 20 minutes, or until the filling is just set and the pastry is golden brown.
5 Serve the quiche hot or cold.

Beignets d'Escargots aux Petales d'Aulx

Snail Fritters with Garlic

INGREDIENTS

Serves 4–6

750 g (1 1/2 lb) potatoes
vegetable oil, for deep-frying
60 g (2 oz) parsley sprigs
18 snails, such as escargots de Bourgogne
2 tbsp walnut oil
90 g (3 oz) butter
12 garlic cloves, cut into thin slices

For the fritter batter

3 eggs, lightly beaten
175 g (6 oz) flour
300 ml (1/2 pint) lager, warmed
salt and freshly ground pepper

PREPARATION

1 Make potato baskets: cut the potatoes into very thin slices. Using wire potato baskets or 2 ladles, line the inside of the larger one with overlapping potato slices. Place the smaller basket or ladle on top and deep-fry in hot vegetable oil, for about 4 minutes until golden. Remove and drain on paper towels. Repeat to make 4 or 6 baskets. Keep warm.
2 Deep-fry the parsley sprigs until bright green and crisp. Remove and drain on paper towels.
3 Make the fritter batter: mix the eggs with the flour until smooth. Add the warm lager and season.
4 Sauté the snails in the walnut oil. Let cool. Melt the butter in a frying pan, add the garlic, and cook until soft; keep warm.
5 Plunge the snails into the fritter batter to coat on all sides. Lift them out, draining off excess batter. Deep-fry the snails in the hot vegetable oil until puffed and golden. Remove with a slotted spoon and drain on paper towels.
6 Arrange the snail fritters in the baskets. Garnish with fried parsley and garlic, and serve immediately.

Snails in Culinary History

Snails have been a popular food for thousands of years. Great heaps of snail shells have been found at prehistoric sites. The Romans kept vast numbers of snails in special "snailers", where they were fattened and sweetened on bran and wine. The Gauls even enjoyed snails as a dessert.

TOURTE JULIA

GUINEA FOWL, PORK, CABBAGE, AND PORT PIE

INGREDIENTS

Serves 6

1 guinea fowl, weighing about 1·5 kg (3 lb), with its liver
2 tsp vegetable oil
200 g (7 oz) mirepoix of vegetables (see page 133)
a bouquet garni
3 tbsp port
300 ml (1/2 pint) veal stock
salt and freshly ground pepper
60 g (2 oz) clarified butter
1/2 green cabbage, weighing about 400 g (14 oz), cut into strips
30 g (1 oz) butter, cut into small pieces

For the pâte brisée

350 g (12 oz) flour
175 g (6 oz) butter
1 egg
2 tbsp water
1 beaten egg, for glazing

For the stuffing

1 egg white
200 g (7 oz) boned pork loin, roughly chopped
1/2 bunch of tarragon
150 ml (5 fl oz) double cream

PREPARATION

1 Make the pâte brisée, and chill the dough for at least 30 minutes (see page 152).

2 Remove the breasts from the guinea fowl, keeping each in one piece. Skin them, and set aside. Remove the legs and bone them. Reserve the leg meat and liver for the stuffing. Coarsely chop the carcass and reserve.

3 Make the sauce: heat the oil in a pan, add the carcass and the leg bones, and sauté until lightly browned. Add the mirepoix and bouquet garni. Sweat for a few minutes, or until the vegetables are soft. *Deglaze* the pan with the port, then add the stock. Bring to a boil and simmer for 20-25 minutes. Strain the sauce, and set aside.

4 Meanwhile, season the guinea fowl breasts and sauté them in half of the clarified butter until they are browned on both sides and half cooked. Remove and set aside.

5 Blanch the cabbage in boiling salted water for 1-2 minutes. Drain well and cook gently in the remaining clarified butter for about 5 minutes, or until very soft. Season well and set aside to cool.

6 Make the stuffing: remove any skin from the guinea fowl leg meat, then put the meat in a food processor with the liver, egg white, pork, and tarragon. Blend just until smooth. Press the mixture through a fine sieve into a bowl. Set the bowl over an ice bath and gradually whisk in the cream. Season the stuffing.

7 Roll out two-thirds of the pâte brisée dough until about 3 mm (1/8 inch) thick. Line an 20-cm (8-inch) diameter springform tin with the dough. Trim off the excess dough, leaving 1·25-cm (1/2-inch) overhanging around the edge to be folded over the pie after it has been filled.

8 Spread the stuffing evenly over the bottom of the pie shell. Cut the guinea fowl breasts into slices and arrange them on top. Cover with the cabbage. Fold in the overhanging dough.

9 Roll out the remaining dough and use to cover the pie. Seal the edges and glaze the top with beaten egg. Cut a steam hole in the centre. Use the trimmings to make decorative shapes, arrange them on the top, and brush with beaten egg.

10 Bake in a preheated oven at 190°C (375°F, Gas 5) for 15 minutes. Reduce the temperature to 170°C (325°F, Gas 3) and bake for a further 20 minutes, or until the crust is golden.

11 Bring the sauce to a boil, lower the heat, and whisk in the butter. Check the seasoning.

12 Serve the pie hot, with the sauce.

IN HER HONOUR

In the 1930s, Le Cordon Bleu in Paris was taken over by Elizabeth Brassart, following the death of Marthe Distel, who had run the school for 50 years, and the curriculum was updated and improved. After World War II, the US government gave the school a grant to teach French cooking to GIs. Among those to receive the prestigious *Grand Diplôme* was a soldier's wife, Julia Child, who became America's favourite French-style chef. Le Cordon Bleu have created this guinea fowl pie in her honour.

Homard et Poireaux Tiedes a la Badiane

Warm Lobster and Leek Salad with Star Anise

INGREDIENTS

Serves 4
court bouillon (see page 51)
2 live lobsters, each weighing about 800 g (1 lb 10 oz)
8 medium leeks, white part only
salt and freshly ground pepper
4 tbsp white wine vinegar
8 star anise
150 ml (5 fl oz) vegetable oil
a few sprigs of dill, for the garnish

PREPARATION

1 Bring the court bouillon to a boil. Add the lobsters and simmer for about 8-9 minutes, or until the shells turn red-orange. Remove from the heat and leave to cool in the liquid.

2 Meanwhile, cook the leeks in boiling salted water just until tender. Drain and refresh in iced water. Cut the leeks lengthwise in half and diagonally into 2·5-cm (1-inch) chevrons.

3 Remove the lobster meat from the shells (see below). Reserve the claws for the garnish.

4 Warm the vinegar with half of the star anise in a small pan for 5-10 minutes. Remove from the heat and leave to infuse until just cool. Bring back to a simmer, then strain the vinegar. Season and gradually whisk in the vegetable oil.

5 Toss the leek chevrons with a little of the warm vinaigrette, then arrange them in the centre of individual plates. Place the lobster slices on the leeks and sprinkle with more vinaigrette. Top with a lobster claw and garnish with the dill.

6 Put the remaining star anise in a spice or pepper mill. Spoon the remaining vinaigrette around the lobster on each plate, then grind a little star anise over each salad.

Star Anise

The small fruit of an evergreen tree of the magnolia family, star anise is a spice from China and Vietnam which has been adopted by Western cuisines. This spice, whose Chinese name "pak kok" means eight points, is very pretty when used as a decoration. Star anise has an appealing licorice taste.

Removing Cooked Lobster Meat From The Shell

If lobster meat is removed carefully, the tail meat can be cut into medallions and the claws will retain their natural beautiful shape.

1 Twist the head and tail apart. Cut along the tail shell and extract the meat.

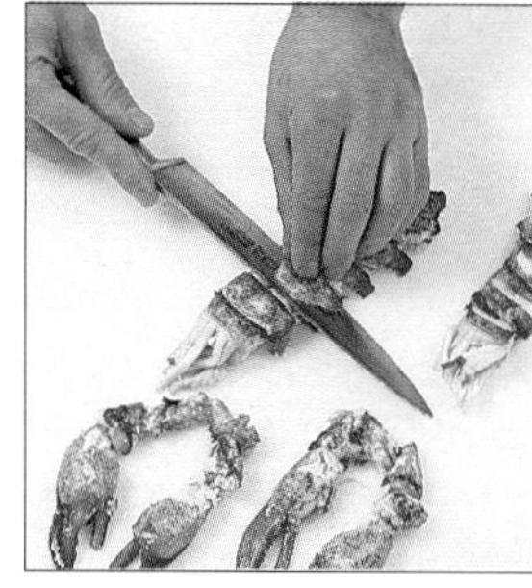

2 Crack the claws and carefully remove the meat in 1 piece. Cut tail meat into thin slices.

Court Bouillon

This aromatic liquid, also called nage *in French, is used for cooking fish and shellfish. Food cooked in this liquid absorbs the flavours of the ingredients.*

♦

- *2·5 litres (4¾ pints) water*
- *200 ml (7 fl oz) dry white wine*
- *125 g (4 oz) carrots, sliced*
- *125 g (4 oz) onions, sliced*
- *4 shallots, chopped*
- *a bouquet garni*
- *1 celery stalk, sliced*
- *2 tsp black peppercorns*

Simmer all the ingredients together in a large deep saucepan or fish kettle, depending on the type of fish to be cooked in it. The flavours should be extracted after 15-20 minutes. The court bouillon should then be left to cool before it is used as a cooking liquid. If it is not cool, the fish or shellfish will immediately firm up when added to the liquid. Strain the court bouillon after cooking fish or shellfish in it, and add it to sauces and soups, or reduce it and use as a sauce for the cooked fish or shellfish.

Huitres en Sabayon au Vin Blanc

Oysters with a White Wine Sauce

INGREDIENTS

Serves 6

36 oysters, in their shells
500 g (1 lb) spinach, stalks removed, chopped
60 g (2 oz) butter
salt and freshly ground pepper
a pinch of cayenne pepper
2 carrots, cut into julienne strips
1·5 kg (3 lb) rock salt, for holding oysters steady

For the sauce

3 shallots, finely chopped
250 ml (8 fl oz) dry white wine
150 ml (5 fl oz) double cream
4 egg yolks
2 tbsp water

For the garnish

1 frisée lettuce
1 lemon, cut lengthwise into wedges
1 cucumber (optional)

PREPARATION

1 Carefully shuck the oysters (see page 137), reserving all their liquor in a bowl. Rinse the oysters under cold water to remove any pieces of shell; set aside. Strain the oyster liquor and set aside. Wash and dry the rounded shells.
2 Cook the spinach in half of the butter until wilted. Season with salt, pepper, and cayenne pepper.
3 Cook the carrot julienne in the remaining butter, in a covered pan, just until tender but still slightly crunchy. Remove from the heat and set aside.
4 Make the sauce: combine the shallots and wine in a saucepan and boil until reduced by three-quarters. Strain and discard the shallots. Add one-third of the oyster liquor and bring back to a boil. Stir in the cream and simmer to reduce by half. Season and set aside.
5 Set a bowl over a pan of simmering water; do not let the bottom of the bowl touch the water. Put the egg yolks and water into the bowl and whisk with an electric mixer until the mixture becomes thick and creamy. Add the creamy wine and oyster reduction. Season and keep warm.
6 Poach the oysters in the remaining liquor for 30 seconds, or until their edges curl. Drain.
7 Arrange the oyster shells on an ovenproof platter filled with rock salt to hold them steady. Put a little spinach in each shell. Top with an oyster and some of the carrots.
8 Spoon the cream sauce over the carrots. Put under a hot grill until the sauce is lightly golden.
9 Serve on individual plates, garnished with frisée lettuce, lemon wedges, and the remaining carrots. Balance the oyster shells on hollowed-out rounds of cucumber, if you like.

Long-Time Favourites

Oysters are very good examples of an ancient food that maintains an important place in modern gastronomy. Many varieties of this succulent mollusc were enjoyed by early civilizations, including the Greeks, Romans, and native Americans.

A spectacular Christmas celebration in New York hosted by the *Alliance Française* in December 1993, inspired Le Cordon Bleu to create this first course.

Mouclade

Mussels in a Rich Cream Sauce

INGREDIENTS

Serves 4
3 litres (5 1/4 pints) mussels
1 onion, finely chopped
60 g (2 oz) butter
250 ml (8 fl oz) dry white wine
250 ml (8 fl oz) single cream
2 tsp mild curry powder
30 g (1 oz) flour
finely chopped parsley, for the garnish

For the liaison
2 egg yolks
75 ml (2 1/2 fl oz) single cream
salt and freshly ground pepper

PREPARATION

1 Clean the mussels: scrape them with a small knife to remove any barnacles, weeds, or "beards". Scrub the mussels under cold running water with a small stiff brush. Discard any mussels that have broken shells or that do not close when tapped.
2 Sweat the onion in half of the butter until softened. Add the mussels and wine and bring to a boil. Cover, and cook until the mussel shells open, shaking the pan from time to time. Remove the mussels and keep them warm.
3 Add the cream and curry powder to the cooking liquid. Mix the remaining butter with the flour to make a beurre manié, and use this to thicken the cooking liquid to the consistency of a light cream (see page 155).
4 Make the liaison: in a small bowl, mix the egg yolks and cream with a little of the cooking liquid. Stir the liaison into the cooking liquid and heat gently, but do not allow to boil. Strain and season.
5 Remove and discard the top shell from each mussel. Put the mussels in soup plates, cover with the sauce, and sprinkle with a little parsley.

Mussels from the Vendee

Two of the most famous French mussel dishes are *mouclade* and *moules marinière*. This particular recipe for mouclade is from the Vendée in western France.

The cultivation of mussels is thought to date back to the latter part of the 13th century, when Patrick Walton, an Irish traveller shipwrecked off the coast of La Rochelle in Charente, discovered that his nets left in the sea quickly became covered with mussels.

Saumon Marine aux Poivres Verts

Marinated Salmon with Green Peppercorns

INGREDIENTS

Serves 10-12
60 g (2 oz) dried green peppercorns
juice of 4 lemons
2 tbsp coarse sea salt
200 ml (7 fl oz) olive oil
1 side of very fresh salmon, with skin, weighing about 1·25 kg (2 1/2 lb)

For the garnish
1 lemon, cut into wedges
a few sprigs of dill
finely chopped chervil

PREPARATION

1 Finely crush the peppercorns with a pestle and mortar or in an electric grinder.
2 Mix the lemon juice and salt. Add the peppercorns and gradually whisk in the oil.
3 With a filleting knife, cut the fresh salmon into slices as you would a side of smoked salmon, but a little thicker. Discard the salmon skin.
4 Spoon half of the peppercorn mixture over the bottom of a shallow non-metallic dish or platter. Lay the slices of salmon on top, overlapping them slightly. Spoon the rest of the marinade evenly over the salmon. Cover and leave to marinate in a cool place for at least 2 hours.
5 Garnish with the lemon wedges, dill, and chervil. Serve with toast, if you like.

Sorbet a la Tomate

Tomato Sorbet with Herbs

INGREDIENTS

Serves 6

800 g (1 lb 10 oz) ripe red tomatoes
75 g (2 1/2 oz) shallots, chopped
150 ml (5 fl oz) water
salt and freshly ground pepper
a pinch of sugar
30 g (1 oz) basil or mint leaves, finely chopped
a few basil or mint leaves, for the garnish

PREPARATION

1 Cut the tomatoes in half and squeeze gently to remove the seeds.
2 Put the tomatoes, shallots, and water in a saucepan. Cook over a low heat until the tomatoes are very soft. Season with salt and pepper, and a pinch of sugar.
3 Press the tomato mixture through a fine sieve set over a bowl. Let the purée cool, then pour into an ice-cream machine and freeze.
4 When the sorbet is nearly frozen, add the chopped basil or mint and mix evenly. Serve in scoops, garnished with basil or mint leaves.

Sorbet au Melon

Melon Sorbet

INGREDIENTS

Serves 10

500 g (1 lb) cantaloupe melon flesh, puréed
125 g (4 oz) caster sugar
30 g (1 oz) liquid glucose
juice of 1 lemon
a few mint leaves, for the garnish

PREPARATION

1 Briefly mix the ingredients together in a blender or food processor. Pour into an ice-cream machine and freeze.
2 Serve the sorbet in scoops, in a melon shell if you like, garnished with mint leaves.

Melon Madness

The tender flesh of the melon has raised passions. Alexandre Dumas, the 19th-century French author of *The Three Musketeers* and *The Count of Monte Cristo*, was so affected by the fruit that he is said to have offered all of his past and future writing for a guaranteed annual supply.

Sorbet au Campari

Campari Sorbet

INGREDIENTS

Serves 20

150 g (5 oz) sugar
150 ml (5 fl oz) water
1 vanilla pod, split
300 ml (1/2 pint) orange juice
100 ml (3 1/2 fl oz) Campari
juice of 1 lime

PREPARATION

1 Combine the sugar, water, and vanilla pod in a saucepan and simmer, stirring, until all the sugar has dissolved. Bring to a boil, remove from the heat, and set aside to cool.
2 When cool, remove the vanilla pod. Add the orange juice, Campari, and lime juice; mix well.
3 Pour the mixture into an ice-cream machine and freeze. Serve the sorbet in scoops.

*M*AIN COURSES

Whether a main-course dish is simple or complex to prepare, classical, regional, rich, or light, the selection of quality ingredients and appropriate cooking techniques are the keys to success.

When planning a menu, choose main-course dishes that match your skills and your budget. It is always sad when a good cook tries something "special", only to find it necessary to substitute ingredients to cut down on cost. It is even worse when a fine recipe is diminished because a sauce was not stirred properly, or the meat was not prepared according to instructions.

Coquilles Saint-Jacques au Brouilly

Scallops with a Red Wine Sauce

INGREDIENTS

Serves 4-6
16 large scallops, with coral if available
salt and freshly ground pepper
12 new potatoes
150 g (5 oz) mangetout
1/2 cauliflower, broken into small florets
200 g (7 oz) small carrots
200 g (7 oz) small turnips
200 g (7 oz) bulbous spring onions
50 g (1 3/4 oz) clarified butter
2 shallots, finely chopped
1/2 bottle Brouilly or other fruity red wine
100 ml (3 1/2 fl oz) veal stock
125 g (4 oz) butter, cut into small pieces
a few sprigs of chervil, for the garnish

PREPARATION

1 Shell and trim the scallops (see below). Cut the white flesh into 3 slices. If there is coral, cook it in boiling salted water for 1 minute. Drain and refresh in a bowl of iced water. Set aside.

2 Cook the potatoes, mangetout, cauliflower, carrots, turnips, and spring onions, separately, in boiling salted water, just until tender. Drain, refresh, and set them aside together in a saucepan.

3 Heat the clarified butter in a non-stick frying pan. Season the scallop slices and sauté briskly for 1–2 minutes. Do this in batches, if necessary. Remove the scallop slices and keep warm. Discard the excess clarified butter.

4 Add the shallots to the pan with the wine. Bring to a boil and reduce to a glaze, then add the stock. Bring back to a boil, and continue to reduce until the sauce is syrupy. Whisk in the butter, season, and keep warm.

5 Reheat the vegetables, with a little butter, if you like. Season to taste.

6 Arrange the vegetables, scallop slices and corals, and sauce attractively on warmed plates. Garnish with chervil and serve immediately.

Shelling and Trimming Scallops

In Europe, scallops are often sold in their shells, with their bright orange corals still attached. It is important to remove the tough muscle from the side of the scallop, or it will make the scallop chewy when cooked.

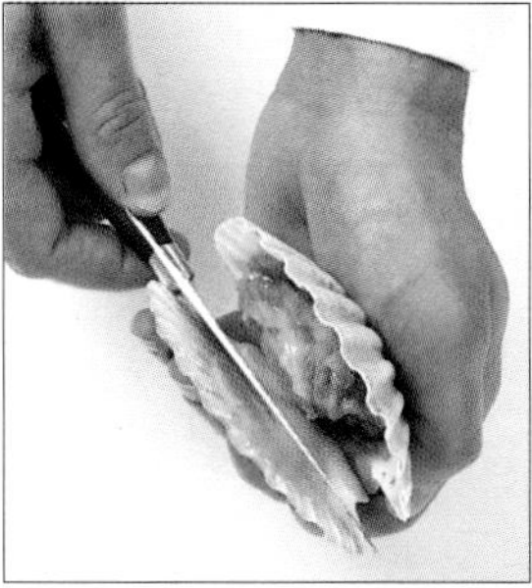

1 Insert a knife between both shells, and slide it around to loosen the flesh. Open the scallop.

2 Extract the flesh and coral from the rounded shell and discard any membranes or dark organs.

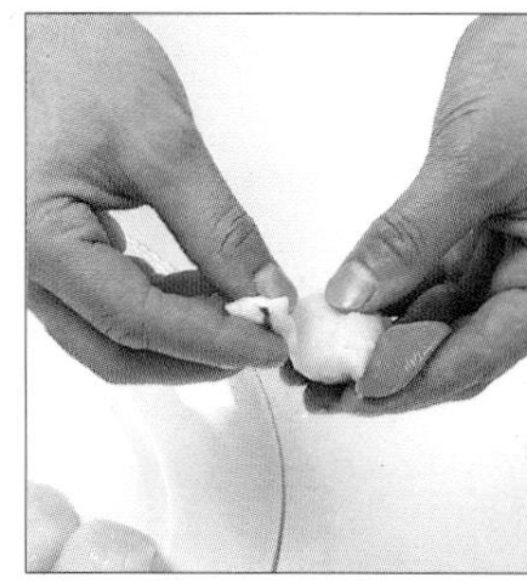

3 Remove the tough muscle from the side of the flesh. Rinse the flesh and coral and set aside.

*W*INES FROM *B*URGUNDY

Many writers left Paris during World War II and took up temporary residence around Lyon. To their delight, they discovered that the local Beaujolais wines were excellent, and they wrote enthusiastically about them. By the time the war ended, Paris was thirsting for Fleurie, Morgon, Chènas, and Brouilly.

Brouilly, made from grapes grown around Montagne de Brouilly, is best drunk young. Its fruity flavour makes it the perfect wine for cooking. Wine should always be boiled when used in cooking – boiling reduces the acid content of the wine and makes it less potent. The wine should not overpower the sauce, just add a hint of flavour.

"DRINK NO LONGER WATER, BUT USE A LITTLE WINE FOR THY STOMACH'S SAKE AND THINE OFTEN INFIRMITIES."

Holy Bible
1 Timothy: chapter 5, verse 23

Fricassee de Langoustines Epicees

Sauteed Spicy Langoustines with Chanterelles

INGREDIENTS

Serves 4

24 medium langoustines
1 tbsp mixed ground spices, such as star anise, cinnamon, cardamom, and cumin
3½ tbsp olive oil
400 g (14 oz) chanterelle mushrooms
60 g (2 oz) butter
1 shallot, finely chopped
salt and freshly ground pepper
100 ml (3½ fl oz) chicken stock
30 g (1 oz) flat-leaf parsley, finely chopped

PREPARATION

1 Peel the langoustines, leaving the last section of shell and tail attached. Put the langoustines in a bowl and add the spices and olive oil. Stir, then leave to marinate for 1 hour.
2 Gently rinse the chanterelles and pat them dry. Sauté them quickly in half of the butter with the shallot and a little salt. Set aside.
3 Just before serving, drain off the spicy oil from the langoustines and sauté them in a non-stick frying pan. Remove the langoustines and keep warm.
4 Deglaze the pan juices with the stock, then boil to reduce by two-thirds. Add the remaining butter, cut into small pieces, whisking vigorously. Strain the sauce through a fine sieve.
5 Quickly reheat the chanterelles with the parsley.
6 Season the langoustines and chanterelles and arrange on plates. Spoon the sauce around them and serve immediately.

Piccata d'Ormeau au Noilly

Escalope of Abalone with Vermouth

INGREDIENTS

Serves 4

1 shelled abalone, weighing about 1 kg (2 lb)
2 eggs
1 tsp vegetable oil
salt and freshly ground pepper
100 g (3½ oz) flour
250 g (8 oz) fine breadcrumbs
300 ml (½ pint) dry vermouth, such as Noilly Prat
2 shallots, chopped
2 tbsp meat glaze (see page 145)
300 g (10 oz) butter, cut into small pieces
200 ml (7 fl oz) clarified butter

For the garnish

½ bunch of chives, snipped
500 g (1 lb) squid ink noodles, cooked (optional)

PREPARATION

1 Clean and trim the abalone. Wrap it in a tea towel and pound it well to make it tender. Cut the abalone into very thin small escalopes.
2 Lightly beat the eggs with the oil and seasoning in a shallow dish. Lightly coat the abalone escalopes with flour, then dip in the egg mixture, and finally coat with breadcrumbs. Set aside.
3 Put the vermouth, shallots, and meat glaze in a saucepan and bring to a boil. Reduce to a glaze. Add the butter, a few pieces at a time, whisking vigorously. Season the sauce and keep warm.
4 Fry the abalone escalopes in the clarified butter until golden brown on both sides.
5 Make large pools of sauce on individual plates. Place the abalone escalopes on top, garnish with the snipped chives, and squid ink noodles, if you like.

Ancient Abalone

Mounds of shells excavated at Catalina Island, off the western coast of the United States, suggest that residents of what we now call California have enjoyed abalone since the fourth millennium BC.

Abalone, or *ormeau* in French, is a large marine gastropod quickly identified by its ear-shaped shell. Varieties are enjoyed in several places, including the Channel Islands and the Mediterranean Sea, where a curious form of abalone has earned it the nickname *Oreilles de Saint-Pierre*, or St. Peter's Ears.

Langouste en Ballotins

Crawfish in Spinach Purses

INGREDIENTS

Serves 4

1 live crawfish or spiny lobster, weighing about 1 kg (2 lb)
4 or 8 large spinach or lettuce leaves
50 g (1 3/4 oz) onion
30 g (1 oz) each of red and green pepper
juice and finely chopped zest of 1 lemon
1 1/2 tsp whole-grain mustard
1 tbsp hazelnut oil
1 tbsp soy sauce
salt and freshly ground pepper
1/2 bunch of chives, snipped
4 parsley or chervil stalks, blanched

For the sauce

2 tomatoes, concassées (see page 136)
juice of 1 lemon
1 tbsp hazelnut oil
a little single cream, to taste

For the garnish

salmon or lumpfish roe
a few sprigs of chervil

PREPARATION

1 Place the crawfish in a pan of boiling water and cook for 6-7 minutes. Drain. Remove the meat from the shell and cut it into cubes. Cover and keep cool.
2 Blanch the spinach leaves. Refresh in a bowl of iced water, pat dry, and set aside.
3 Cut the onion and peppers into small dice.
4 Combine the lemon juice, mustard, oil, soy sauce, and seasoning in a bowl and whisk to mix. Add the lemon zest, diced onion and peppers, and chives. Chill in the refrigerator.
5 Make the sauce: put the tomatoes in a blender. With the machine running, add the lemon juice, oil, and seasoning. Mix in a little cream. Chill.
6 Season the crawfish, then mix with the diced onion and pepper mixture. Divide among the spinach leaves. (You will need 1 or 2 per serving, or even 3 each if the leaves are very small.) Form each into a small purse shape and tie with a blanched parsley or chervil stalk.
7 Make pools of sauce on individual plates and set the spinach purses on top. Garnish with salmon or lumpfish roe and chervil before serving.

Calamars a l'Orientale

Squid with Chilli and Soy Sauce

INGREDIENTS

Serves 4

2 squid, each weighing about 300 g (10 oz)
2 tbsp vegetable oil
2 tbsp sugar
2 garlic cloves, finely chopped
10 g (1/3 oz) green chilli, seeded and diced
2 tbsp soy sauce
salt and freshly ground pepper
oven-baked rice (see page 89), to serve

PREPARATION

1 Prepare the squid: separate the pouch and the tentacles. Discard the tentacles. Pull out the clear bone from inside the pouch and pull off the black membrane covering the pouch and fins. Cut the pouch into rings.
2 Heat the oil in a frying pan. Add the squid rings and cook for 3 minutes.
3 Add the sugar and cook until caramelized, stirring from time to time.
4 Add the garlic, chilli, and soy sauce, and mix well. Cook for 10 minutes over a very low heat, stirring occasionally. Season with salt and pepper.
5 Serve the squid rings hot, with rice.

Japanese Influence

The above recipe can also be referred to as *calamars d'Yedo*, which means "squid from Tokyo". The capital of Japan was called Yedo until 1868.

The art of making soy sauce is probably as old as the art of Japanese cooking. Many recipes exist, with variations benefiting from the addition of ginger, mushrooms, or anchovies. All, however, are based on a nutritious fermentation of the simple soya bean.

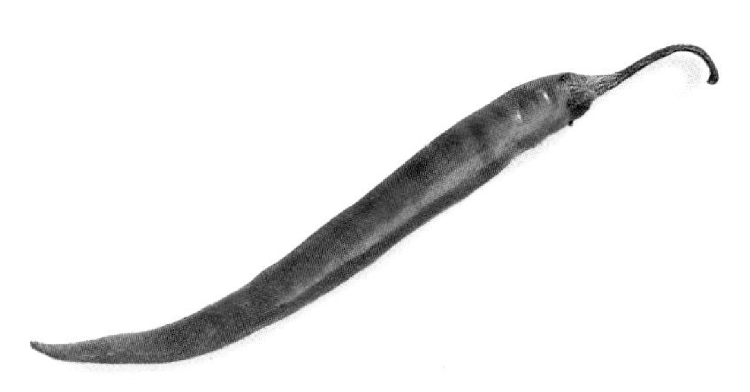

Paupiettes de Saumon au Beurre Blanc

Stuffed Salmon Rolls with White Butter Sauce

INGREDIENTS

Serves 6
1 salmon, weighing about 1·5 kg (3 lb)
a little butter
3 shallots, finely chopped
100 ml (3½ fl oz) dry white wine
200 ml (7 fl oz) fish stock
a few tarragon leaves, for the garnish
pilaff rice (see page 61), to serve

For the stuffing
9 scallops, white flesh only
2 egg whites
100 ml (3½ fl oz) double cream
¼ bunch of chervil, finely chopped
¼ bunch of tarragon, finely chopped
salt and freshly ground pepper
a pinch of cayenne pepper

For the sauce
200 ml (7 fl oz) white wine vinegar
3 shallots, chopped
a bouquet garni
300 g (10 oz) butter, cut into small pieces

PREPARATION

1. Make the stuffing: put the scallops in a food processor and blend until smooth. Add the egg whites and blend briefly. Turn into a bowl and set in a bowl of iced water. Gradually whisk in the cream. Add the chopped herbs, salt and pepper, and the cayenne.
2. Fillet and skin the salmon (see page 139). Cut the salmon fillets into long thin rectangles. Make paupiettes with the salmon rectangles and the stuffing (see below).
3. Put the salmon paupiettes into a buttered pan with the shallots, wine, and fish stock. Cook in a preheated oven at 170°C (325°F, Gas 3), for 10-15 minutes.
4. Remove the paupiettes, season with salt and pepper, and keep warm. Strain the cooking liquid into a saucepan.
5. Make the sauce: add the vinegar, shallots, and bouquet garni to the cooking liquid and boil until well reduced. Discard the bouquet garni. Gradually whisk in the butter, a few pieces at a time. Check the seasoning.
6. Arrange the salmon paupiettes and sauce attractively on plates, and garnish with tarragon leaves. Serve with pilaff rice.

Making Fish Paupiettes

Here, paupiettes are very thinly cut fish fillets which have stuffing spread over them before being rolled into neat cylinders. Sometimes, paupiettes are just thinly cut fish fillets folded over a mousse.

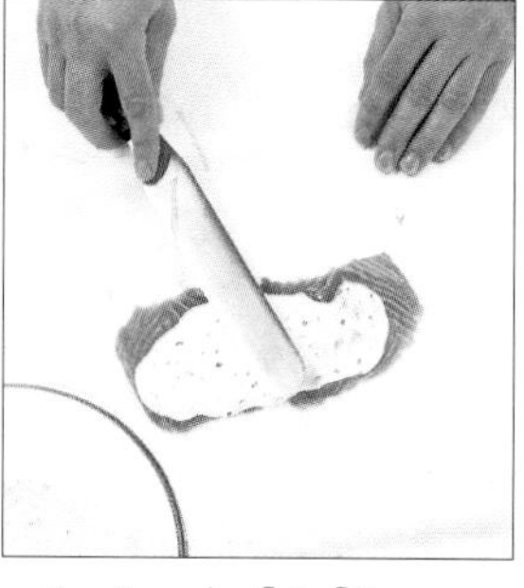

1 Lay the fish fillets on a sheet of non-stick paper. Spread a layer of stuffing over each fillet.

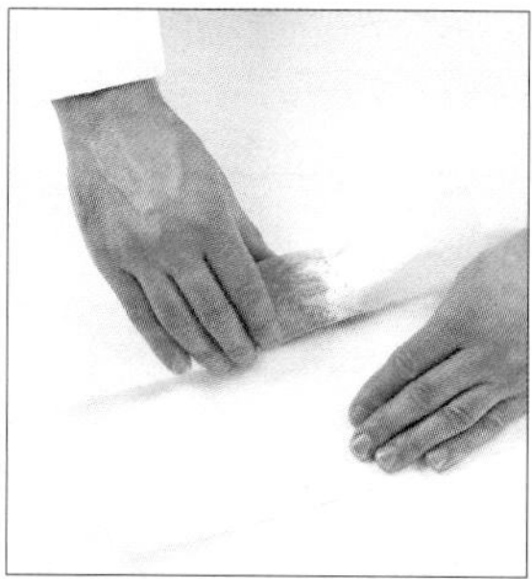

2 Use the non-stick paper to help roll up the paupiettes. Roll from the short end of the paper.

3 Twist the ends of the paper to secure the paupiettes. Chill for 30 minutes. Remove paper.

Pilaff Rice

Rice that is cooked by the pilaff method should be fluffy and not stick together. Here, it is garnished with sweetcorn, carrots, peas, and courgettes.

- *30 g (1 oz) butter*
- *1 onion, finely chopped*
- *300 g (10 oz) long-grain rice*
- *500 ml (16 fl oz) hot chicken stock*
- *a bouquet garni*
- *salt and freshly ground pepper*

For the garnish

- *125 g (4 oz) sweetcorn*
- *125 g (4 oz) carrots, diced*
- *125 g (4 oz) peas*
- *1 courgette, cut into thin slices*

Melt the butter in a saucepan, add the onion and sauté until soft. Add the rice and cook for 2 minutes, or until all the grains are transparent. Add the hot stock with the bouquet garni and salt and pepper. Cover and bring to a boil. Lower the heat and simmer, without stirring, for about 20 minutes, or until the rice is tender and all the liquid has been absorbed. If the pilaff is too firm, add more liquid. Season the rice. Cook all the vegetables in boiling salted water until tender, drain, then add the sweetcorn, carrots, and peas to the rice. Garnish with the courgette slices.

Turbot Poele aux Cepes et Pleurottes

Fried Turbot with Ceps and Oyster Mushrooms

INGREDIENTS

Serves 8

1 turbot, weighing 2-2·5 kg (4-5 lb), filleted and skinned
300 ml (1/2 pint) veal stock
salt and freshly ground pepper
175 g (6 oz) flour
100 ml (3 1/2 fl oz) vegetable oil
160 g (5 1/2 oz) butter
800 g (1 lb 10 oz) ceps, cleaned and sliced
500 g (1 lb) oyster mushrooms, cleaned and sliced
3 tbsp finely chopped shallots
3 tbsp chopped flat-leaf parsley

PREPARATION

1 Cut 8 neat, even pieces from the turbot fillets, each weighing about 160 g (5 1/2 oz). Set aside.
2 Boil the veal stock until it has reduced to a glaze. Keep warm.
3 Season the turbot pieces and coat them lightly with flour. Heat the oil with one-third of the butter, add the turbot pieces, and fry until golden.
4 Meanwhile, in another pan, cook the ceps and oyster mushrooms in a little butter. Halfway through, add the shallots and parsley. Season.
5 Arrange the turbot and mushrooms on warmed individual plates. Quickly melt the remaining butter in a pan, cook until browned (*beurre noisette*), and then drizzle over the turbot. Serve immediately, with the veal glaze.

Filets de Morue Fraiche aux Feves

Fillet of Cod with Broad Beans

INGREDIENTS

Serves 8

1 cod fillet, weighing about 1·5 kg (3 lb), skinned
50 g (1 3/4 oz) coarse sea salt
500 g (1 lb) broad beans
3 1/2 tbsp olive oil
200 g (7 oz) baby onions
60 g (2 oz) butter
30 g (1 oz) sugar

For the sauce

10 garlic cloves
salt and freshly ground pepper
100 g (3 1/2 oz) butter
200 g (7 oz) mirepoix of vegetables (see page 133)
2 tomatoes, concassées (see page 136)
a bouquet garni
1 strip of lemon zest
300 ml (1/2 pint) dry white wine
1 tsp white peppercorns, crushed
juice of 1 lemon

PREPARATION

1 Sprinkle the fish evenly with the sea salt. Leave in a cool place for at least 2 hours.
2 Meanwhile, prepare the garlic purée for the sauce: cook the garlic in salted water with 15 g (1/2 oz) of the butter until tender. Drain and purée.
3 Cook the broad beans in boiling salted water until tender. When cool, slip off the skins. Keep warm.
4 Rinse the fish in cold water and pat dry. Heat the oil in a baking dish. Put in the fish and turn to coat with oil. Roast in a preheated oven at 200°C (400°F, Gas 6) for 20 minutes.
5 Meanwhile, caramelize the onions in a little salted water with the butter and sugar. Keep warm.
6 Make the sauce: put the mirepoix and tomatoes into a saucepan. Add water to cover, a little salt, the bouquet garni, and lemon zest. Bring to a boil, and simmer until tender. Add the wine and peppercorns and bring back to a boil.
7 Purée the sauce mixture in a blender or food processor until smooth and slightly thick. Work through a sieve, then reheat with the garlic purée, the remaining butter, and the lemon juice.
8 Season the fish and cut it into slices. Make pools of sauce on individual plates, and top with the fish, broad beans, and onions.

Supremes de Saumon Roti en Croute d'Amandes

Salmon in an Almond Crust with Red Butter Sauce

INGREDIENTS

Serves 6
6 pieces of salmon fillet, each weighing about 150 g (5 oz)
salt and freshly ground pepper
60 g (2 oz) clarified butter
a few sprigs of chervil, for the garnish

For the beurre rouge
4 tbsp red wine
2 shallots, finely chopped
3 tbsp fish stock
300 g (10 oz) butter, cut into small pieces
a pinch of sugar

For the almond crust
50 g (1 3/4 oz) ground almonds
50 g (1 3/4 oz) breadcrumbs
60 g (2 oz) butter, softened
1 egg, lightly beaten
2 tbsp finely chopped parsley
1 tsp almond oil

PREPARATION

1 Begin to make the *beurre rouge*: combine the red wine and shallots in a saucepan, bring to a boil, and cook until reduced to a syrupy glaze.
2 Meanwhile, mix together the ingredients for the almond crust.
3 Sprinkle the pieces of fish with salt and pepper. Fry the fish on one side only in the clarified butter just until firm. Remove from the heat. Press the crust mixture on to the uncooked side of each piece of fish to make an even coating.
4 Place the fish, crust-side up, under a hot grill and cook until the crust is lightly browned and the fish just firm.
5 Add the fish stock to the reduced red wine and continue to reduce. Whisk in the butter, a few pieces at a time. Season with salt, pepper, and a pinch of sugar. Strain through a fine sieve.
6 Place the pieces of fish in the centre of warmed individual plates and surround with beurre rouge. Garnish with chervil and serve immediately.

Pompanos a la Mediterraneenne

Pompanos in Garlic Sauce

INGREDIENTS

Serves 8
8 pompanos or red snappers, each weighing about 500 g (1 lb), cleaned
a little salt
200 g (7 oz) dried chiles serranos *or other very hot chillies, finely chopped*
500 ml (16 fl oz) olive oil
24 garlic cloves, sliced
500 g (1 lb) butter
24 garlic cloves, puréed
200 g (7 oz) fresh chiles serranos *or other very hot green chillies, finely chopped*

PREPARATION

1 Season the fish with the salt, then roll in the chopped dried chillies. Fry in olive oil until cooked and golden brown on both sides.
2 Meanwhile, gently fry the sliced garlic in the butter just until golden. Remove with a slotted spoon and drain on paper towels.
3 Reheat the butter and mix in the garlic purée and chopped fresh chillies.
4 Drain the fish on paper towels and arrange on a platter. Spoon over the garlic and chilli butter and scatter the golden garlic slices on top. Serve immediately.

Hot and Spicy

The fiery sauce of this rich stew echoes its South American origins. Any dried and fresh chillies can be used, but hot *serrano* chillies are the most appropriate. The stew can be made with either pompano, an excellent fish found in the waters between Florida and the coast of Venezuela, or red snapper, a member of the bass family found in the Mediterranean Sea.

Filets de Rougets en Ecailles Croustillantes

Fillets of Red Mullet with Potato Scales

This elegant dinner party recipe is a favourite of the former chef of Le Doyen and Carré d'Or restaurants in Paris, Chef Boucheret, who wrote the recipe for his advanced course at Le Cordon Bleu.

INGREDIENTS

Serves 4

4 red mullet, each weighing about 200 g (7 oz)
1 egg yolk, lightly beaten
200 g (7 oz) new potatoes
a little clarified butter

For the sauce

2 oranges
200 ml (7 fl oz) dry white wine
2 shallots, chopped
100 ml (3 1/2 fl oz) double cream
125 g (4 oz) butter, cut into small pieces
1 carrot, cut into small dice
2 tbsp Cointreau

For the garnish

broccoli cream (see page 65)
a few broccoli florets, lightly cooked
a few carrot julienne *strips, cooked*

PREPARATION

1 Scale the fish, then fillet them, leaving the skins attached (see page 139). Carefully remove all bones, and set the fillets aside.
2 Prepare the sauce: pare the zest from the oranges and cut it into fine dice; set aside. Squeeze the juice from the oranges into a saucepan, and boil it until reduced to a glaze.
3 Reduce the wine with the shallots in another saucepan. Add the cream and reduce again, then whisk in the butter, a few pieces at a time. Strain through a fine sieve and add the orange glaze, orange zest, carrot dice, and Cointreau. Keep the sauce warm.
4 Dip the skin side of the fish in the egg yolk. Prepare and layer the potato scales (see below).
5 Cook the fish on the potato-coated sides, in a non-stick frying pan, just until done.
6 Make pools of sauce on individual plates and set 2 fish fillets on top. Garnish with broccoli cream and florets, and carrot julienne.

Preparing and Layering Potato Scales

Potato scales are a novelty that look attractive and taste delicious. Brushing them with clarified butter before cooking helps keep them from discolouring, and also helps the potato scales stick together.

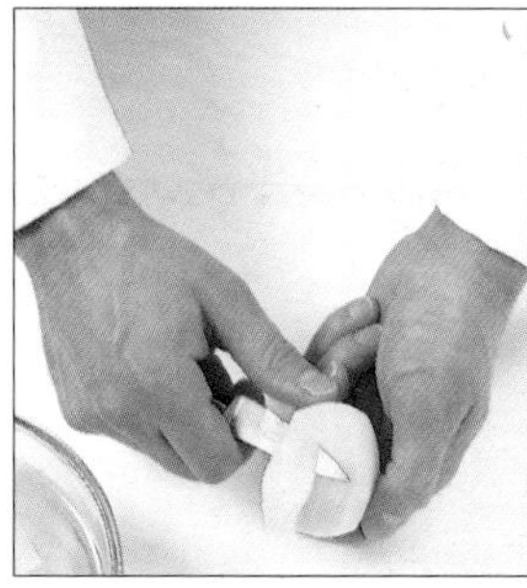

1 Peel the potatoes and use a sharp knife to round off the edges. A pastry cutter can also be used.

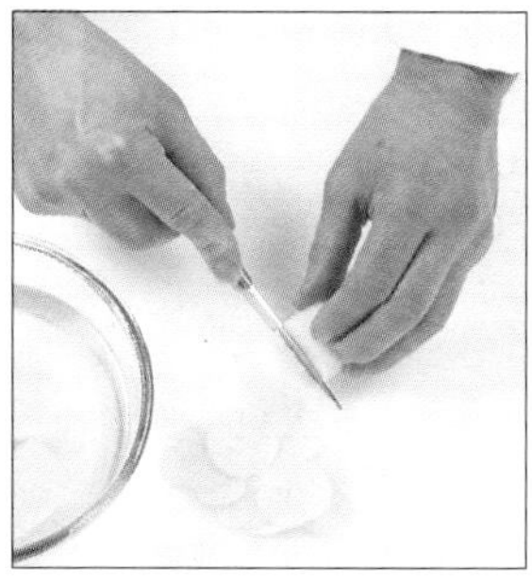

2 Slice the rounded potatoes into very thin rounds. A vegetable peeler can also be used.

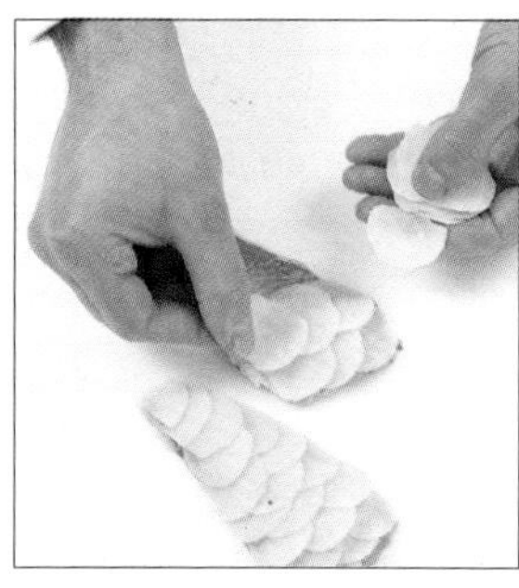

3 Place the potatoes, slightly overlapping, on the fish fillets. Brush with clarified butter.

Broccoli Cream

This "cream" is a basic vegetable purée set with eggs so that it becomes firm. The same method can be used for other vegetables and is especially good with Jerusalem artichokes, spinach, and carrots.

Serves 4

- *melted butter, for mould*
- *100 g (3½ oz) broccoli*
- *1 egg yolk*
- *½ whole egg*
- *3½ tbsp whipping cream*
- *a pinch of freshly grated nutmeg*
- *salt and freshly ground pepper*

Brush an ovenproof mould with melted butter, and chill until set. Place a round of non-stick paper in the bottom and brush with melted butter. Cook the broccoli in boiling salted water for 7 minutes, or until tender. Drain the broccoli and purée in a food processor. Mix the purée with all the remaining ingredients. Place in the prepared mould. Bake in a *bain marie* in a preheated oven at 180°C (350°F, Gas 4) for 10 minutes, or until lightly set. Use 2 dessertspoons to scoop out the broccoli cream in *quenelle* shapes. Alternatively, turn the broccoli cream on to a plate, remove the non-stick paper, and cut the cream into slices.

Sole Murat

Fried Strips of Sole with Artichoke and Potato Dice

INGREDIENTS

Serves 4

4 soles, each one weighing
350-400 g (12-14 oz), cleaned
2 globe artichokes
juice of 1 1/2 lemons
300 g (10 oz) potatoes, diced
75 g (2 1/2 oz) clarified butter
a little flour, for coating
125 g (4 oz) butter
2 shallots, finely chopped
4 tbsp meat jus (see page 145)
salt and freshly ground pepper
finely chopped parsley, for the garnish

PREPARATION

1 Fillet the soles (see page 139). Cut the sole fillets into long thin strips, or *goujonettes*.
2 Turn the artichokes (see page 134), and remove the chokes. Cut the artichoke hearts into small dice. Sprinkle the dice with a little lemon juice to prevent discoloration.
3 Sauté the diced potatoes in a little of the clarified butter until golden and tender. Keep warm.
4 In another pan, sauté the artichoke dice in a little of the clarified butter until tender. Keep warm.
5 Coat the sole goujonettes lightly in flour and fry in the remaining clarified butter until golden.
6 Melt 15 g (1/2 oz) of the butter in a saucepan and sweat the shallots. Stir in the meat jus and the remaining lemon juice. Whisk in the remaining butter, cut into small pieces, and season to taste.
7 Serve the sole with the potato and artichoke dice, and the sauce, in shallow soup plates. Sprinkle with chopped parsley.

Mulets Rotis Menagere

Grey Mullet with Vermouth, Mushrooms, and Herbs

INGREDIENTS

Serves 6

6 grey mullet, each weighing 300 g (10 oz), cleaned
50 g (1 3/4 oz) shallots, chopped
250 ml (8 fl oz) dry white wine
2 tbsp dry vermouth, such as Noilly Prat
150 g (5 oz) button mushrooms, sliced
10 black peppercorns
a little salt
6 sprigs of thyme
6 bay leaves
300 g (10 oz) butter, cut into small pieces
juice of 1/2 lemon
3 tbsp finely chopped parsley
1 bunch of chives, snipped

For the parsley potatoes

750 g (1 1/2 lb) new potatoes
75 g (2 1/2 oz) butter
finely chopped parsley

PREPARATION

1 Arrange the whole fish in a single layer in a baking dish. Add the chopped shallots, wine, vermouth, sliced mushrooms, black peppercorns, and salt. Place a thyme sprig and a bay leaf on top of each fish. Bake in a preheated oven at 200°C (400°F, Gas 6) for 20 minutes, or until the fish is tender.
2 Meanwhile, cook the unpeeled potatoes in boiling salted water for about 12 minutes, or just until tender. Drain well, and toss in the butter and chopped parsley. Keep warm.
3 Transfer the fish to a serving dish and keep warm. Strain the fish cooking liquid into a saucepan and bring to a boil. Reduce by half.
4 Whisk the butter into the reduced cooking liquid, a few pieces at a time. Add the lemon juice. At the last moment, add the herbs.
5 Coat the fish with the sauce and serve with the parsley potatoes.

The Meaning of Menagere

The elegance of this recipe and its simple name are a playful contradiction. When applied to cooking, *ménagère* usually indicates basic dishes prepared with accessible and relatively inexpensive ingredients. This dish appears to be an exception to the rule.

Filets de Sole a la Portugaise

Sole Fillets with Tomatoes, Mushrooms, and Onions

INGREDIENTS

Serves 4

4 soles, each weighing about 400 g (14 oz), cleaned
3 onions, 1 chopped and 2 sliced
1 carrot, chopped
150 g (5 oz) butter
500 ml (16 fl oz) water
100 ml (3½ fl oz) dry white wine
a bouquet garni
350 g (12 oz) tomatoes, concassées (see page 136)
125 g (4 oz) mushrooms, sliced
½ bunch of chives, snipped
a pinch of cayenne pepper
salt and freshly ground pepper
15 g (½ oz) flour
finely chopped parsley, for the garnish

PREPARATION

1 Fillet the soles (see page 138); reserve the bones.

2 Sweat the chopped onions and carrot in 15 g (½ oz) of the butter until soft. Add the fish bones, the water, half of the wine, and the bouquet garni. Bring to a boil, and simmer for 20 minutes, skimming occasionally.

3 Meanwhile, cook the sliced onions in 30 g (1 oz) of the butter until golden. Add the tomatoes and mushrooms and cook for 15 minutes, stirring occasionally. Remove from the heat, add the chives, and keep warm.

4 Strain the fish stock and return it to the pan. Boil until reduced by half.

5 Season the sole with the cayenne, salt and pepper to taste. Roll the fillets up, and stand them upright side-by-side in a flameproof serving dish. Add the reduced fish stock and the remaining wine, and poach in a preheated oven at 180°C (350°F, Gas 4) for 10-12 minutes. Pour off the liquid and reserve. Cover the fish and keep warm.

6 Melt 30 g (1 oz) of the butter in a saucepan and stir in the flour. Cook, stirring, for 1-2 minutes. Add the reserved cooking liquid, bring to a boil, and cook until the sauce is smooth, stirring constantly. Whisk in the remaining butter, cut into small pieces. Check the seasoning.

7 Spoon the warm vegetables into the fish rolls, cover with sauce, and glaze under a hot grill for a few minutes. Serve hot, sprinkled with parsley.

Saint-Pierre Braise au Coriandre

John Dory Braised with Coriander

INGREDIENTS

Serves 4

150 g (5 oz) butter
2 shallots, chopped
1 John Dory, weighing about 1·25 kg (2½ lb), cleaned
1 bunch of coriander, chopped, with stalks reserved
20 coriander seeds
300 ml (½ pint) dry white wine
200 ml (7 fl oz) fish stock
1·25 kg (2½ lb) tomatoes, peeled and sliced
turned cucumber (see page 135), for the garnish
salt and freshly ground pepper
300 ml (½ pint) double cream

PREPARATION

1 Brush a large ovenproof dish with 45 g (1½ oz) of the butter and scatter the shallots over the bottom. Set the John Dory in the dish and add the stalks from the fresh coriander and the coriander seeds. Pour over the wine and stock.

2 Cook in a preheated oven at 180°C (350°F, Gas 4) for 10-12 minutes.

3 Lift the fish from the liquid and remove the skin.

4 Return the fish to the dish. Arrange the tomato slices on top of the fish to resemble scales. Place in the oven to finish cooking, about 10 minutes.

5 Meanwhile, sauté the cucumber in 30 g (1 oz) of the butter for 2-3 minutes. Season and keep warm.

6 Transfer the fish to a serving dish and keep warm. Strain the cooking liquid into a saucepan. Bring to a boil, and boil until reduced. Whisk in the cream and the remaining butter, cut into small pieces. Season the sauce and, at the last minute, add the chopped coriander leaves.

7 Spoon the sauce over the fish, garnish with the cucumber, and serve.

The Parable of John Dory

John Dory, or *Saint-Pierre*, is a long, oval fish identifiable by a large black spot on either side of its body. Legend has it that these spots are the thumbprints of St. Peter who, after netting the fish and hearing it moan as it lay in the bottom of his boat, felt pity and cast it back into the Sea of Galilee. While it is true that John Dory makes a moaning sound when out of the water, the Sea of Galilee is a freshwater lake and would be an unlikely habitat for this sea fish.

Boudin de Saumon au Vin de Chinon

Salmon Sausage with Red Wine Sauce

"Cooking is an art; it demands hard and sometimes distasteful work, but on the whole, it is the creative side that prevails."

Constance Spry and Rosemary Hume
The Constance Spry Cookery Book

The Chinon–Rabelais Connection

When you select a bottle of Chinon wine for this recipe, give some thought to its history. The grapes for the wine are grown around the Loire surrounding the Fort de Coudray at Chinon, where Joan of Arc demanded that Charles VII (the Dauphin) force the English from France.

Later, a native son of Chinon, François Rabelais (1483-1553), became one of France's most important satirists and humanists, shocking the church and government with his brave publications; he was also a great gastronome and food writer. His mother, Anne Frapin, is an ancestor of André Cointreau, president and chairman of Le Cordon Bleu.

INGREDIENTS

Serves 8

625 g (1 1/4 lb) salmon fillet, skinned and all small bones removed
3 eggs
500 ml (16 fl oz) crème fraîche
1/2 bunch of tarragon, finely chopped
1/2 bunch of chervil, finely chopped
1/2 tsp mace
salt and freshly ground pepper
1·8 metres (6 feet) pig's intestinal lining or synthetic sausage casing

For the sauce

100 g (3 1/2 oz) mirepoix of vegetables (see page 133)
100 g (3 1/2 oz) butter
a bouquet garni
about 400 g (14 oz) salmon bones
1 tsp peppercorns, crushed
500 ml (16 fl oz) good red wine, such as Chinon
200 ml (7 fl oz) brown veal stock
2 tsp meat glaze (see page 145)

For the garnish

4 courgettes, cut into large parisienne (see page 135)
200 g (7 oz) horns of plenty (wild black mushrooms), cleaned
1 shallot, finely chopped
30 g (1 oz) butter
salmon roe

PREPARATION

1 Make the sausage filling: purée the salmon and eggs in a food processor until smooth. Press through a fine sieve into a bowl. Set this bowl in a bowl of iced water and gradually whisk in the crème fraîche. Add the chopped herbs, mace, and salt to taste. Cover and set aside in a cool place.

2 Make the sauce: sweat the mirepoix in 30 g (1 oz) of the butter. Add the bouquet garni, salmon bones, peppercorns, and wine, and bring to a boil. Simmer for 25 minutes.

3 Meanwhile, prepare the garnish: cook the courgette balls in a little boiling salted water just until tender. Drain and keep warm. Sauté the mushrooms and shallot in the butter. Set aside and keep warm.

4 Strain the red wine stock and return it to the pan. Boil until reduced by half. Add the veal stock and the meat glaze. Boil again to reduce until syrupy, then whisk in the remaining butter, cut into small pieces. Check the seasoning, and keep the sauce warm.

5 Prepare the salmon sausages (see below).

6 Lower the sausages into a large saucepan of simmering water. Poach for about 6 minutes.

7 Lift out the sausages, remove the casing, and cut into slices. Put the mushrooms in the centre of individual plates, place the sausage slices on top of the mushrooms, and spoon over the sauce. Garnish with the courgette balls, and salmon roe. Serve immediately.

PREPARING SALMON SAUSAGES

Sausages are held together in a casing. Traditionally, these casings were the intestinal linings of animals, but synthetic casings are now available from selected butchers. Casings should be soaked for 1-2 hours before use to make them pliable.

1 Clean the casing by gently passing cold water through it. Tie one end with string.

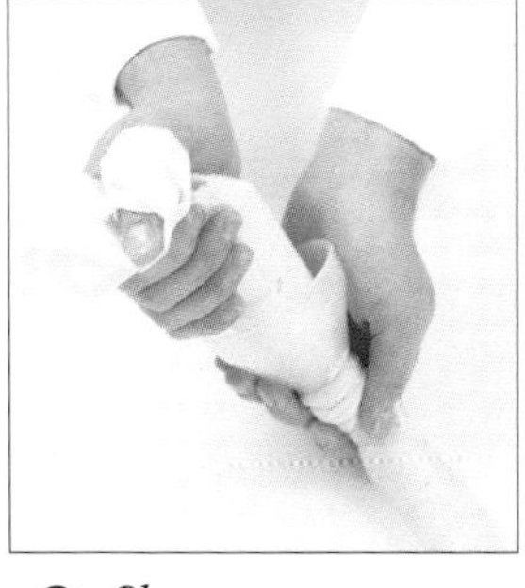

2 Place some sausage filling in a piping bag, and pipe through a funnel into the casing.

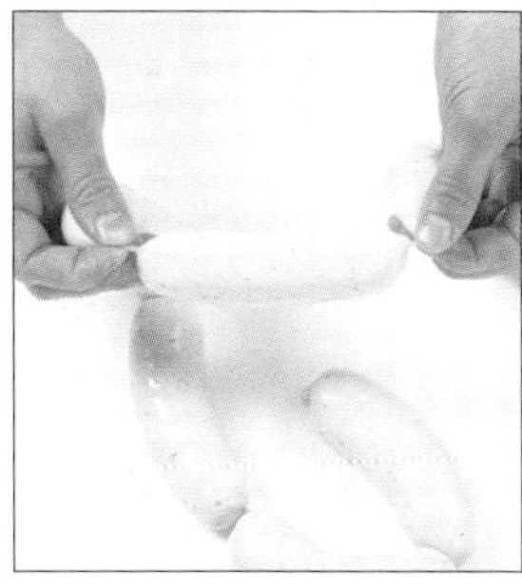

3 Twist the sausage at regular intervals. Tie the open end of the casing with string.

Truites Farcies a l'Oignon au Vin

Trout Stuffed with Onions and Braised in Red Wine

INGREDIENTS

Serves 6

625 g (1 1/4 lb) onions, finely sliced
90 g (3 oz) butter
salt and freshly ground pepper
a little sugar
3 tbsp finely chopped parsley
750 ml (1 1/4 pints) red wine
3 shallots, chopped
a bouquet garni
6 trout, each weighing 200-250 g (7-8 oz), cleaned and boned from the back (see page 138)
400 ml (14 fl oz) veal stock
18 button mushrooms, turned (see page 134)
juice of 1/2 lemon

For the chive potatoes

875 g (1 3/4 lb) potatoes, turned (see page 135)
75 g (2 1/2 oz) butter
1 bunch of chives, snipped

PREPARATION

1 Cook the onions gently in 50 g (1 3/4 oz) of the butter until they are very soft, but not coloured. Season with salt and pepper, and the sugar, to taste. Remove from the heat and stir in the chopped parsley. Let cool slightly.

2 Combine the wine, shallots, and bouquet garni in a saucepan and boil to reduce by half.

3 Open the boned trout and season the inside. Divide the onions among the trout. Reshape the fish and arrange them in a single layer in a buttered ovenproof dish.

4 Pour the veal stock and wine reduction over the fish and braise in a preheated oven at 180°C (350°F, Gas 4) for 10-15 minutes.

5 Meanwhile, cook the mushrooms with the lemon juice and enough water to cover. Drain well.

6 Prepare the chive potatoes: cook the potatoes in boiling salted water just until tender. Drain well.

7 When the trout are ready, transfer them to a warmed serving dish, cover, and set aside. Strain the cooking liquid into a saucepan and boil until syrupy. Whisk in the remaining butter, cut into small pieces. Add the mushrooms and season.

8 Pour the sauce over the trout. Serve immediately, with the potatoes tossed in the butter and chives.

Darnes de Colin, Pates au Basilic, Sauce Pistou

Hake Steaks with Basil Pasta and Tomato Pistou

INGREDIENTS

Serves 8

1 hake, weighing about 2 kg (4 lb), cleaned
salt and freshly ground pepper
125 ml (4 fl oz) olive oil

For the basil pasta

400 g (14 oz) flour
4 eggs
2 tsp olive oil, more for cooking noodles
1/2 bunch of basil, chopped
30 g (1 oz) butter

For the tomato pistou

100 ml (3 1/2 fl oz) olive oil
375 g (12 oz) tomatoes, concassées (see page 136)
3 garlic cloves, chopped
175 ml (6 fl oz) double cream
1/2 bunch of basil, chopped
150 g (5 oz) butter, cut into small pieces

PREPARATION

1 Cut the hake into steaks (see page 139), season them, shape into rounds, and secure each one with string.

2 Make the basil pasta: sift the flour into a bowl and add the eggs, oil, basil, and a little salt. Mix together to make a dough, then knead until smooth. Wrap and chill for at least 30 minutes.

3 Meanwhile, make the pistou: heat the oil in a saucepan and add the tomatoes, garlic, and seasoning. Cover with a round of buttered non-stick paper and cook until thick. Set aside.

4 Make the basil noodles by passing the dough through a pasta machine.

5 Season the hake steaks and sauté in hot olive oil for 10 minutes, or just until cooked, turning once. Remove the string and the central bone from the fish; keep warm.

6 Cook the noodles with a little olive oil in boiling salted water. Drain and sauté in butter for 1 minute.

7 Reheat the pistou and stir in the cream, chopped basil, and butter.

8 Serve the hake steaks on a bed of the noodles with the pistou spooned over.

Pave de Daurade au Beurre d'Algue

Sauteed Sea Bream with Seaweed Butter

INGREDIENTS

Serves 4

4 sea bream fillets with skin,
each weighing about 150 g (5 oz)
salt and freshly ground pepper
400 ml (14 fl oz) dry white wine
50 g (1 3/4 oz) onion, chopped
1 tbsp tomato purée
a little olive oil

For the seaweed butter

200 g (7 oz) edible seaweed, blanched
350 g (12 oz) butter, softened
juice of 1 lemon
75 g (2 1/2 oz) stoned black olives, chopped

For the garnish

750 g (1 1/2 lb) egg noodles
1 tomato, diced

PREPARATION

1 Make a slit in the skin of each fish fillet. Season the fillets and set aside.
2 Put the wine, onion, and tomato purée in a saucepan. Boil until reduced to a glaze.
3 Meanwhile, make the seaweed butter: put all the ingredients into a blender or food processor and purée until smooth.
4 Whisk the seaweed butter into the wine and tomato glaze. Season the sauce, and keep warm.
5 Heat a lightly oiled non-stick frying pan, add the fish fillets and cook gently, on the skin side only, just until done.
6 Meanwhile, cook the egg noodles with a little olive oil in boiling salted water for about 5 minutes. Drain well.
7 Make pools of sauce on individual plates and set the fish fillets on top. Garnish with the tomato dice. Serve immediately, with the egg noodles.

A Vegetable From the Sea

Seaweed is a major ingredient in Japanese cooking, and there are many different edible varieties available, such as wakame, nori, and kelp. When it is used in fish recipes, it contributes a beautiful green colour.

Seaweed is extremely nutritious – it is full of vitamins, minerals, and protein.

Ailes de Raie au Safran

Skate Wings with a Saffron Vinaigrette

INGREDIENTS

Serves 6

1·5 kg (3 lb) skate wings
200 ml (7 fl oz) white wine vinegar
200 ml (7 fl oz) court bouillon (see page 51)
1 kg (2 lb) egg noodles, cooked and tossed
in finely chopped parsley, to serve

For the saffron vinaigrette

4 oranges
2 pink grapefruit
1 lemon
300 ml (1/2 pint) olive oil
10 g (1/3 oz) saffron threads
30 g (1 oz) pink peppercorns
2-3 drops of Tabasco sauce, to taste
a pinch of celery seasoning

PREPARATION

1 Place the skate wings and vinegar in a bowl of iced water. Leave to *dégorge* for about 6 hours. Drain the skate, and dry on paper towels.
2 Cook the skate wings in the court bouillon, for 8-10 minutes. Remove the skate flesh from the cartilage and the skin. Divide into 6 portions.
3 Make the vinaigrette: squeeze the juice from the citrus fruits and mix with the oil and saffron. Mix in the remaining ingredients.
4 Put each portion of skate on a bed of noodles. Spoon over the vinaigrette and serve.

Supremes de Volaille Farcis Doria

Stuffed Chicken Breasts with Herbs and Cucumber

INGREDIENTS

Serves 8
8 chicken suprêmes, *each weighing about 200 g (7 oz)*
1 litre (1 3/4 pints) chicken stock, for poaching
2 cucumbers
45 g (1 1/2 oz) butter
snipped chives, for the garnish

For the stuffing
1 shallot, finely chopped
15 g (1/2 oz) butter
2 chicken legs, skinned and boned
1 egg white
200 ml (7 fl oz) crème fraîche
45 g (1 1/2 oz) fresh white breadcrumbs
15 g (1/2 oz) mixed herbs, finely chopped
salt and freshly ground pepper

For the sauce
60 g (2 oz) butter
75 g (2 1/2 oz) shallots, finely chopped
100 ml (3 1/2 fl oz) dry white wine
500 ml (16 fl oz) chicken stock
60 g (2 oz) mushrooms, chopped (optional)
400 ml (14 fl oz) double cream

Chicken Supremes

A suprême of chicken is a skinless chicken breast, with the wing bone still attached. Removing suprêmes from a whole chicken follows a similar technique to removing a duck breast (see page 141), but instead of only the breast meat being removed, the flesh is separated from the carcass through the wing joint.

PREPARATION

1 Make the stuffing: sweat the shallot in the butter until soft, then let cool. Grind the meat from the chicken legs in a food processor. Add the shallot and egg white, and grind again until very smooth. Put the mixture in a bowl set over an ice bath, and stir in the crème fraîche and breadcrumbs. Add the herbs and season.

2 Remove any rib or backbone from each chicken breast. Clean the tip of the wing bone.

3 Stuff the chicken breasts (see page 73).

4 Prepare the sauce: melt 15 g (1/2 oz) of the butter in a pan, add the shallots, and cook until soft. Add the wine and boil to reduce by half. Pour in the stock and add the mushrooms (if using). Bring back to a boil and reduce until syrupy. Set aside.

5 Wrap the chicken packages with aluminium foil and poach gently in the chicken stock for 15-20 minutes. Keep warm in the stock.

6 Cut the cucumbers into 4-cm (1 1/2-inch) sections. Cut into quarters and remove and discard the seeds. Turn the cucumber pieces by paring them in a quick curving movement (see page 135). Blanch in boiling water for 1-2 minutes. Drain and refresh. Set aside.

7 Strain the sauce and return it to the pan. Add the cream and boil to a coating consistency. Whisk in the remaining butter, cut into small pieces. Check the seasoning. Keep warm.

8 Sauté the turned cucumber in the butter until tender but not coloured.

9 Unwrap the chicken and cut into slices. Place the chicken on individual plates and spoon over the sauce. Garnish with the cucumber and chives.

Stuffing Chicken Breasts

A variety of different stuffings works well with chicken. Fresh herbs are a colourful addition and any type can be used. Tarragon, parsley, chervil, and chives are particularly good with chicken.

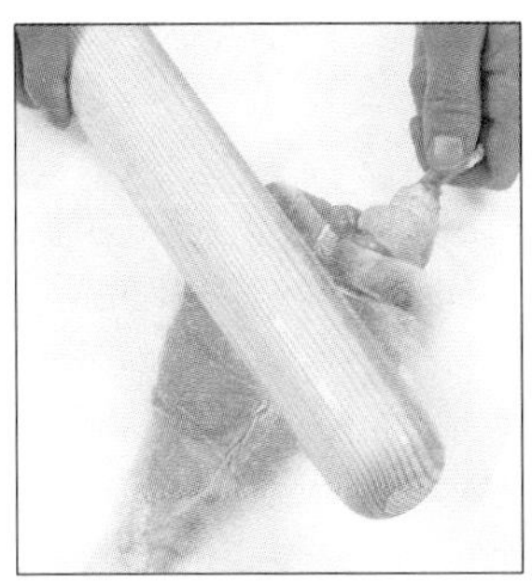

1 Remove the fillets from the breasts. Flatten both the fillets and the breasts between non-stick paper.

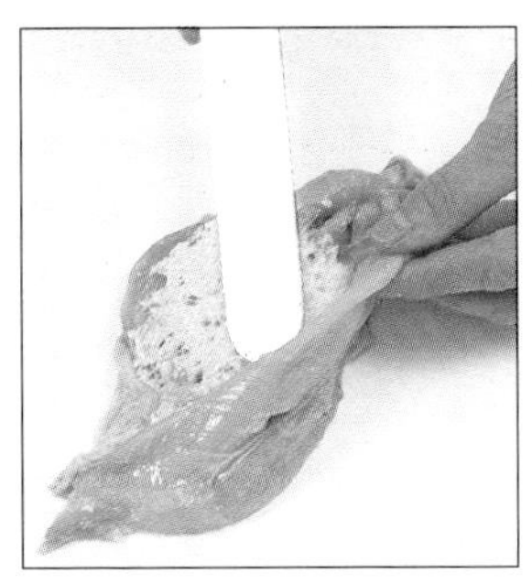

2 Cut a pocket in each breast, season, and fill with the stuffing. Replace the fillets on top.

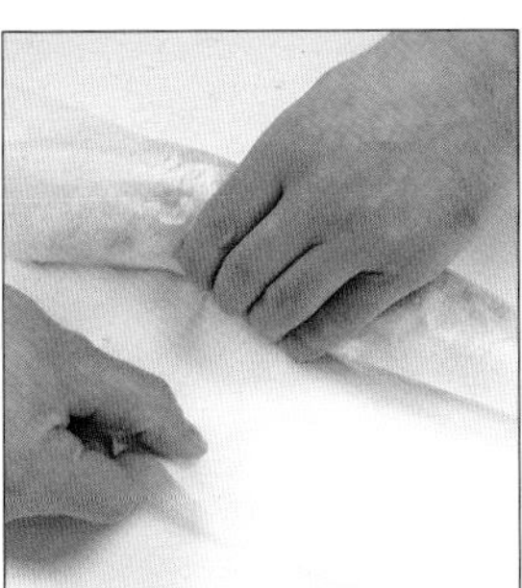

3 Roll up each breast in non-stick paper. Secure the ends of the packages with kitchen string.

Poulet a la Franchinoise

Chicken in Coconut Milk

INGREDIENTS

Serves 6

300 g (10 oz) freshly grated coconut or
90 g (3 oz) desiccated coconut
500 ml (16 fl oz) boiling water
1 chicken, jointed into 6 pieces (see page 140)
salt and freshly ground pepper
a pinch of cayenne pepper
2·5 cm (1 inch) cinnamon stick
a pinch of ground coriander
1 saffron thread, soaked in 2 tbsp hot water
2 egg yolks

For the spicy basmati rice

30 g (1 oz) butter
300 g (10 oz) basmati rice
4 whole cloves
2·5 cm (1 inch) cinnamon stick

PREPARATION

1 Soak the coconut in the boiling water: if using fresh coconut, soak for 20-30 minutes; if using desiccated coconut, soak for 1½ hours.

2 Pour the coconut pulp into a muslin-lined sieve set over a bowl, and strain the "milk". Squeeze the muslin to extract all the milk; discard the pulp.

3 Season the chicken pieces with salt and pepper and a pinch of cayenne. Put the chicken in a sauté pan and add the coconut milk, cinnamon, coriander, and saffron. Simmer for about 40 minutes. Remove the chicken and keep warm.

4 Prepare the rice: melt the butter in a saucepan, and stir in the rice, spices, and water to cover. Season and simmer, covered, for 15 minutes.

5 Mix the egg yolks with a little of the coconut sauce; stir into the coconut sauce to thicken. Return the chicken to the pan and serve immediately, with the spicy basmati rice.

Coq au Vin d'Alsace

Chicken Braised in White Wine

INGREDIENTS

Serves 4

1 chicken, weighing about 2 kg (4 lb), jointed into 8 pieces (see page 140)
60 ml (2 fl oz) vegetable oil
30 g (1 oz) flour
250 ml (8 fl oz) chicken stock
salt and freshly ground pepper
250 ml (8 fl oz) double cream

For the marinade

1 litre (1¾ pints) white wine, preferably from Alsace
200 g (7 oz) mirepoix of vegetables (see page 133)
2 garlic cloves, crushed
a bouquet garni
12 white peppercorns

For the garnish

150 g (5 oz) button mushrooms
45 g (1½ oz) butter
juice of ½ lemon
20 baby onions
a pinch of sugar
8 croûtes (see page 88)

PREPARATION

1 Combine the marinade ingredients in a large bowl. Add the chicken pieces. Cover and leave to marinate in a cool place for at least 24 hours.

2 Drain the chicken, reserving the marinade. Pat the chicken pieces dry with paper towels.

3 Heat the oil in a flameproof casserole, and sauté the chicken until brown. Sprinkle with the flour.

4 Strain the marinade, reserving both vegetables and liquid. Add the vegetables to the casserole and brown lightly. Pour in the marinade liquid and the stock, season, and bring to a boil. Reduce the heat, cover, and let simmer for 1 hour.

5 Meanwhile, prepare the garnish. Cook the mushrooms in 15 g (½ oz) of the butter and the lemon juice. Cook the onions in the remaining butter, the sugar, and water to cover. Shake the pan to make sure the onions caramelize evenly.

6 When the chicken is ready, remove it to a warmed serving dish and set aside. Strain the sauce into a saucepan and bring to a boil. Reduce until syrupy, then add the cream, and check the seasoning.

7 Add the mushroom and onion garnish to the sauce, then spoon over the chicken. Arrange 2 croûtes on each serving, and serve immediately.

Magret de Canard a la Pistache

Duck Breasts with Pistachios

INGREDIENTS

Serves 4

1 large mallard duck
salt and freshly ground pepper

For the sauce

300 g (10 oz) mirepoix of vegetables (see page 133)
a bouquet garni
100 ml (3½ fl oz) Amaretto
1 litre (1¾ pints) veal stock
3½ tbsp red wine vinegar
150 g (5 oz) pistachio paste, or pistachios puréed in a food processor
150 g (5 oz) butter, cut into small pieces

For the garnish

125 g (4 oz) shelled and skinned pistachios
250 g (8 oz) cooked carrots, puréed
300 g (10 oz) cooked sweet potato flesh, mixed with 200 g (7 oz) chestnut purée
400 g (14 oz) cooked peas (optional)
8 pea pods, blanched (optional)

PREPARATION

1 Remove the breasts from the duck (see page 141) and set aside. Chop up the remaining duck carcass.

2 Make the sauce: put the carcass in a pan with the mirepoix and bouquet garni. Cook, stirring, until brown. *Deglaze* with half the Amaretto. Add the stock, and water to cover. Bring to a boil, and reduce until syrupy. Strain and set aside.

3 Generously salt the duck breasts on the fat side. Cook them, fat-side down, in a heavy-based frying pan over low heat for 12 minutes. Three-quarters of the way through the cooking, turn the duck breasts over to seal the other side.

4 Remove the breasts and keep warm. Deglaze the pan with the remaining Amaretto and the vinegar. Add the duck stock and bring to a boil. Thicken the sauce with the pistachio paste, then whisk in the butter, a few pieces at a time. Check the seasoning.

5 Slice the breasts and arrange on individual plates. Pour the sauce around and garnish with pistachios, carrot purée, and sweet potato and chestnut purée. Peas served in their blanched pods can also be used for garnish.

Poulet Marine a la Moutarde

Marinated Chicken with Mustard

INGREDIENTS

Serves 4

1 chicken, weighing about 1 kg (2 lb)
180 ml (6 fl oz) lemon juice
75 ml (2½ fl oz) olive oil
sea salt and freshly ground pepper
3½ tbsp Dijon mustard

PREPARATION

1 With the breast of the bird down, split open the chicken by cutting along both sides of the backbone. Cut along the carcass, removing and discarding all the bones except the leg and wing tips. Open the chicken out flat, skin-side up, and press it down with the heel of your hand to flatten.

2 Mix the lemon juice and oil, pour over the chicken, and leave to marinate for 2 hours.

3 Grill the chicken with the skin towards the heat for about 15 minutes. Baste with the marinade from time to time.

4 Turn the chicken over and baste well. Cook for a further 15 minutes, or until the juices run clear.

5 Remove the chicken from the heat and brush with mustard. Season and return to the grill until the mustard melts into the bird.

6 Serve the chicken cut into 4 pieces.

POT AU FEU DE PINTADE

BRAISED GUINEA FOWL WITH BABY VEGETABLES

INGREDIENTS

Serves 8
3 litres (5 1/4 pints) chicken stock
15 g (1/2 oz) star anise
2 guinea fowl, trussed (see page 140)
200 g (7 oz) green beans
salt and freshly ground pepper
2 celery hearts, quartered
16 baby onions
24 baby carrots
16 pieces of celeriac, turned (see page 135)
16 baby leeks
16 baby turnips
16 new potatoes, turned (see page 135)
1 small Savoy cabbage
8 thick slices of beef marrow (optional)
2 tbsp sea salt (optional)

For the pasta dough
200 g (7 oz) flour
a pinch of salt
2 eggs

For the ravioli filling
liver and heart from the guinea fowl, fried and diced
60 g (2 oz) chicken livers, fried and diced
30 g (1 oz) butter
60 g (2 oz) mixed herbs, finely chopped
20 g (2/3 oz) breadcrumbs
1 garlic clove, finely chopped

For the vinaigrette
100 ml (3 1/2 fl oz) white wine vinegar
1 tsp Dijon mustard
1/2 tsp ground pepper
2 tsp salt
1/2 garlic clove, crushed
1 sprig of thyme
45 g (1 1/2 oz) mixed herbs, finely chopped
300 ml (1/2 pint) vegetable oil
3 1/2 tbsp walnut oil

PREPARATION

1 Make the pasta dough: mix the ingredients in a food processor until they come together. Knead lightly, then chill for 30 minutes. Make and fill the ravioli (see page 77); poach in 250 ml (8 fl oz) of the stock. Drain and keep warm.
2 Set 500 ml (16 fl oz) of the stock aside for cooking the vegetables. Put the remaining stock in a large pot and add the star anise. Bring to a boil. Add the guinea fowl and simmer gently, covered, for 35-40 minutes.
3 Meanwhile, cook the beans in boiling salted water, and all the remaining vegetables, individually, in the reserved stock. Drain well. Cut the cabbage into 8 wedges. Keep warm.
4 Make the vinaigrette: mix together all the ingredients in the order given.
5 If using beef marrow, poach gently in a little extra stock. Sprinkle with sea salt. Keep warm.
6 Drain the guinea fowl, season, and carve them so that the thighs can be served with the drumsticks, and the tip of the breast with the wing end. Arrange the pieces on warmed plates. If you like, reduce a little of the stock and use it to moisten the guinea fowl.
7 Divide the vegetables among the plates and dress with the vinaigrette. Serve with the warm ravioli, and the beef marrow, if you like.

PINTADE

Guinea fowl, or *pintade* in French, is native to Africa. It is a small bird which has similarities in flavour with pheasant and chicken. It has darker, leaner flesh than chicken, and this can dry out easily if overcooked.

Today, guinea fowl can be obtained in most large cities at any time of year. In France, before guinea fowl was widely available, it was traditionally sold six weeks after Easter, at Whitsun.

Making and Filling Ravioli

Ravioli, with a filling that includes the offal from guinea fowl, make a beautiful garnish. This step-by-step method can be adapted for a variety of different stuffings.

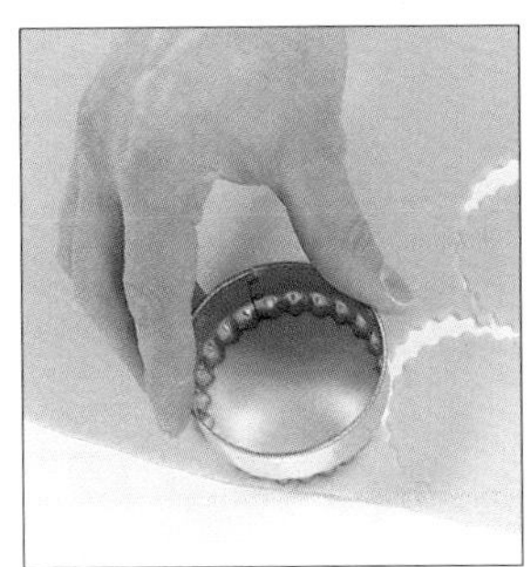

1 Roll out the pasta dough and cut into rounds with a fluted pastry cutter, or a pasta wheel.

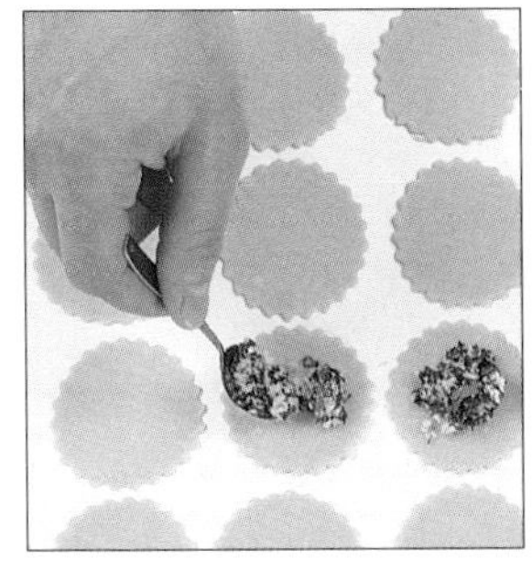

2 Mix the filling ingredients. Place a little mixture in the centre of half the pasta shapes.

3 Cover with the plain pasta, and seal the edges with a little water.

Cuisses de Dinde Farcies Boulangere

Stuffed Turkey Legs with Boulangere Potatoes

INGREDIENTS

Serves 6
6 turkey legs
salt and freshly ground pepper
100 ml (3½ fl oz) olive oil
2 shallots, finely chopped
2 garlic cloves, finely chopped
600 ml (1 pint) dry white wine
500 ml (16 fl oz) chicken stock
blond roux (see page 155), made from
60 g (2 oz) each butter and flour
120 ml (4 fl oz) double cream
500 g (1 lb) carrots, diced and cooked, for the garnish

For the stuffing
150 g (5 oz) bacon, diced
300 g (10 oz) fresh wild mushrooms, diced
1 apple, peeled and diced
100 g (3½ oz) butter
2 shallots, finely chopped
1 garlic clove, finely chopped
200 g (7 oz) skinless, boneless chicken breast
1 egg
1 bunch of flat-leaf parsley, finely chopped

For the boulangère potatoes
1 kg (2 lb) potatoes, sliced
150 ml (5 fl oz) vegetable oil
500 g (1 lb) large onions, sliced
100 g (3½ oz) butter
500 ml (16 fl oz) chicken stock
a bouquet garni

PREPARATION

1 Make the stuffing: blanch the diced bacon in boiling water; drain and set aside. Sauté the diced mushrooms and apple in half the butter until tender and the excess liquid has evaporated. In another pan, sweat the shallots and garlic in the remaining butter until soft. Leave to cool.

2 Put the chicken in a food processor and work until smooth. Turn into a bowl and set over an ice bath. Gradually beat in the egg. Add the mushroom mixture, bacon, shallots, garlic, and parsley; mix together well. Season and set aside.

3 Bone the turkey legs, leaving a little of the leg bone attached (see page 141). Season the legs and fill with the stuffing. Wrap the skin under the legs and secure with wooden cocktail sticks.

4 Heat the olive oil in a sauté pan, add the turkey legs and cook until brown. Add the shallots and garlic. *Deglaze* with 400 ml (14 fl oz) of the wine and add the stock. Simmer for 25 minutes.

5 Meanwhile, make the boulangère potatoes: sauté the potatoes in hot oil until golden. Drain well. Sauté the onions in the butter until soft. Layer the potatoes and onions in a baking dish. Add the stock and bouquet garni. Bake in a preheated oven at 180°C (350°F, Gas 4) for 1 hour.

6 Melt the butter in a saucepan and stir in the flour. Add the cooking liquid from the turkey legs and the remaining wine, and bring to a boil. Simmer for 20 minutes. Strain the sauce and return to the pan. Stir in the cream and check the seasoning.

7 Serve garnished with the carrots.

The Bird from the Indies

For some time after the early explorations, the New World was known as the Spanish Indies. As a result, the birds imported to Europe were known as *coq d'Inde* (Indian cock) by the French. This name was eventually corrupted to *dinde*, or *dindon*. In Italy, the bird became known as *galle d'India,* and in Germany it was named *Indianische henn*. Seafaring traders imported these birds to Britain from Seville, but many of them set off from Turkey in the eastern Mediterranean before collecting their cargo. Hence the name "turkey-birds".

Canette Rotie en Croute, Baies Cordon Bleu

Duckling Baked in a Herb and Peppercorn Crust

INGREDIENTS

Serves 4
2 shallots, peeled
a bouquet garni
1 duckling, weighing about 1·5 kg (3 lb)

For the dough
30 g (1 oz) mixed peppercorns
30 g (1 oz) herbes de Provence
1 kg (2 lb) flour
500 g (1 lb) coarse sea salt
300 g (10 oz) egg whites

For the Mireille potatoes
400 g (14 oz) potatoes, cut into julienne *strips*
150 g (5 oz) clarified butter
salt and freshly ground pepper
4 artichoke hearts, cooked and cut into julienne *strips*
200 g (7 oz) cooked ham, cut into julienne *strips*

For the sauce
2 shallots, finely chopped
90 g (3 oz) butter, cut into small pieces
1 bottle red wine from Bordeaux, such as Margaux
1 tbsp meat glaze (see page 145)
1 litre (1 3/4 pints) chicken stock

PREPARATION

1 Put the shallots and bouquet garni inside the duckling. Brown the duckling on all sides in a frying pan. Transfer to a baking dish and roast in a preheated oven at 180°C (350°F, Gas 4) for 15 minutes. Leave to cool.

2 Make the dough: grind the peppercorns with the herbes de Provence in a spice mill. Turn into a bowl, and add the flour, salt, and egg whites. Mix to a smooth dough, adding a little water if necessary.

3 Roll out the dough into a round 1 cm (3/8 inch) thick. Wrap the dough around the duckling, moulding it into shape. Place in a clean baking dish and bake for 45 minutes.

4 Meanwhile, prepare the potatoes: cook them in most of the butter until tender. Remove from the heat and season. Spread half of the potatoes in a cast-iron pan. Add the artichoke and ham strips, and cover with the remaining potatoes. Spoon over the remaining butter and bake for 30-35 minutes.

5 Make the sauce: sweat the shallots in a little butter, add the wine and meat glaze, and boil until reduced. Add the chicken stock and bring back to a boil. Reduce until syrupy. Strain the sauce through a fine sieve into a clean pan. Whisk in the butter, a few pieces at a time. Check the seasoning.

6 Serve the duckling, removing its crust, with the sauce in a sauceboat. Turn the potatoes upside-down on to a serving plate to accompany the duckling.

Pigeon Roti aux Navets Jus aux Morilles

Roast Pigeon with Turnips and Morel Sauce

INGREDIENTS

Serves 6
6 pigeons, each weighing about 400 g (14 oz)
175 g (6 oz) clarified butter
18 baby turnips
15 g (1/2 oz) butter
a pinch of sugar
60 g (2 oz) mushrooms, roughly chopped
1 shallot, chopped
300 ml (1/2 pint) chicken stock
125 g (4 oz) morels (wild mushrooms)
a few sprigs of flat-leaf parsley, for the garnish

PREPARATION

1 Sauté the pigeons in 150 g (5 oz) of the clarified butter until they are brown on all sides. Place the pigeons in a flameproof casserole and roast in a preheated oven at 220°C (425°F, Gas 7) for 20 minutes. They should still be a little pink.

2 Meanwhile, place the turnips, butter, sugar, and enough water to cover in a saucepan, and simmer until caramelized and tender. Arrange the turnips on individual plates. Keep warm.

3 Carve the pigeons and place the breast and leg pieces on top of the turnips. Keep warm.

4 Make the sauce: sauté the pigeon bones, mushrooms, and shallot in the casserole. *Deglaze* the casserole with the stock. Strain into a saucepan and reduce until syrupy.

5 Quickly sauté the morels in the remaining clarified butter. Add the sauce and check the seasoning.

6 Spoon the sauce over the pigeon, and garnish with parsley. Serve immediately.

Cailles Roties Grand-Mere

Roast Quail with Vegetable Cakes

INGREDIENTS

Serves 4
8 quails, each barded with 1 piece of bacon, and trussed (see page 140)
175 g (6 oz) butter
salt and freshly ground pepper
100 ml (3½ fl oz) dry white wine
300 ml (½ pint) veal stock

For the garnish
300 g (10 oz) streaky bacon, cut into small strips
300 g (10 oz) button mushrooms, halved
250 g (8 oz) baby onions
a pinch of sugar
a few sprigs of parsley

For the vegetable cakes
1 kg (2 lb) potatoes
150 g (5 oz) carrots
125 g (4 oz) turnips
100 ml (3½ fl oz) vegetable oil

"Strange to see how a good dinner and feasting reconciles everybody."

Samuel Pepys (1633-1703)

PREPARATION

1 Sauté the quails in one-third of the butter until golden brown on all sides. Season and transfer to a large flameproof casserole. Roast in a preheated oven at 180°C (350°F, Gas 4) for about 15 minutes.

2 Meanwhile, prepare the garnish: blanch the bacon, drain, and sauté in 20 g (⅔ oz) of the butter until golden brown. Sauté the mushrooms in another 20 g (⅔ oz) of the butter until golden brown. Cook the onions in a little salted water, sugar, and 20 g (⅔ oz) of the butter, until tender and caramelized. Keep the garnish warm.

3 Remove the quails from the casserole and keep warm. Pour off any excess fat and *deglaze* the casserole with the wine. Add the stock and boil to reduce by half. Whisk in the remaining butter, cut into small pieces. Check the seasoning. Keep the sauce warm.

4 Make the vegetable cakes (see below).

5 Place the quails on the vegetable cakes, allowing 2 per serving. Arrange the garnish next to the quails, spoon over the sauce, and finish with the parsley. Serve immediately.

Making Vegetable Cakes

This is an alternative way to present shredded vegetables. The starch from the potato helps bind the vegetables together during cooking. The cakes both look attractive and act as a garnishing bed for other ingredients.

1 Shred the vegetables in a food processor, using a shredding attachment. Season the mixed vegetables.

2 Shape the vegetables into 8 cakes and fry in hot oil until golden. Turn the cakes over.

3 Continue frying until the cakes are golden on the underside, then lift out, and drain on paper towels.

GAME OR POULTRY?

Quails are small migratory birds, originally found in Europe, Australia, and North America, where they were considered to be wild or game birds, and were hunted almost to extinction. As a result of this, several native species of quail are now protected by law. Once man realized the value of quails as a source of food, they were domesticated in a similar way to other types of poultry.

Gigue de Chevreuil Sauce Diane

Marinated Haunch of Venison with Chestnuts

INGREDIENTS

Serves 10

1 haunch of venison, weighing about 2 kg (4 lb)
400 g (14 oz) mirepoix of vegetables (see page 133)
a bouquet garni
a little vegetable oil
100 ml (3½ fl oz) red wine vinegar
100 ml (3½ fl oz) dry white wine
1 litre (1¾ pints) veal stock
12 black peppercorns, crushed
75 g (2½ oz) butter, cut into small pieces
100 ml (3½ fl oz) double cream

For the marinade

1 litre (1¾ pints) red wine
a bouquet garni
200 g (7 oz) mirepoix of vegetables
2 garlic cloves, finely chopped
salt and freshly ground pepper

For the garnish

1 kg (2 lb) chestnuts, shelled and peeled
120 ml (4 fl oz) chicken stock
1 celery stalk, chopped
a pinch of sugar
10 apples
juice of 1 lemon
90 g (3 oz) butter
60 g (2 oz) cranberries

PREPARATION

1 Mix together all the ingredients for the marinade. Add the haunch of venison. Cover, and leave to marinate in a cool place for at least 24 hours.

2 Remove the venison, strain the marinade, and reserve the liquid.

3 Put the venison in a flameproof casserole with the mirepoix, bouquet garni, and a little oil. Roast in a preheated oven at 220°C (425°F, Gas 7) for 50 minutes, basting from time to time.

4 While the venison is roasting, prepare the garnish: cook the chestnuts in the stock with the celery, sugar, and a little salt until tender; drain and set aside. Peel the apples, cut in half, and remove the cores. Rub all over with lemon juice to prevent discoloration. Put the apples in a baking dish and dot with 30 g (1 oz) of the butter. Set aside. Stew the cranberries in 30 g (1 oz) of the butter and a little water just until tender. Set aside.

5 Remove the venison from the casserole and keep warm. Pour off the fat, then *deglaze* the casserole with the vinegar. Boil until evaporated. Add the wine and the marinating liquid and boil until reduced by half. Add the stock and reduce for about 20 minutes, or until the sauce is well-flavoured.

6 Meanwhile, put the prepared apples in the oven and bake for 20 minutes, or until tender.

7 Remove the sauce from the heat and stir in the crushed peppercorns. Leave to infuse for 3 minutes, then strain into a saucepan. Check the seasoning. Whisk in the butter and then the cream.

8 Reheat the chestnuts in the remaining butter until glazed. Reheat the cranberries and spoon into the apple halves.

9 Carve the haunch of venison and serve on a platter, garnished with the chestnuts and filled apples. Serve the sauce in a sauceboat.

From the Hunt

The word "venison" derives from the Latin *venatio*, meaning hunt. As a result, French recipes calling for venison may refer to meat from any large game animal. There is one exception, however; when the hindquarter of the animal is specifically mentioned, as in this recipe, venison should be used rather than other types of game.

Diana, ancient goddess of the hunt, lends her name to the cream-and-pepper sauce traditionally served with venison, which has now become popular as a sauce for beef steaks.

Faisan Cuit en Cocotte au Repere

Pheasant Casserole

INGREDIENTS

Serves 2

250 g (8 oz) clarified butter
1 pheasant, trussed (see page 140)
salt and freshly ground pepper
12 small potatoes
8 baby onions
45 g (1 1/2 oz) bacon, cut into small pieces
a little vegetable oil
12 button mushrooms
2 tbsp Madeira
150 ml (5 fl oz) veal stock
100 g (3 1/2 oz) flour

PREPARATION

1 Divide the clarified butter into quarters. Sauté the pheasant in one-quarter of the clarified butter until brown. Transfer to a flameproof casserole, season, and set aside.
2 Peel the potatoes and trim into pieces about 3 cm (1 1/4 inches) long. Turn the potatoes by paring them in a quick curving movement (see page 135). Blanch the potatoes and drain well. Brown in one-quarter of the butter. Transfer the potatoes to the casserole.
3 Lightly brown the onions in one-quarter of the butter. Cover, and sweat over a low heat, until tender. Transfer to the casserole.
4 Blanch the bacon and drain. Sauté in a little oil until lightly browned. Add to the casserole.
5 Sauté the mushrooms in the remaining butter until lightly browned. Add to the casserole.
6 Place the casserole over a high heat and *deglaze* with the Madeira. Add the stock.
7 Mix the flour with water to make a sealing dough. Cover the casserole and seal. Cook in a preheated oven at 170°C (325°F, Gas 3) for 1-1 1/2 hours.
8 Remove the sealing dough and serve the pheasant straight from the casserole.

En Cocotte

A round or oval cooking pan with a tight-fitting lid, a cocotte is ideal for long, slow cooking, such as braising. Traditional cocotte pans are made of cast iron, but modern versions are also available in enamel, aluminium, or glazed ceramic.

Lapin Mijote aux Carottes Fondantes

Simmered Rabbit with Carrots

INGREDIENTS

Serves 4

8 rabbit legs, each weighing about 200 g (7 oz)
salt and freshly ground pepper
125 g (4 oz) flour
100 ml (3 1/2 fl oz) vegetable oil
150 g (5 oz) butter
75 g (2 1/2 oz) shallots, finely chopped
1·5 litres (2 1/2 pints) red wine
a bouquet garni
400 ml (14 fl oz) veal stock
750 g (1 1/2 lb) carrots, cut into small sticks
250 g (8 oz) baby onions
a pinch of sugar
500 g (1 lb) button mushrooms

PREPARATION

1 Sprinkle the rabbit with salt and pepper, then the flour. Sauté the rabbit in a flameproof casserole in the oil and half the butter until golden brown. Remove and set aside.
2 Sweat the shallots in the casserole until soft. Pour off the excess fat, and add the wine and bouquet garni. Return the rabbit to the casserole and simmer for about 20 minutes.
3 Add the veal stock and simmer gently for a further 20 minutes, or until the rabbit is cooked.
4 Meanwhile, cook the carrots in boiling salted water. Drain and add to the rabbit.
5 Cook the onions with 30 g (1 oz) of the butter, the sugar, and water to cover, until caramelized. Sauté the mushrooms in the remaining butter.
6 Serve the rabbit with the onions and mushrooms.

Entrecote au Thym Comme en Provence

Sirloin Steaks Provençal Style

INGREDIENTS

Serves 6

6 sirloin steaks, each weighing about 150 g (5 oz)
salt and freshly ground pepper
750 g (1 1/2 lb) potatoes
100 ml (3 1/2 fl oz) vegetable oil
24 cherry tomatoes, peeled
3 tbsp strong mustard
vegetable compote (see page 85), to serve

For the sauce

200 ml (7 fl oz) Madeira
300 ml (1/2 pint) veal stock
1/2 small bunch of thyme
20 g (3/4 oz) butter

The Herb of Happiness

Thyme is an aromatic herb, originally from southern Europe. It is used in many Provençal soups, stews, and sauces. Some people believe that thyme has more flavour when it is grown on its native soil. Throughout history it has been associated with strength and happiness, and it was widely used by the ancient Greeks and Romans.

PREPARATION

1 Trim and season the steaks; set aside.

2 Cut the potatoes into parisienne (see below). Sauté the balls in 3 tbsp of hot oil until golden. Keep the potatoes warm.

3 Make the sauce: boil the Madeira until reduced. Add the stock and reduce until syrupy. Whisk in the butter, cut into small pieces, to thicken the sauce slightly. Add the thyme leaves and keep the sauce warm.

4 Heat the cherry tomatoes in a steamer.

5 Heat the remaining oil in a pan and sauté the steaks until well-browned on both sides. They should be slightly rare in the centre. Cover the steaks with mustard.

6 Spoon some vegetable compote in the centre of each plate and set a steak on top. Surround with a ring of sauce and garnish with the potatoes and cherry tomatoes. Serve immediately.

Cutting Potatoes into Parisienne

These potatoes are an elegant garnish for any dish. The term "parisienne" refers to their round shape – obtained by using a melon baller. It may also suggest that a dish is made with button mushrooms or artichoke hearts.

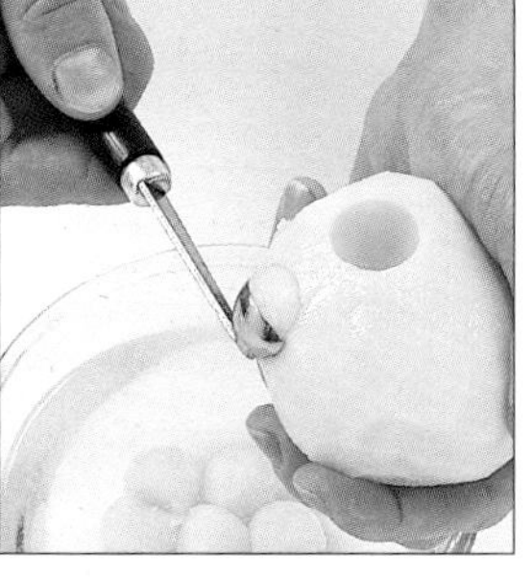

1 Peel the potatoes, then use a melon baller to cut the potatoes into even-sized balls.

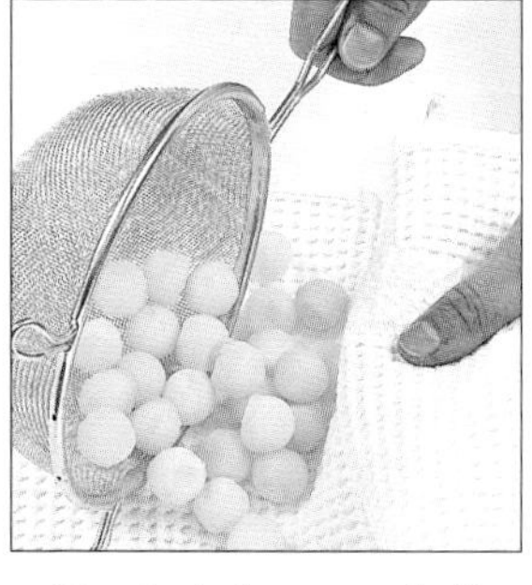

2 Cook the potato balls in boiling salted water just until tender. Drain well, and dry thoroughly.

Vegetable Compote

This is a mixture of vegetables reduced almost to a sauce, from the Provence region of France. Peppers, courgettes, and tomatoes are used abundantly in this region, as is olive oil.

- *200 g (7 oz) onions, diced*
- *a little olive oil*
- *1 red pepper*
- *1 yellow pepper*
- *1 green pepper*
- *300 g (10 oz) courgettes*
- *salt and freshly ground pepper*
- *4 tomatoes, concassées (see page 136)*
- *2 garlic cloves, finely chopped*
- *a bouquet garni*

Cook the onions gently in a little olive oil until soft and tender. Meanwhile, core and seed the peppers and cut them into small dice. Cut the courgettes into small dice. Add the pepper and courgette dice to the onions, mix in a little more olive oil, and cook until the peppers are just tender. Season and add the tomatoes concassées, finely chopped garlic, and the bouquet garni. Leave all the compote ingredients to cook over a low heat for 10 minutes, or until all the vegetables are tender.

Tournedos Montagnarde

Fillet Steaks with Goat's Cheese and Pine Nuts

INGREDIENTS

Serves 8

1 kg (2 lb) beef fillet, cut into 8 mignon *steaks*
250 g (8 oz) soft goat's cheese
2 egg yolks

For the sauce

6 shallots, finely chopped
90 g (3 oz) butter
120 ml (4 fl oz) red wine
180 ml (6 fl oz) Madeira
300 ml (1/2 pint) veal stock
salt and freshly ground pepper
60 g (2 oz) pine nuts, lightly toasted
1/2 bunch of chives, snipped

For the garnish

350 g (12 oz) fresh wild mushrooms, such as horns of plenty
1 shallot, finely chopped
150 g (5 oz) butter
1 kg (2 lb) green beans
1 kg (2 lb) carrots, turned (see page 135)

For the croûtes

8 slices of white bread, cut into rounds
30 ml (1 fl oz) olive oil
2 garlic cloves, crushed

PREPARATION

1 Make the sauce: sweat the chopped shallots in 30 g (1 oz) of the butter until soft. *Deglaze* with the red wine and boil to reduce. Add the Madeira and stock, and boil to reduce until syrupy. Season, then whisk in the remaining butter, cut into small pieces. Keep the sauce warm.

2 For the garnish, sauté the mushrooms and shallots in the butter just until tender. Cook the green beans and the carrots, separately, in boiling salted water just until tender. Drain and keep warm.

3 Sauté the steaks on both sides in a non-stick pan. Transfer them to a baking sheet. Mix the goat's cheese with the egg yolks and spoon on top of the steaks. Place in a preheated oven at 220°C (425°F, Gas 7) for 6-8 minutes, until glazed.

4 Meanwhile, make the *croûtes*: fry the slices of bread in the olive oil and garlic. Drain the croûtes on paper towels.

5 Serve each steak on a croûte. Add the pine nuts and chives to the sauce and spoon around the steaks. Garnish with the vegetables.

Filet de Boeuf Louis XIV

Fillet of Beef with Foie Gras, Truffles, and Macaroni Gratin

INGREDIENTS

Serves 6

1 centre-cut beef fillet, weighing about 1 kg (2 lb)
salt and freshly ground pepper
150 g (5 oz) liver mousse (mousse de foie gras)
6 slices of truffle
1 tbsp meat glaze (see page 145)
1 large piece of pork caul
3 1/2 tbsp vegetable oil
45 g (1 1/2 oz) butter
7 tbsp port
300 ml (1/2 pint) veal stock
watercress, for the garnish

For the macaroni gratin

150 g (5 oz) macaroni
1/2 onion, finely chopped
45 g (1 1/2 oz) butter
100 g (3 1/2 oz) Gruyère cheese, grated
3 eggs, lightly beaten
180 ml (6 fl oz) double cream
a few slices of truffle, finely chopped

PREPARATION

1 Trim the fillet, reserving the trimmings. Cut the fillet lengthwise in half, without cutting completely through the meat.
2 Season the fillet and stuff it with the liver mousse. Coat the slices of truffle in meat glaze and arrange them on the mousse.
3 Reshape the whole fillet. Wrap in caul and tie with string. Set aside in a cool place until ready to cook.
4 Make the macaroni gratin: cook the macaroni in boiling salted water just until tender. Drain and refresh. Set aside.
5 Cook the onion in the butter until soft. Remove from the heat and add the macaroni and Gruyère cheese. Mix together the eggs and cream and stir into the macaroni mixture. Season to taste, and add the chopped truffle.
6 Turn the macaroni mixture into a buttered charlotte mould or individual buttered brioche moulds. Set in a *bain marie* and bake in a preheated oven at 180°C (350°F, Gas 4) for 20-25 minutes. When ready, leave to rest for 5-10 minutes before turning out for serving.
7 Cook the fillet: brown the trimmings from the meat in the oil and 15 g (1/2 oz) of the butter in a roasting tin. Remove the trimmings and discard. Add the fillet and brown on all sides. Transfer to the oven and roast for 15-18 minutes. The meat should be rare or medium, as preferred.
8 Remove the fillet and keep warm. Pour off all the excess fat from the roasting tin. *Deglaze* the tin with the port, then add the stock. Bring to a boil, stirring to dissolve the juices and sediment in the bottom of the tin. Simmer until reduced by half. Strain through a fine sieve into a saucepan. Whisk in the remaining butter, cut into small pieces, to thicken the sauce. Check the seasoning.
9 Slice the fillet to serve. Garnish with watercress, the macaroni gratin, and the sauce.

A Dish Fit for a King

Louis XIV is well known for the impact he had on French cooking, revolutionizing the country's kitchen equipment and the cultivation of fruit and vegetables. He is also remembered for the amount of food he consumed at his elaborate banquets. It is fitting that his name is associated with this rich and delicious combination of beef, pasta, and cheese.

Boeuf Bourguignon

Beef in Red Wine

INGREDIENTS

Serves 6

750 g (1 1/2 lb) boneless stewing beef, such as neck
30 g (1 oz) flour
100 g (3 1/2 oz) clarified butter
2 tsp tomato purée
750 ml (1 1/4 pints) beef stock

For the marinade

1 litre (1 3/4 pints) red wine
200 g (7 oz) mirepoix of vegetables (see page 133)
2 garlic cloves, finely chopped
12 black peppercorns

For the garnish

150 g (5 oz) baby onions
60 g (2 oz) butter
salt and freshly ground pepper
a pinch of sugar
150 g (5 oz) mushrooms
150 g (5 oz) bacon, cut into small strips
1 tbsp vegetable oil
parsley, finely chopped
6 croûtes (see page 88)

PREPARATION

1 Cut the beef into large cubes. Mix all the marinade ingredients in a bowl and add the beef. Cover and leave to marinate for at least 12 hours.
2 Remove the beef, reserving the marinade. Pat the beef cubes dry and sprinkle with the flour. In a flameproof casserole, sauté the beef in the clarified butter until well-browned on all sides.
3 Strain the marinade, keeping both the vegetables and the liquid. Add the vegetables and the tomato purée to the beef and brown lightly. Add the marinade liquid and boil until reduced by half.
4 Add the beef stock and bring back to a boil. Cover and simmer over a low heat for 1 1/2 hours.
5 Meanwhile, prepare the garnish: put in a pan with the onions and half of the butter, and just enough water to cover. Add the sugar and seasoning, and simmer for 8-10 minutes until golden. Sauté the mushrooms in the remaining butter. Put the bacon in a pan of cold water, bring to a boil, drain, and refresh. Sauté in the oil, until golden. Drain and add to the onions and mushrooms.
6 Transfer the beef to a serving dish, garnish with the onions, mushrooms, and bacon, and sprinkle with parsley. Serve with the croûtes.

Veau Saute a la Marengo

Veal, Tomato, and Mushroom Stew

The dish is said to take its name from the Battle of Marengo in 1800, when Napoleon Bonaparte's chef first created it in celebration of the French victory over the Austrians. Here, we show the classic recipe with its traditional garnish of crayfish, deep-fried eggs, and croûtes.

INGREDIENTS

Serves 4

1 kg (2 lb) boned breast of veal, cut into chunks
100 ml (3½ fl oz) olive oil
1 onion, chopped
a little flour
100 ml (3 ½ fl oz) veal stock
500 g (1 lb) tomatoes, concassées (see page 136)
1 tbsp tomato purée
1 garlic clove, finely chopped
250 g (8 oz) button mushrooms, quartered
a bouquet garni
a pinch of freshly grated nutmeg
salt and freshly ground pepper

For the garnish

2 slices of white bread
2 tbsp olive oil
oven-baked rice (see page 89)
4 crayfish, cooked (see page 26)
4 deep-fried eggs (see page 146)
finely chopped parsley

PREPARATION

1 Sauté the veal chunks in hot olive oil in a flameproof casserole until lightly browned. Add the onion and cook until soft. Sprinkle with a little flour and stir well, then cook for 5 minutes.
2 Stir in the stock, tomatoes, tomato purée, garlic, mushrooms, bouquet garni, nutmeg, and seasoning. Cook, covered, over a low heat, for about 1 hour.
3 Meanwhile, make heart-shaped *croûtes* (see below), toasting them in a preheated oven at 190°C (375°F, Gas 5).
4 Serve the veal with the oven-baked rice. Garnish with croûtes, crayfish, eggs, and parsley.

A New Marengo

Charles Poulain, chef des cuisines of the prestigious *Automobile Club de France*, was one of Marthe Distel's first chef-instructors and contributors to *La Cuisinière Cordon Bleu* magazine. This is his version of classic Veal Sauté à la Marengo, which was originally published in the magazine in 1896.

Making Heart-Shaped Croutes

Croûtes are an appealing crunchy garnish for stews, soups, and salads. They can be oven-toasted or fried in olive oil. A heart is just one of the many shapes that can be prepared.

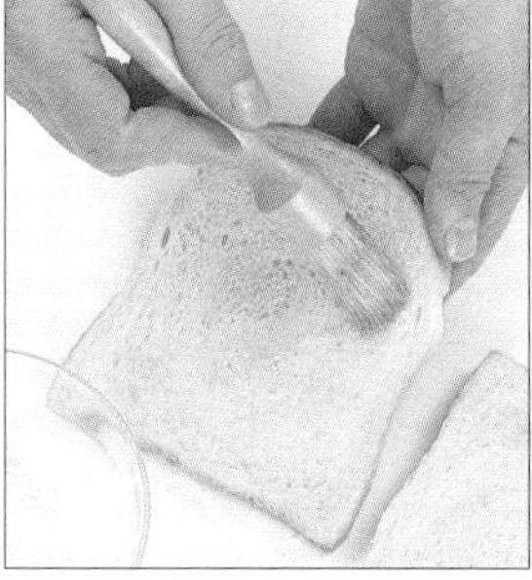

1 Use a pastry brush to spread a little olive oil evenly over both sides of each slice of bread.

2 Use a pastry or aspic cutter, depending on the size required, to stamp out heart shapes.

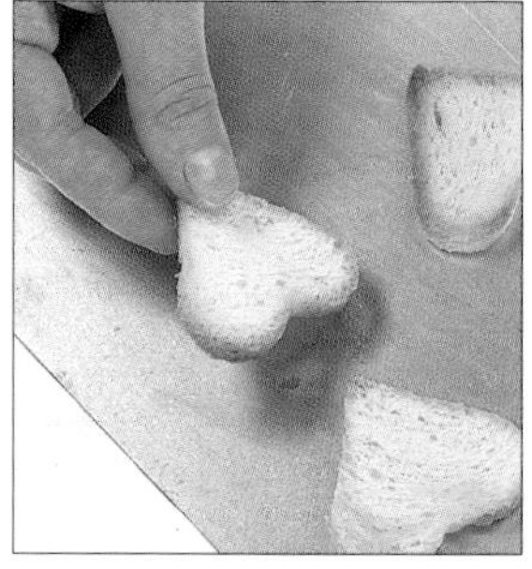

3 Toast the croûtes on a baking tray in the oven for 5-10 minutes, turning once to brown both sides.

Oven-Baked Rice

Basmati rice is a long-grain rice that cooks more quickly than other varieties. It is the best-flavoured rice for general use.

- *45 g (1 1/2 oz) butter*
- *1 shallot, finely chopped*
- *200 g (7 oz) basmati rice*
- *350 ml (12 fl oz) hot white veal stock*
- *a bouquet garni*
- *salt and freshly ground pepper*

Melt the butter in a flameproof casserole, add the shallot and sauté until soft. Add the rice and cook for 2 minutes, or until all the butter has been absorbed and the grains are transparent. Add the stock with the bouquet garni, salt, and pepper. Cover the casserole and bring to a boil. Place in a preheated oven at 180°C (350°F, Gas 4) for about 25 minutes, or until the rice is tender and all of the liquid has been absorbed. If the rice is too firm at this stage, add more liquid to the casserole. Remove the rice from the oven and leave to rest for 5 minutes before serving. To shape the rice into timbales, pack it into ramekins and turn out on to individual plates.

Escalopes de Veau Vallee d'Auge

Veal Escalopes with Apples and Calvados

INGREDIENTS

Serves 6

6 veal escalopes, each weighing about 175 g (6 oz)
4 tsp vegetable oil
60 g (2 oz) clarified butter
3 shallots, chopped
500 g (1 lb) mushrooms, sliced
3½ tbsp Calvados
300 ml (½ pint) crème fraîche
salt and freshly ground pepper

For the garnish

6 apples, peeled, cored, and cut into rings
60 g (2 oz) clarified butter
finely chopped parsley

PREPARATION

1 Pound the escalopes (see page 142). Sauté them in the oil and butter until lightly browned.
2 Add the shallots and mushrooms. Cook until the veal is tender and vegetables soft. *Deglaze* the pan with Calvados, then stir in the crème fraîche.
3 Remove the escalopes and keep warm. Boil the sauce to reduce to a thicker consistency. Season.
4 Sauté the apple rings in the remaining clarified butter just until tender.
5 Spoon the sauce over the escalopes and serve garnished with the apples and parsley.

The Best of Normandy

A fertile region of northern France, Normandy is famous for the quality of its agricultural produce. Three of the best – veal from the Auge valley, apples, and Calvados (made from distilled cider) – are combined in this classic recipe.

Longe de Veau Braisee a l'Angevine

Loin of Veal with Smoked Ham and Sorrel

INGREDIENTS

Serves 10

1 boned loin of veal, weighing about 2·5 kg (5 lb)
2 tbsp vegetable oil
salt and freshly ground pepper
100 g (3½ oz) butter
400 g (14 oz) onions and carrots, diced
150 g (5 oz) bacon, cut into small strips
1 tbsp curry powder
1 tbsp flour
300 ml (½ pint) dry white wine, such as Jasnières
300 ml (½ pint) white veal stock
100 ml (3½ fl oz) crème fraîche
1 egg yolk
100 g (3½ oz) smoked ham, cut into julienne *strips*
10 large sorrel leaves, cut into julienne *strips*
watercress, for the garnish

PREPARATION

1 Sauté the veal in hot oil in a flameproof casserole for 10 minutes, turning the meat so that it is well-coloured on all sides. Season and roast in a preheated oven at 200°C (400°F, Gas 6) for 1 hour, or until cooked.
2 Pour off excess fat from the casserole, then add the butter, onions and carrots, and the bacon. Roast for a further 10 minutes, watching to be sure the vegetables do not colour too much.
3 Add the curry powder and flour and stir to mix well with the vegetables and melted butter. *Deglaze* with the wine. Cover the loin of veal with foil and return to the oven. Roast for a further 20 minutes, basting from time to time.
4 Remove the loin of veal and keep warm. Add the stock to the casserole and bring to a boil on top of the stove, stirring well. Boil to reduce the sauce by one-third.
5 Mix the crème fraîche and egg yolk together. Add to the sauce and stir in gently. Do not boil. Stir in the ham and sorrel. Check the seasoning.
6 Carve the loin of veal into thin slices and arrange on a warmed serving platter. Cover the veal slices with the sauce and garnish with watercress.

Foie de Veau a la Bordelaise

Braised Calf's Liver with Fresh Ceps

INGREDIENTS

Serves 8-10

1 calf's liver, weighing 1-1·5 kg (2-3 lb), trimmed
150 g (5 oz) pork fat, cut into 5-cm (2-inch) strips and chilled in iced water
250 ml (8 fl oz) dry white wine
3 carrots, chopped
a bouquet garni
750 g (1 1/2 lb) fresh ceps, chopped
400 g (14 oz) onions, chopped
100 g (3 1/2 oz) shallots, chopped
200 g (7 oz) butter
1 piece of pork caul, weighing about 300 g (10 oz)
300 ml (1/2 pint) brown veal stock
30 g (1 oz) beurre manié (see page 155)

For the Duchess potatoes

500 g (1 lb) potatoes
salt and freshly ground pepper
45 g (1 1/2 oz) butter
3 egg yolks
a pinch of freshly grated nutmeg

PREPARATION

1 Lard the liver: sew the pork fat strips into the liver with a trussing needle. Put the liver in a bowl with the wine, carrots, and bouquet garni. Cover and leave to marinate overnight.

2 Sauté the ceps with the onions and shallots in a little butter until tender.

3 Drain the liver, reserving the marinade, and pat dry. Brown it in a little of the butter.

4 Wrap the liver and ceps together in the caul. Braise the liver with the reserved marinade and the stock in a flameproof casserole for 30 minutes.

5 Meanwhile, prepare the Duchess potatoes: put the potatoes in a pan of cold salted water, bring to a boil, and boil until tender. Drain and mash the potatoes. Beat in the butter, egg yolks, nutmeg, and seasoning. Put the mixture into a piping bag fitted with a star nozzle, and pipe swirls on to a buttered baking sheet. Put the potato swirls under a hot grill until lightly browned on top.

6 Remove the liver and keep warm. Strain the cooking liquid and boil until reduced to a glaze. Thicken with beurre manié. Serve the liver sliced, with the sauce and potatoes.

Escalopes de Veau Chasseur

Veal Escalopes in a Mushroom and Wine Sauce

INGREDIENTS

Serves 6

6 veal escalopes, each weighing about 175 g (6 oz)
salt and freshly ground pepper
1 tbsp clarified butter
250 g (8 oz) mushrooms, sliced
1 tbsp vegetable oil
1 shallot, chopped
3 tbsp dry white wine
2 tbsp tomato purée
150 ml (5 fl oz) veal stock
2 tsp meat glaze (see page 145)

For the garnish

500g (1 lb) fresh noodles, cooked (optional)
finely chopped parsley

PREPARATION

1 Pound the escalopes (see page 142) and season. Melt the butter in a pan, add the escalopes, and sauté until lightly browned on both sides and just cooked. Remove from the pan and keep warm.

2 Add the mushrooms to the butter with the oil and cook until golden brown. Add the shallot and cook for 1 minute, then moisten with the wine. Boil to reduce by half.

3 Stir in the tomato purée, stock, and meat glaze, to make a rich sauce.

4 Place the escalopes on a bed of noodles, if you like. Spoon the sauce over the escalopes, sprinkle with parsley, and serve.

An Updated Classic

Devised by master chef Henri Paul Pellaprat (1869-1950), one of the most influential figures in the history of Le Cordon Bleu, this classic recipe has been revised by Chef Jean-Claude Herchembert. During Pellaprat's 30 years as an instructor at the school, he wrote a number of highly influential articles and books, including *L'Art Culinaire Moderne* (first edition 1935) and *La Cuisine Familiale et Pratique*. Chasseur, or hunter's, sauce is always made with mushrooms, shallots, and tomatoes.

Carre d'Agneau Persille

Rack of Lamb with Parsley and Garlic Crust

With its juicy fork-tender meat, rack of lamb is incomparable for its succulence. In this superb yet simple recipe, the lamb's great flavour is complemented by Dijon mustard and a crunchy parsley and garlic crust. A colourful ratatouille is the perfect accompaniment.

INGREDIENTS

Serves 6

2 best ends of neck of lamb, each with 6 ribs
salt and freshly ground pepper
2 tbsp vegetable oil
500 ml (16 fl oz) brown veal stock or water
1 bunch of watercress, for the garnish
ratatouille Niçoise (see page 93), to serve

For the parsley and garlic crust

90 g (3 oz) fresh white breadcrumbs
45 g (1 1/2 oz) butter, softened
60 g (2 oz) parsley, finely chopped
salt and freshly ground pepper
8 garlic cloves, finely chopped
2 tbsp Dijon mustard

PREPARATION

1 Prepare the best ends of neck of lamb for roasting (see page 143) and season.
2 Heat the oil in a roasting tin, add the lamb, and cook until lightly browned on all sides. Remove the lamb and let cool slightly.
3 Make the parsley and garlic crust (see below).
4 Return the lamb to the tin and roast in a preheated oven at 220°C (425°F, Gas 7) for 15-20 minutes, or until the crust is brown; the meat should still be pink in the centre. Remove the lamb from the tin and keep warm.
5 Pour off all the excess fat from the tin, leaving behind the sediment and cooking juices. Put the tin on top of the stove, and *deglaze* with the stock or water. Boil until reduced and concentrated, then strain into a saucepan and keep warm.
6 Carve the lamb into cutlets and arrange on warmed plates with ratatouille. Spoon the sauce over the meat. Garnish each serving with watercress sprigs, and serve immediately.

Making Parsley and Garlic Crust

Coating the fat side of rack of lamb with a crust both flavours the meat and keeps it moist while it is being cooked. It also makes an attractive presentation.

1 Beat the breadcrumbs in a bowl with the butter, parsley, garlic, and salt and pepper to taste.

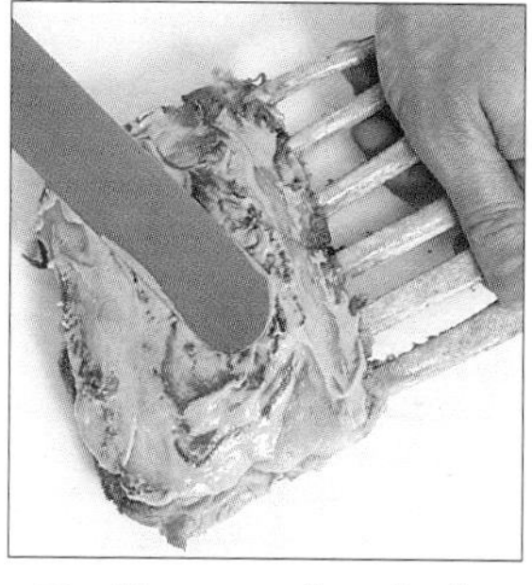

2 Using a palette knife, spread the fat side of the lamb evenly with the Dijon mustard.

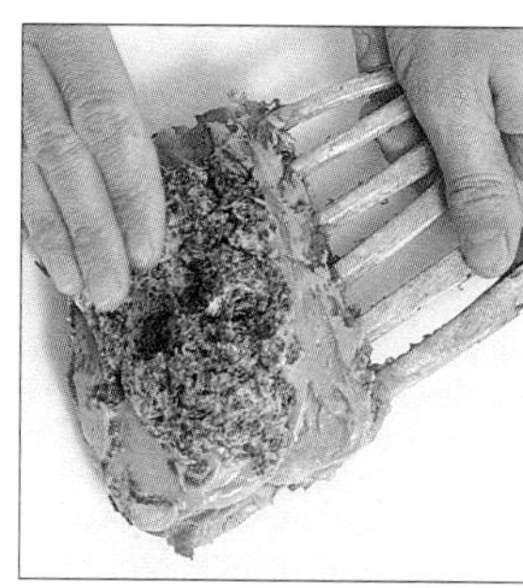

3 Cover the mustard with the parsley and garlic mixture, pressing it down firmly on to the mustard.

Ratatouille Niçoise

The colours and flavours of this vegetable dish – a classic from the city of Nice in Provence, evoke the sunny climate of that region. Make it ahead of time – it improves with reheating.

♦

♦ 1 aubergine ♦ 250 g (8 oz) courgettes ♦ salt and freshly ground pepper ♦ 90 ml (3 fl oz) olive oil ♦ 1 onion, finely sliced ♦ 3 peppers (green, red, and yellow), finely sliced ♦ 3 medium tomatoes, concassées (see page 136) ♦ 1 tbsp tomato purée ♦ 3 garlic cloves, finely chopped ♦ a bouquet garni

Slice the aubergine and courgettes into sticks about 4 cm (1 1/2 inches) long and 6 mm (1/4 inch) wide. Sprinkle the aubergine and courgettes with salt, and let stand for 20-30 minutes, to draw out the bitter juices. Rinse under cold running water, drain, and pat dry. Heat the oil in a heavy saucepan over a high heat, add the onion and peppers, and cook until softened. Add the aubergine, courgettes, and all the remaining ingredients. Stir gently, season, then simmer over a low heat, without stirring, for 20 minutes. Discard the bouquet garni and adjust seasoning before serving.

Gigot d'Agneau du Boulanger

Leg of Lamb in a Brioche Crust

INGREDIENTS

Serves 8
1 boned leg of lamb
salt and freshly ground pepper
1 tbsp olive oil
250 g (8 oz) mirepoix of vegetables (see page 133)
a bouquet garni
300 ml (1/2 pint) veal stock
120 ml (4 fl oz) double cream
150 g (5 oz) butter, cut into small pieces
1 bunch of watercress, for the garnish

For the brioche dough
500 g (1 lb) flour
1 tbsp salt
15 g (1/2 oz) fresh yeast
1 tbsp hot milk
6 eggs
250 g (8 oz) butter, softened
1 beaten egg, for glazing

For the braised lettuce
4 lettuces, cut into strips
250 g (8 oz) mirepoix of vegetables
75 g (2 1/2 oz) butter
300 ml (1/2 pint) brown veal stock

PREPARATION

1 Make the brioche dough: sift the flour and salt on to a work surface and make a large well in the centre. Dissolve the yeast in the hot milk and put into the well with the eggs. Gradually incorporate the flour to make a sticky dough. Knead lightly and place in an oiled bowl for 1 1/2-2 hours, until it has risen. Add the softened butter to the dough and knead until it is completely incorporated, at least 10 minutes. The dough should be elastic to the touch. Return the dough to an oiled bowl, cover, and let it rise in the refrigerator overnight.

2 Trim the lamb, reserving any trimmings. Season, and tie the meat into a neat shape with string, taking care not to tie it too tightly.

3 Roast the lamb in the olive oil in a preheated oven at 200°C (400°F, Gas 6) for about 40 minutes, turning it so that it browns evenly. Halfway through cooking, add any lamb trimmings to the roasting tin together with the mirepoix and bouquet garni. Continue roasting until the lamb is cooked rare.

4 Remove the leg of lamb and set aside to cool. Pour excess fat from the tin. *Deglaze* with the stock, then strain into a saucepan, and set aside.

5 Remove the brioche dough from the refrigerator and knead lightly. Roll out the brioche dough to about 2-cm (3/4-inch) thickness. Brush all over with beaten egg.

6 Remove the string from the leg of lamb. Set the lamb in the centre of the dough, and wrap the dough neatly around the meat.

7 Turn the wrapped leg over so the dough seam is underneath, and set on a buttered baking tray. Leave to rise for about 45 minutes.

8 Meanwhile, blanch the lettuce in boiling salted water for about 3 minutes. Drain and refresh. Sweat the mirepoix in the butter until soft. Add the lettuce and moisten with the stock. Braise for 30 minutes. Season.

9 Brush the brioche crust all over with egg glaze. Place in the oven and bake for about 45 minutes.

10 Reheat the sauce gently. Add the cream and reduce until syrupy. Whisk in the butter and season.

11 Serve the leg of lamb in its crust with the braised lettuce and the sauce. Garnish with watercress.

The Gigot of Lamb

A *gigot* is a French cut of lamb, resembling an ancient, elongated stringed instrument known as *gigu*. A gigot is traditionally the hind leg of lamb and the muscles beyond it. It is usually sold on the bone, but this can be easily removed with a sharp knife.

Canon d'Agneau en Crepinette au Persil

Lamb Fillet with Chicken and Parsley Mousse

INGREDIENTS

Serves 4–6

2 fillets of lamb, trimmed
2½ tbsp vegetable oil, more for deep-frying
salt and freshly ground pepper
1 bunch of flat-leaf parsley
500 g (1 lb) skinless, boneless chicken breasts
2 egg whites
350 ml (12 fl oz) crème fraîche
1 piece of pork caul, weighing about 500 g (1 lb), halved
1 litre (1¾ pints) chicken stock
60 g (2 oz) butter

For the garnish

500 g (1 lb) carrots, turned (see page 135)
500 g (1 lb) turnips, turned (see page 135)
250 g (8 oz) petits pois
30 g (1 oz) butter

PREPARATION

1 Brown the lamb fillets on all sides in the oil. Remove from the pan. Season and leave to cool.
2 Deep-fry the parsley in vegetable oil until bright green. Drain on paper towels, then purée in a food processor, reserving a few sprigs for garnish.
3 Put the chicken and egg whites in a food processor and purée until smooth. Turn into a bowl set over an ice bath. Gradually whisk in the crème fraîche. Season and mix in the parsley purée.
4 Spread out 1 piece of the caul on a cloth. Cover evenly with half the chicken mousse. Set 1 lamb fillet on top and wrap up in the caul. Repeat for the second fillet. Chill for 1 hour.
5 Cook the vegetables for the garnish, separately, in boiling salted water just until tender. Drain and set them aside together.
6 Boil the stock until well reduced. Keep hot.
7 Sauté the lamb in the butter over a low heat, turning to lightly brown on all sides. Transfer to a preheated oven at 180°C (350°F, Gas 4) for about 5 minutes. Remove from the oven and leave to rest for 5 minutes. Meanwhile, quickly toss the vegetable garnish in hot butter.
8 Cut the lamb into thin slices, arrange around the edge of a platter, and pile the vegetable garnish in the centre. Spoon the reduced stock over the meat.

Croquets d'Agneau a l'Infusion de Menthe

Lamb Croquettes with a Fresh Mint Infusion

INGREDIENTS

Serves 6

3 fillets of lamb, trimmed
3½ tbsp vegetable oil
salt and freshly ground pepper
6 sheets of phyllo pastry
2 egg whites, lightly beaten
1 bunch of fresh mint, stalks removed
30 button mushrooms
75 g (2½ oz) clarified butter
juice of ½ lemon
400 g (14 oz) spinach, stalks removed

For the sauce

2 tbsp honey
100 ml (3½ fl oz) dry vermouth, such as Noilly Prat
300 ml (½ pint) chicken stock
60 g (2 oz) butter, cut into small pieces
2 tbsp mint leaves, cut into julienne *strips*
2 tbsp whole-grain mustard

PREPARATION

1 Sauté the lamb fillets in a little oil until lightly browned on all sides. Season and leave to cool.
2 Brush one sheet of phyllo pastry with beaten egg white and set another sheet on top. Brush it with egg white and cover with mint leaves. Set a lamb fillet near one edge and roll up, tucking in the ends neatly. Repeat for the remaining fillets.
3 Heat a little more oil and quickly sauté the phyllo-covered fillets. Transfer to a baking tray and finish the cooking in a preheated oven at 180°C (350°F, Gas 4) for about 10 minutes.
4 Meanwhile, cook the mushrooms in half the clarified butter with the lemon juice.
5 Cook the spinach in the remaining clarified butter until tender; drain, then purée the spinach in a food processor. Drain the purée in a sieve to remove excess liquid. Season and keep warm.
6 Make the sauce: cook the honey until it turns a light brown. *Deglaze* with the vermouth, then add the stock and reduce until syrupy. Whisk in the butter, and add the mint julienne and mustard.
7 Place the spinach purée on individual plates. Slice the lamb fillets and put on the plates. Garnish with the mushrooms and spoon over the honey sauce.

Carre de Porc a la Franc-Comtoise

Roast Loin of Pork with Kidney and Herb Stuffing

INGREDIENTS

Serves 6

1 loin of pork with 6 rib bones
1 tbsp vegetable oil
200 g (7 oz) mirepoix of vegetables (see page 133)
6 garlic cloves, finely chopped
300 ml (1/2 pint) dry white wine
500 ml (16 fl oz) brown veal stock
salt and freshly ground pepper

For the kidney stuffing

3 pork kidneys, diced
100 g (3 1/2 oz) butter
3 skinless, boneless chicken breasts
2 egg whites
100 ml (3 1/2 fl oz) double cream
30 g (1 oz) mixed herbs, finely chopped

For the garnish

1 celeriac, peeled and diced
300 ml (1/2 pint) double cream
300 g (10 oz) butter
4 apples, turned (see page 135)
300 g (10 oz) carrots, cut into julienne strips
a few sprigs of chervil

PREPARATION

1 Make the kidney stuffing (see below).

2 Stuff the pork by cutting a 2-cm (3/4-inch) flap in the meat, following the curve of the loin. Do not cut completely to the bone. Stuff the loin, replace the flap of meat, and secure with string.

3 Sauté the pork in hot oil in a roasting tin until golden brown on all sides. Add the mirepoix and garlic and roast in a preheated oven at 180°C (350°F, Gas 4) for 35-40 minutes. Remove the pork, cover with foil, and set aside. *Deglaze* the pan with the wine and the stock and reduce until syrupy. Season and set aside.

4 Prepare the garnish: cook the celeriac in boiling salted water until tender. Drain well and purée. Whisk in the cream, half the butter, and season. Sauté the apples in the remaining butter until tender. Put the carrot julienne into a pan of cold salted water, bring to a boil, and simmer until tender. Drain. Keep the garnish warm.

5 Remove the string from the pork and cut the stuffed pork into slices, leaving a bone in each. Put the slices on plates and garnish with celeriac purée, apples, and carrots. Spoon some of the sauce over the meat and finish with chervil.

Making Kidney Stuffing

Pork kidneys are often mixed with other ingredients in stuffings, pies, and stews. This stuffing brings flavour, colour, and juiciness to an otherwise plain loin of pork.

1 Sauté the kidneys in the butter just until sealed. Remove with a slotted spoon and pat dry on paper towels.

2 Purée the chicken in a food processor. Press through a sieve into a bowl set over an ice bath.

3 Mix in the egg whites and gradually add the cream, kidneys, herbs, and seasoning to taste.

The Region of Franche-Comte

The excellent quality and diversity of agricultural produce from Franche-Comté, come together in this stuffed pork dish. The rustic chalets on the foothills of the Alps are the purveyors of dairy produce, meat, and fruity Arbois wines. Despite their rural appearance, the small farms have organized themselves into cooperatives, and combined their resources into modernizing machinery and farming procedures.

A shared border with the French cantons of Switzerland enriches the variety of dishes enjoyed in the mountains of the region. The charcuterie, in particular, is especially highly prized.

Chou Farci Entier a l'Auvergnate

Cabbage Stuffed with Pork, Mushrooms, and Herbs

INGREDIENTS

Serves 6
1 large green cabbage
2 sheets of pork caul
200 g (7 oz) mirepoix of vegetables (see page 133)
1 litre (1 3/4 pints) brown veal stock
a bouquet garni

For the stuffing
1 onion, chopped
2 shallots, chopped
3 garlic cloves, finely chopped
100 g (3 1/2 oz) butter
250 g (8 oz) mushrooms, finely diced
1 bunch of parsley, finely chopped
1/2 bunch of tarragon, finely chopped
salt and freshly ground pepper
2 slices of bread, crusts removed and diced
3 1/2 tbsp milk
150 g (5 oz) pork fat
400 g (14 oz) boned pork shoulder or neck
1 egg, lightly beaten

PREPARATION

1 Carefully pull the leaves from the head of cabbage. Trim off the hard stalks. Blanch the leaves in boiling salted water for 3-8 minutes, or until tender. Drain and refresh. Dry on paper towels.
2 Make the stuffing: sweat the onion, shallots, and garlic in the butter until soft. Add the mushrooms and cook until the mixture is quite dry, stirring frequently. Leave to cool, then stir in the parsley and tarragon. Season with salt and pepper.
3 Moisten the diced bread with the milk, then add to the herb mixture.
4 Mince or finely chop the pork fat and pork meat. Add to the herb mixture with the egg. Mix well.
5 Arrange a layer of the largest, greenest cabbage leaves on a tea towel. Spread a layer of stuffing over the leaves. Cover with another layer of cabbage leaves, then add more of the stuffing. Continue layering in this way, working through to the small, pale inner leaves.
6 Shape the layered cabbage leaves into a neat ball by gathering up the edges of the tea towel and twisting.
7 Wrap the cabbage in the sheets of pork caul.
8 Put the mirepoix, stock, and bouquet garni in a casserole and place the cabbage on top. Cover and braise in a preheated oven at 170°C (325°F, Gas 3) for about 1 hour.
9 Transfer the stuffed cabbage to a warmed serving dish and keep warm. Strain the cooking liquid into a saucepan and boil to reduce until syrupy. Serve the liquid as a sauce with the cabbage.

Carre de Porc Apicius

Spiced Roast Pork

INGREDIENTS

Serves 6
30 g (1 oz) ground cumin
1 tsp ground ginger
1 tsp dried thyme
1 tsp ground coriander
1 loin of pork with 6 rib bones
a pinch of salt
200 g (7 oz) mirepoix of vegetables (see page 133)
250 ml (8 fl oz) water
1 tbsp potato flour

PREPARATION

1 Trim the fat from the pork loin. Mix together the cumin, ginger, thyme, and coriander. Rub over the pork, cover, and leave to marinate overnight.
2 Sprinkle the pork with salt, then roast in a preheated oven at 180°C (350°F, Gas 4) for about 1 1/2 hours. Halfway through the cooking, add the mirepoix and the water.
3 Remove the pork and keep warm. Strain the cooking liquid, skim off excess fat, and boil to reduce. Sprinkle the potato flour into the cooking liquid and whisk vigorously until thickened.
4 Cut the pork into chops and serve immediately, with the sauce spooned over.

An Ancient Recipe

Pork was one of the favourite meats in both ancient Greece and Rome. The above recipe for Spiced Roast Pork has been translated and adapted from the culinary writings of the second Apicius in culinary history, Marcus Gavius, born c. AD 25, whose work was documented in 10 cookbooks, containing a wealth of information on the preparation of pork.

Echine de Porc au Cresson

Pork Sauteed with Watercress

INGREDIENTS

Serves 6–8
1 kg (2 lb) boned loin of pork
3 1/2 tbsp vegetable oil
500 ml (16 fl oz) chicken stock
salt and freshly ground pepper
4 bunches of watercress, stalks removed
juice of 1 lemon

For the egg-fried rice
200 g (7 oz) rice
45 g (1 1/2 oz) petits pois
2 eggs, beaten
45 g (1 1/2 oz) ham, cut into julienne *strips*

PREPARATION

1 Cut the pork loin into thin slices. Sauté the pork slices in most of the oil until they are golden brown on all sides.
2 Pour off the excess fat from the pan, then *deglaze* with the stock. There should be enough stock to cover the pork. Season and simmer for 10 minutes.
3 Add the watercress and lemon juice, and seasoning. Boil to reduce until almost dry.
4 Meanwhile, prepare the egg-fried rice: cook the rice in boiling salted water until tender. Drain the rice, if necessary, and put in a wok or frying pan with the remaining oil. Stir-fry the rice with the petits pois, eggs, and ham.
5 Place the egg-fried rice on a serving dish and spoon over the pork and watercress.

Choucroute d'Alsace

Sauerkraut with Pork and Sausages

INGREDIENTS

Serves 12
500 g (1 lb) bacon, cut into small strips
6 small bacon chops
500 g (1 lb) salt pork
2 pork knuckles
3 kg (6 lb) sauerkraut, uncooked
300 g (10 oz) lard
200 g (7 oz) mirepoix of vegetables *(see page 133)*
a bouquet garni
30 g (1 oz) juniper berries
12 white peppercorns
500 ml (16 fl oz) white wine from Alsace
2 litres (3 1/2 pints) chicken stock
6 Strasbourg sausages
6 smoked sausages
6 thick slices of cooked ham, cut into strips
cooked turned potatoes *(see page 135)**, for the garnish*

PREPARATION

1 Blanch the bacon strips, bacon chops, salt pork, and pork knuckles separately in boiling water. Drain well.
2 Wash the sauerkraut under cold running water. Drain and squeeze out any excess moisture.
3 Heat the lard in a large flameproof casserole and brown the bacon. Add the sauerkraut, bacon chops, salt pork, pork knuckles, mirepoix, bouquet garni, juniper berries, and peppercorns. Moisten with the wine and stock. Cover and cook over a low heat, for about 3 hours.
4 About 10 minutes before the choucroûte is ready, add the Strasbourg and smoked sausages and the ham strips, pushing them down into the mixture.
5 Serve hot on a platter, with turned potatoes.

Alsacienne Cuisine

Over the centuries, many foods from neighbouring countries have influenced the development of French cooking. The chefs of Alsace, in eastern France, were strongly influenced by German ideas and ingredients. Their most famous dish, *choucroûte*, or sauerkraut, uses cured cabbage, various cuts of pork, sausages, and the local wine – four of the region's most highly prized ingredients.

Longe de Porc Farci au Miel

Roast Loin of Pork with Honey Stuffing

INGREDIENTS

Serves 8–10

250 ml (8 fl oz) red wine
45 g (1½ oz) honey
2 bay leaves
¼ tsp cayenne pepper
100 g (3½ oz) fresh breadcrumbs
2 kg (4 lb) boned loin of pork
salt and freshly ground pepper

For the garnish

300 g (10 oz) wild rice
300 g (10 oz) peas
a few sprigs of parsley

PREPARATION

1 Boil the wine with the honey, bay leaves, and cayenne, and reduce until syrupy. Discard the bay leaves. Add the breadcrumbs and mix well.
2 Slit the pork loin in half, not cutting completely through the meat, and stuff it with the honey and crumb mixture. Roll up the pork loin and tie it into a neat shape with string. Wrap in foil.
3 Roast in a preheated oven at 180°C (350°F, Gas 4) for about 1½ hours. Unwrap for the last 20 minutes.
4 Meanwhile, cook the rice in boiling salted water until *al dente*. Cook the peas in a separate pan of boiling salted water, drain, and keep warm.
5 Slice the pork and sprinkle with pepper. Serve with the wild rice and the peas. Garnish with the sprigs of parsley.

Roti de Porc a l'Anglaise

Roast Pork with Sage Stuffing

INGREDIENTS

Serves 8–10

1 loin of pork, weighing about 2·5 kg (5 lb)
150 g (5 oz) mirepoix of vegetables (see page 133)
750 ml (1¼ pints) brown veal stock
a bouquet garni
400 g (14 oz) apples, peeled and diced (see page 148)
30 g (1 oz) butter
30 g (1 oz) sugar

For the stuffing

75 g (2½ oz) onion, chopped
75 g (2½ oz) butter
2 egg yolks
1 bunch of sage, chopped
3 tbsp finely chopped parsley
150 g (5 oz) fresh breadcrumbs
salt and freshly ground pepper

PREPARATION

1 Blanch the pork in boiling water for 15 minutes. Drain and dry on paper towels.
2 Put the pork in a roasting tin with the mirepoix and roast in a preheated oven at 200°C (400°F, Gas 6) for 1½ hours. After 1 hour, add the stock and bouquet garni.
3 Meanwhile, make the stuffing: sweat the onion in the butter until soft. Leave to cool, then mix with the remaining ingredients and season. Roll the mixture into a neat log shape and wrap in foil. Cook with the pork for the last 15 minutes of roasting.
4 Cook the apples with the butter and sugar until very tender. Stir occasionally.
5 Remove the pork and keep warm. Discard excess fat from the tin, then boil the liquid to reduce to a gravy. Strain and season.
6 Carve the pork and serve with slices of stuffing, the gravy, and the apples.

Anglo-French Cuisine

This recipe is a French salute to authentic English cooking, which has traditionally combined sweet and savoury flavours to great effect. Roast pork with apples is a perfect demonstration of how delicious these contrasting ingredients can be.

DESSERTS

The last course of a meal is arguably the most important. When choosing a dessert, consider the previous courses, the season of the year, and the special preferences of your family and guests. Desserts made of fresh fruit at its best always enhance a meal. Heavy main dishes suggest light desserts – perhaps a meringue, or wine sorbet. Special thought given to the dessert course will lighten spirits and lift conversation.

Terrine de Fruits a la Gelee de Miel

Fresh Fruit and Honey Jelly Terrine

This is a beautiful dessert for warm weather. The fruits are colourful and taste delicious when set in honey jelly. A raspberry coulis highlights the layers within the jelly, and is the perfect accompaniment for many desserts.

INGREDIENTS

Serves 8-10

zest of 1 orange, cut into julienne strips
250 g (8 oz) strawberries
1 punnet of raspberries
1 bunch of black seedless grapes
1 punnet of blackberries
45 g (1 1/2 oz) candied orange peel, finely chopped
raspberry coulis (see page 103), to serve

For the honey jelly

1 tbsp honey
750 ml (1 1/4 pints) water
150 g (5 oz) sugar
zest of 1 orange and 1 lemon
8 mint leaves, plus more for the garnish
12 leaves of gelatine, soaked in cold water

PREPARATION

1 Make the honey jelly: put the honey, water, sugar, zest, and mint in a saucepan and bring almost to a boil, stirring to dissolve the sugar. Remove from heat, and set aside for 10 minutes.

2 Strain the infused liquid into a pan. Drain the gelatine, and melt in the liquid. Leave to cool.

3 Blanch the orange julienne in boiling water for 1 minute. Drain and refresh. Let cool.

4 Layer the fruits (keeping some for the garnish), the orange julienne, and candied orange peel in a terrine mould, measuring 25 x 7·5 x 8·5 cm (10 x 3 x 3 1/2 inches). Fill the mould with the jelly. Place a piece of wood covered with foil on top of the terrine; this weight will compress the terrine, making it easier to slice. Chill in the refrigerator until firm.

5 Remove the weight. Turn out and slice the fruit terrine (see below). Serve with the raspberry coulis, and garnish with mint leaves and the reserved fruits.

Turning Out and Slicing a Fruit Terrine

Terrines that are set in gelatine but are not lined can be turned out and sliced as illustrated. Lined terrines may need to be loosened with a heated sharp knife.

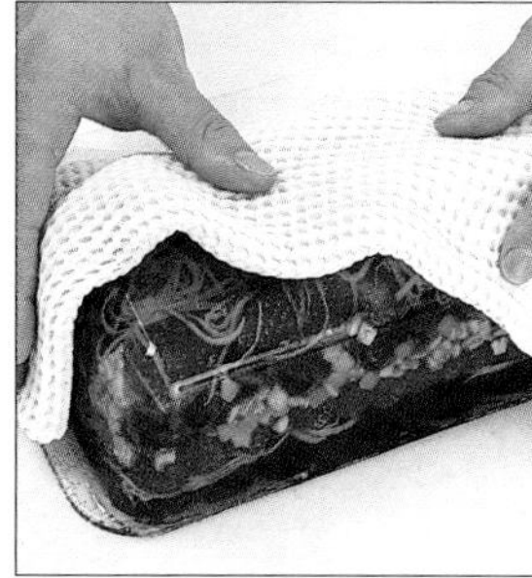

1 Place a board on top of the mould and invert. Wrap a hot tea towel around the sides of the mould.

2 The heat should break the airlock on the sides. Carefully lift the mould off the terrine.

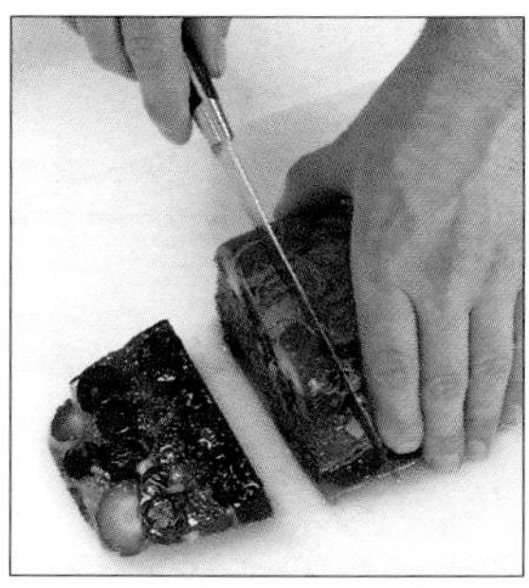

3 Use a gentle sawing motion to cut the terrine into slices with a sharp chef's knife.

Raspberry Coulis

♦ 500 g (1 lb) raspberries ♦ 100 g (3½ oz) icing sugar ♦ juice of 1 lemon ♦ 1 tbsp honey, melted (optional) ♦ 2 tbsp framboise (raspberry liqueur), optional

♦

Crush the raspberries in a large non-metallic bowl and mix with the icing sugar and lemon juice. Add the melted honey and liqueur, if you like. Press through a sieve into another bowl. Discard the raspberry seeds. Keep the coulis in a cool place.

Les Babas

Rum-Soaked Yeast Cakes with Fresh Fruit

INGREDIENTS

Serves 10

45 g (1 1/2 oz) fresh yeast
4 tsp warm water
250 g (8 oz) flour
1 tsp salt
2 tsp caster sugar
2-3 eggs, beaten
45 g (1 1/2 oz) butter, softened
30 g (1 oz) currants
125 g (4 oz) apricot jam, melted and sieved, to glaze

For the syrup

400 g (14 oz) sugar
1 litre (1 3/4 pints) water
zests of 1 orange and 1 lemon
100 ml (3 1/2 fl oz) rum
a few drops of vanilla essence

For the decoration

Chantilly cream (see page 150)
strawberries, raspberries, kiwi fruit slices, grapes, pineapple pieces, and orange segments

PREPARATION

1 In a large bowl, mix the yeast with the warm water until smoothly blended. Add the flour, salt, sugar, and eggs, and mix to make a dough; add a little more water if needed. Knead the dough for at least 5 minutes. Cover and leave to rise in a warm place until it has doubled in bulk.

2 Add the softened butter and currants to the dough, and knead lightly to knock out the air. Place the dough in 10 buttered baba moulds and leave to rise to the top of the moulds.

3 Bake the babas in a preheated oven at 170°C (325°F, Gas 3) for 30-35 minutes. Remove from the oven and let cool in the moulds.

4 Make the syrup: combine the sugar, water, and zests in a saucepan and slowly bring to a boil, stirring to dissolve the sugar. Remove from the heat and add the rum and vanilla.

5 Turn the babas out on to a wire rack set over a tray. Ladle the hot syrup over them to moisten. Continue until all the syrup has been absorbed, then brush the babas with the melted apricot jam.

6 Fill the centres of the babas with Chantilly cream and decorate with fresh fruit.

Fantaisie Croquante aux Melons

Melon Fantasy

INGREDIENTS

Serves 6

1 watermelon, 1 cantaloupe, and 1 honeydew melon
100 ml (3 1/2 fl oz) sweet dessert wine
45 g (1 1/2 oz) caster sugar
1 tbsp grenadine (pomegranate sugar syrup)
mint leaves, cut into julienne *strips, for the decoration*

For the croquante

125 g (4 oz) honeydew melon, puréed and sieved
120 ml (4 fl oz) milk
3 egg yolks
60 g (2 oz) caster sugar
30 g (1 oz) flour
6 sheets of phyllo pastry
60 g (2 oz) butter, melted

PREPARATION

1 Prepare the *crème pâtissière* for the croquante: put the sieved melon and the milk in separate pans and bring both to a boil. Beat the egg yolks with the sugar until the mixture is thick. Mix in the flour, then the melon juice followed by the milk. Pour this mixture into a clean pan and cook, stirring, for 2-3 minutes, or until the melon custard is thick. Pour into a bowl and let cool.

2 Meanwhile, halve the melons and discard the seeds. Cut the flesh into balls with a melon baller.

3 Combine the wine, sugar, and grenadine in a saucepan and slowly bring to a boil, stirring to dissolve the sugar. Boil, without stirring, until reduced to a thick syrup. Let cool, then add the melon balls. Leave until ready to serve.

4 Put the cold crème pâtissière in a piping bag fitted with a large plain nozzle. Place a sheet of phyllo on the work surface and brush it generously with melted butter. Pipe a thick sausage-shape of crème pâtissière on the pastry, just off centre. Roll the pastry up around the crème pâtissière, tucking in the sides to enclose it completely. Set the croquante on a buttered baking tray and brush it with melted butter. Make 5 more croquantes in the same way.

5 Bake the croquantes in a preheated oven at 200°C (400°F, Gas 6) for 2-3 minutes. Let cool.

6 Arrange the croquantes and macerated melon balls on chilled plates, with the grenadine syrup. Decorate with mint and serve.

Crepes Suzette a la Cointreau

Crepes with Orange and Cointreau

INGREDIENTS

Serves 4
10 sugar cubes
1 orange
1 lemon
90 ml (3 fl oz) Cointreau
125 g (4 oz) butter, cut into small pieces

For the crêpe batter
125 g (4 oz) flour
2 eggs
250 ml (8 fl oz) milk
60 g (2 oz) butter, cooked until brown
15 g (1/2 oz) caster sugar
finely grated zest of 1/2 orange and 1/2 lemon

PREPARATION

1. Make the crêpe batter: sift the flour into a bowl. Make a well in the centre of the flour and break the eggs into the well. Add one-third of the milk and gradually mix the wet ingredients into the flour until smooth. Whisk in the remaining milk, the browned butter, sugar, and grated orange and lemon zests. Leave to rest for 30 minutes.
2. Meanwhile, rub 5 of the sugar cubes all over the orange, to take up the oil from the zest. Rub the remaining sugar cubes all over the lemon.
3. Make about 16-20 crêpes (see page 147).
4. Pare the zest from the orange and lemon, using a citrus zester, then squeeze their juice.
5. Melt the sugar cubes in a large frying pan and stir in the zest and juice. Taking the crêpes one at a time, turn them in this sauce to coat both sides, then fold into quarters. Arrange the crêpes on warmed individual plates.
6. Add the Cointreau to the sauce, whisk in the butter, and serve spooned over the crêpes.

The Origin of Crepes Suzette?

The exact creator of *Crêpes Suzette* is widely debated among food historians. Henri Carpentier, the chef for the Rockefeller family in the early 1900s, claimed to have invented the dish in 1895, during his time at the Café de Paris in Monte Carlo, as a treat for a companion of the Prince of Wales. However, records show he was not old enough to have performed such a feat of gastronomy.

Soupe de Fruits Exotiques au Poivre

Exotic Fruit Salad with Green Peppercorns

INGREDIENTS

Serves 5
1 tbsp green peppercorns, in brine
100 g (3 1/2 oz) sugar
100 ml (3 1/2 fl oz) water
3 passionfruit
juice of 2 oranges
1 baby pineapple, peeled and diced (see page 148)
8 lychees, peeled and stoned
4 kiwi fruit, peeled and diced
1 mango, peeled, stoned, and sliced (see page 149)
1 papaya, peeled, seeded, and sliced
3 guavas, peeled and diced
passionfruit, mango, or lime sorbet, to serve (optional)

PREPARATION

1. Put the green peppercorns in a sieve and rinse under cold running water.
2. Meanwhile, combine the sugar and water in a saucepan and bring slowly to a boil, stirring to dissolve the sugar.
3. Add the peppercorns to the syrup. Halve the passionfruit and scoop the pulp into the syrup. Add the orange juice. Bring back to a boil and skim off any foam from the surface.
4. Pour the syrup into a bowl and let cool. Add all the prepared fruit. Cover and chill.
5. Divide the fruit and syrup among chilled plates, and serve with a scoop of sorbet, if you like.

Mousse au Citron

Lemon Mousse with Lemon Balm Syrup

INGREDIENTS

Serves 4-6

175 g (6 oz) egg whites
175 g (6 oz) caster sugar
400 ml (14 fl oz) lemon juice
400 ml (14 fl oz) double cream, whipped
200 ml (7 fl oz) natural yogurt
9 leaves of gelatine, soaked in cold water

For the lemon balm syrup

200 g (7 oz) sugar
200 ml (7 fl oz) water
1 bunch of lemon balm, chopped

For the decoration

2 lemons
2 pink grapefruits
2 limes
2 oranges
200 g (7 oz) sugar
200 ml (7 fl oz) water
a few sprigs of lemon balm
1 punnet of strawberries

PREPARATION

1 Whisk the egg whites with the sugar to a stiff meringue. Fold in the lemon juice, whipped cream, and the natural yogurt.

2 Drain the gelatine, and melt it in 1 tbsp boiling water. Cool, then add to the mousse mixture.

3 Put the mousse mixture into a piping bag fitted with a star nozzle and pipe into 4-6 oiled individual ring moulds. Cover and chill for about 4 hours, until set.

4 Prepare the lemon balm syrup: combine the sugar and water in a saucepan and slowly bring to a boil, stirring to dissolve the sugar. Add the lemon balm and let cool.

5 Make the decoration: pare the zest from all the citrus fruits with a citrus zester; set the zest aside. Peel the fruits and cut out the segments (see page 149). Combine the sugar and water in a saucepan and slowly bring to a boil, stirring until the sugar dissolves. Use the sugar syrup to candy the citrus zest (see page 107).

6 Serve the mousses unmoulded in the centre of individual plates. Strain the lemon balm syrup, and spoon around each mousse. Decorate with the citrus segments, candied citrus zest, lemon balm sprigs, and strawberries.

Lemon Balm

Also known as *citronnelle* or *melissa*, lemon balm adds a distinctive yet delicate taste to salads, soups, sauces, and fruit desserts. In this recipe for lemon mousse, its delicate lemon-like flavour balances the slightly sharp tones of mint and raspberry.

This light, modern dessert also makes the most of the fresh flavour and bright juicy flesh of citrus fruits.

Candying Citrus Zest

Easy to candy, citrus zest adds flavour to creamy desserts, as well as being an attractive decoration. An assortment of different citrus fruits can be used to create a medley of colour.

1 Blanch the citrus zest in boiling water for 1 minute, drain, and refresh in cold water; drain again.

2 Add the citrus zest to the sugar syrup and simmer until the zest is translucent, 8-10 minutes.

3 Remove the citrus zest with a fork and spread out on non-stick paper. Leave to cool before using.

Charlotte aux Framboises

Raspberry Charlotte

INGREDIENTS

Serves 6–8

125 g (4 oz) raspberries, plus more for the decoration
30 g (1 oz) pistachios, chopped, for the decoration
raspberry coulis (see page 103), to serve

For the sponge mixture

4 eggs, separated
125 g (4 oz) caster sugar
125 g (4 oz) flour, sifted

For the syrup

60 g (2 oz) sugar
4 tbsp water
1 tbsp framboise (raspberry liqueur)

For the mousse

200 g (7 oz) sugar
90 ml (3 fl oz) water
20 g (2/3 oz) glucose
4 egg whites
4 tsp framboise
4 leaves of gelatine, soaked in cold water
250 g (8 oz) raspberries, puréed and sieved
150 ml (5 fl oz) whipping cream

For the raspberry glaze

175 g (6 oz) raspberry jam
1 tbsp framboise

PREPARATION

1 Make the sponge: whisk the egg whites and sugar until stiff. Fold in the egg yolks and the flour. Line a baking tray with non-stick paper. With a plain nozzle, pipe the mixture on to the paper in a 15-cm (6-inch) round and in fingers 5 cm (2 inches) long. Bake in a preheated oven at 170°C (325°F, Gas 3) for about 12 minutes. Cool.

2 Make the syrup: combine the sugar and water in a saucepan and bring slowly to a boil, stirring to dissolve the sugar. Stir in the framboise.

3 Line the bottom of a charlotte mould with the sponge round and put the sponge fingers around the edges. Moisten with the syrup and set aside.

4 For the mousse, make a syrup with the sugar, water, and glucose, then boil to hard-ball stage, 120°C (250°F) on a sugar thermometer. Meanwhile, whisk the egg whites to soft peaks. Gradually pour the syrup on to the egg whites, whisking constantly. Continue whisking until the meringue is cool. Heat the framboise in a pan, drain the gelatine, and melt it in the liqueur. Stir into the raspberry purée.

5 Whip the cream until thick. Carefully mix the raspberry purée with the meringue, then fold in the whipped cream. Pour the mousse into the lined mould, adding a layer of raspberries in the middle. Cover and chill until set.

6 Make the glaze: melt the raspberry jam with the framboise. Sieve the mixture and let cool slightly.

7 Remove the charlotte from the mould. Arrange raspberries on top and cover with glaze. Sprinkle over the pistachios. Serve with raspberry coulis.

Charlotte

The English fruit dessert known as "charlotte" was a warm, fruit-filled case of butter and bread, which was probably devised in honour of Queen Charlotte, the wife of King George III.

The more elaborate and elegant French charlotte, on which this recipe is based, requires a mould of sponge, filled with a light mousse. Its inventor, Antonin Carême, was one of France's greatest chefs. Born into poverty in Paris during the late 18th century, Carême displayed an unusual gift for understanding the connection between beauty for the eye and the palate. He is known for his application of architectural design to pastry, and for his work as a food theoretician: more than a hundred sauces and soups bear his name. His fame took him to England, where he served the Prince Regent, the future George IV, and to Russia, to work for Tzar Alexander I.

MOUSSE CHAMPAGNE AUX FRUITS FRAIS

CHAMPAGNE AND ALMOND GATEAU

INGREDIENTS

Serves 8

1 small pineapple, peeled and diced (see page 148)
125 g (4 oz) raspberries, plus more for the decoration
Chantilly cream (see page 150), for the decoration

For the dacquoise sponge

75 g (2 1/2 oz) icing sugar
150 g (5 oz) ground almonds
30 g (1 oz) flour
8 egg whites

For the Champagne mousse

250 g (8 oz) sugar
250 ml (8 fl oz) water
zest of 1 orange
10 egg yolks
250 ml (8 fl oz) Champagne
6 1/2 leaves of gelatine, soaked in cold water
350 ml (12 fl oz) double cream, whipped

PREPARATION

1 Make the dacquoise sponge: sift together the sugar, almonds, and flour. Whisk the egg whites to stiff peaks and fold in the sifted ingredients. Divide the mixture into thirds, and place on baking trays lined with non-stick paper. Spread evenly into rounds. Bake in a preheated oven at 150°C (300°F, Gas 2) for about 30 minutes. Leave to cool.

2 Make the mousse: put the sugar, water, and orange zest in a saucepan and slowly bring to a boil, stirring to dissolve the sugar. Remove the zest. Whisk the egg yolks in a bowl until thick. Add the hot syrup to the egg yolks in a steady stream, whisking constantly. Place the bowl over a pan of simmering water and whisk until thick and creamy. Remove from the heat and continue whisking until cool.

3 Heat the Champagne, drain the gelatine, and melt it in the Champagne. Stir into the egg-yolk mixture; leave to cool. Fold in the cream.

4 Put 1 dacquoise round on a plate. Spread half the Champagne mousse over it and scatter on half the fruit. Add another round and cover with the remaining mousse and fruit. Top with the third round and press on gently. Smooth the edges of the gâteau with a palette knife. Chill until set.

5 Serve the gâteau chilled, decorated with raspberries and Chantilly cream.

SOUFFLE SABRINA

PASSIONFRUIT AND STRAWBERRY SOUFFLE

INGREDIENTS

Serves 8

250 ml (8 fl oz) milk
30 g (1 oz) flour
60 g (2 oz) butter
4 eggs, separated
60 g (2 oz) caster sugar
45 g (1 1/2 oz) passionfruit pulp, sieved
45 g (1 1/2 oz) strawberries, puréed and sieved
1 tsp cornflour

For the macaroons

100 g (3 1/2 oz) icing sugar
75 g (2 1/2 oz) ground almonds
30 g (1 oz) cocoa powder
20 g (2/3 oz) flour
4 egg whites
50 g (1 3/4 oz) caster sugar

PREPARATION

1 Make the macaroons: line a baking tray with non-stick paper. Sift together the icing sugar, almonds, cocoa powder, and flour. Whisk the egg whites with the caster sugar to a stiff meringue. Fold in the sifted ingredients. Pipe the mixture into rounds on the baking trays, and bake in a preheated oven at 200°C (400°F, Gas 6) for 10 minutes. Let the macaroons cool.

2 Put the milk in a saucepan and bring to a boil. Meanwhile, mix the flour and butter together to make a paste. Remove the milk from the heat. Add the paste to the hot milk, in small pieces, whisking constantly. Cook for 1 minute, stirring, to thicken the milk. Remove from the heat.

3 Whisk the egg yolks and half the sugar together until thick. Add to the hot milk and mix well. Divide the custard equally between 2 soufflé dishes. Add the passionfruit pulp to 1 dish and the strawberry purée to the other.

4 Sift the remaining sugar with the cornflour. Whisk the egg whites with the sugar and cornflour mixture to a stiff meringue. Divide equally between the 2 fruit custards and fold in gently.

5 Bake in a preheated oven at 220°C (425°F, Gas 7) for 7-8 minutes, or until lightly browned.

6 Serve immediately, with the macaroons.

Tarte Fine Chaude au Beurre de Miel

Warm Apple and Almond Tart with Honey Butter

INGREDIENTS

Serves 6–8
250 g (8 oz) pâte brisée (see page 152)
6 firm apples, such as Granny Smith
juice of 1 lemon

For the almond cream
30 g (1 oz) icing sugar, sifted
30 g (1 oz) butter, softened
50 g (1¾ oz) ground almonds, sifted
½ beaten egg
3 tbsp single cream, for glazing

For the honey butter
2 tbsp honey
45 g (1½ oz) butter
1½ tbsp Calvados
3 tbsp dry white wine

For the decoration
1 punnet of raspberries
a few mint leaves

PREPARATION

1 Line a 23-cm (9-inch) fluted flan tin with the pâte brisée (see page 152). Chill the pastry shell in the refrigerator.

2 Make the almond cream: combine the icing sugar and butter, and beat until creamy. Gradually add the almonds and beaten egg.

3 Spread half the almond cream in a smooth layer in the pastry shell.

4 Peel the apples, reserving the peel. Core and halve them lengthwise; coat with lemon juice.

5 Cut the apple halves into thin slices and arrange decoratively in concentric circles on top of the almond cream. Bake the tart on a preheated baking tray in an oven at 200°C (400°F, Gas 6) for 20 minutes.

6 Meanwhile, use the reserved apple peel to make the honey butter (see page 111). Keep warm.

7 Mix the remaining almond cream with the single cream, for the glaze. When the tart is cooked, spread this mixture smoothly over the apples. Place under a hot grill until golden.

8 Put the tart on a serving plate and decorate with the raspberries and mint leaves. Serve sliced, accompanied by the honey butter.

As Sweet as Honey

Apples and almonds combine to give this tart a truly wonderful flavour, and the honey and Calvados in the accompanying honey butter sauce are the perfect complement. Honey is one of the oldest culinary treasures known to man. In Rome, honey was a sign of wealth and a symbol of happiness. Wines and rich banquet dishes, such as Roast Loin of Pork with Honey Stuffing (see page 100), were flavoured with honey.

Honey has important medicinal properties. First recognized by the physicians of Greece and Rome, and used throughout the Middle Ages, its properties still continue to stimulate interest.

Making Honey Butter

Honey butter is the perfect sauce to accompany rich, flaky French pastries. The use of tart apple peel is intentional; it counterbalances the sweet and buttery ingredients in the sauce.

1 Place apple peel in a saucepan with the honey, butter, Calvados, and wine. Stir to mix.

2 Gently cook the mixture until the apple peel is soft. Strain the liquid and discard the peel.

3 Bring the honey mixture to a boil and cook until it has reduced by half and looks syrupy.

Sable Fondant aux Fruits Secs

Dried Fruit and Candied Carrot Tart with a Cola Sauce

INGREDIENTS

Serves 8

18 prunes, stoned
18 dried apricots, stoned
18 dates, stoned
2 tbsp raisins
120 ml (4 fl oz) Cointreau
3 tbsp apricot jam, melted and sieved, to glaze
3 tbsp shelled and peeled pistachios
1 tbsp sesame seeds
1 tbsp toasted flaked almonds

For the candied carrots

500 g (1 lb) sugar
500 ml (16 fl oz) water
2 carrots, sliced
1 vanilla pod, split

For the pastry

175 g (6 oz) icing sugar, sifted
300 g (10 oz) butter, softened
500 g (1 lb) flour
a pinch of salt
1 whole egg
1 beaten egg, for glazing

For the cola sauce

350 ml (12 fl oz) cola drink
60 g (2 oz) butter, cut into small pieces
1 tsp cornflour, mixed with a little cola drink

PREPARATION

1 Put the prunes, apricots, dates, raisins, and Cointreau in a bowl. Leave to macerate overnight.
2 Candy the carrots: combine the sugar and the water in a saucepan and bring to a boil, stirring to dissolve the sugar. Add the carrots and vanilla, and simmer for 15 minutes, or just until tender. Remove the carrots and reduce the syrup by half. Return the carrots to the syrup; leave overnight.
3 Make the pastry: work the sugar with the butter until evenly blended and smooth. Mix in the flour, salt, and egg. Knead the ingredients together until smooth, and chill for 30 minutes.
4 Roll out the dough until 6 mm (1/4 inch) thick and cut into a large round. Glaze with the beaten egg. Bake in a preheated oven at 170°C (325°F, Gas 3) for 25 minutes. Leave to cool.
5 Brush the apricot jam over the pastry round. Drain the macerated dried fruit and the carrots and dry on paper towels. Place in neat lines over the pastry round. Scatter over the pistachios, sesame seeds, and flaked almonds.
6 Make the cola sauce: boil the cola until reduced by half. Whisk in the butter and then the cornflour, until the sauce thickens.
7 Cut the tart into slices and serve with the sauce.

Tarte au Brocciu

Sweet Cheese Tart

INGREDIENTS

Serves 6-8

500 g (1 lb) Brocciu or other mild sheep's cheese
5 eggs, lightly beaten
250 g (8 oz) caster sugar
juice of 1 lemon

For the pâte sucrée

250 g (8 oz) flour
125 g (4 oz) butter
a pinch of salt
45 g (1 1/2 oz) caster sugar
2 egg yolks
3 tbsp water

PREPARATION

1 Make the pâte sucrée and use to line a 25-cm (10-inch) fluted flan tin (see pages 152-3). Chill the pastry shell in the refrigerator.
2 Bake the shell blind: prick the base with a fork. Place a crumpled piece of non-stick paper inside, fill with dried beans, and bake in a preheated oven at 220°C (425°F, Gas 7) for at least 10 minutes. Reduce the temperature to 180°C (350°F, Gas 4), remove the paper and dried beans, and bake for a further 5 minutes.
3 Mix together the cheese, eggs, sugar, and lemon juice. Pour into the pastry shell. Bake for about 30 minutes, until set. Serve warm or cool.

"The French will only be united under the threat of danger. Nobody can simply bring together a country that has 265 kinds of cheeses."

Charles de Gaulle (1890-1970)

Tarte Tatin aux Mangues

Upside-Down Mango Tartlets

INGREDIENTS

Serves 8

4 mangoes, peeled, and cut on both sides of the stones
250 g (8 oz) sugar
150 g (5 oz) butter, cut into small pieces
2 tbsp toasted shredded coconut, for the decoration

For the coconut ice cream

1 litre (1 3/4 pints) milk
9 egg yolks
200 g (7 oz) caster sugar
200 ml (7 fl oz) Malibu (white Caribbean rum with coconut)

For the puff pastry

250 g (8 oz) flour
250 g (8 oz) butter
1 tsp salt
1 tsp lemon juice
120 ml (4 fl oz) water

For the apple compote

1 kg (2 lb) apples, peeled and diced (see page 148)
45 g (1 1/2 oz) butter
45 g (1 1/2 oz) apricot jam

The Birth of Tarte Tatin

Culinary legend has it that two Tatin sisters ran a small hotel and restaurant in the French region of Sologne. Times were hard and good help expensive. On a particularly busy day, one of the sisters forgot to put the pastry in her flan tin before adding the apples, so she cut the pastry and arranged it as a lid over the fruit before putting it in the oven. To serve, she tipped the tart on to a plate, allowing the juices to pool around the browned, crisp pastry. Her customers were delighted, and a tradition was born. However, the dish did not become popular until it was served at Maxim's restaurant in Paris.

In keeping with Le Cordon Bleu's philosophy of inventing new dishes from traditional ones, this modern version of *Tarte Tatin* is truly international, including tropical mango and coconut. This recipe was created by Le Cordon Bleu for a banquet in honour of the Royal Viking Lines.

PREPARATION

1 Make the coconut ice cream: put the milk in a heavy-based saucepan and bring to a boil. In a bowl, whisk the egg yolks with the sugar until thick. Whisk a little hot milk into the egg yolks, then return the mixture to the remaining milk in the pan. Gently cook, stirring, until the custard thickens enough to coat the back of a wooden spoon. Strain into a bowl and leave to cool.

2 Stir the Malibu into the cool custard. Freeze in an ice-cream machine until firm.

3 Make the puff pastry (see page 154).

4 Make the apple compote: put the apples and butter in a saucepan, cover, and cook until soft. Add the apricot jam and stir until it has melted.

5 Butter eight 8-10 cm (3-4 inch) non-stick moulds, and coat with sugar. Place 2 mango halves, rounded-side down, in the bottom of each, and cover with compote.

6 Roll out the dough to a 3-mm (1/8-inch) thickness, and cut out rounds about 1·25 cm (1/2 inch) larger than the tops of the moulds. Cover each filled mould with a pastry round, gently pushing the edge of the round down inside the mould. Bake the tartlets in a preheated oven at 200°C (400° F, Gas 6) for about 25 minutes.

7 Make the caramel: place the sugar in a heavy-based pan and cook until the sugar dissolves and becomes golden brown. Take the pan from the heat and whisk in the butter.

8 Turn out each tartlet, pastry-side down, and spoon the caramel on top. Sprinkle with the toasted coconut. Serve warm, with the ice cream.

Miroir Passion

Passionfruit Dessert

This is an exotic light dessert that combines classic French pastry techniques with a modern tropical favourite – passionfruit. The more traditional miroir is made with cassis – the blackcurrant syrup that is popular throughout France.

Passionfruit

The edible fruit of the passion flower, passionfruit, is frequently used in the filling of a classic Pavlova. Passion flowers are favoured by many French gardeners, who find blooms of this climbing vine reminiscent of the French overseas colonies of Martinique, Guadeloupe, and French Guiana.

INGREDIENTS

Serves 6–8
150 ml (5 fl oz) milk
5 egg yolks
100 g (3½ oz) sugar
3 leaves of gelatine, soaked in cold water
150 g (5 oz) passionfruit pulp, sieved
250 ml (8 fl oz) double cream, whipped
apricot jam, melted and sieved, to glaze

For the Genoese sponge
4 eggs
125 g (4 oz) caster sugar
125 g (4 oz) flour, sifted

For the syrup
45 g (1½ oz) sugar
45 ml (1½ fl oz) water
1 tbsp passionfruit juice (optional)

For the decoration
4 passionfruit (2 seeded and 2 cut into quarters)
a few mint leaves

"COOKING IS LIKE LOVE. IT SHOULD BE ENTERED INTO WITH ABANDON OR NOT AT ALL."

Harriet Van Horne

PREPARATION

1 Make the Genoese sponge: put the eggs and sugar in a bowl set over a pan of simmering water and whisk until the mixture is thick and makes a ribbon trail when the whisk is lifted. Remove from the pan of hot water and continue whisking until cold. Gradually fold in the flour.

2 Pipe the sponge mixture into two 23-cm (9-inch) rounds on a baking tray lined with non-stick paper. Bake in a preheated oven at 180°C (350°F, Gas 4) for 10 minutes, or until firm to the touch. Leave to cool on a wire rack.

3 Make the mousse: put the milk in a heavy saucepan and bring to a boil. In a bowl, beat the egg yolks with the sugar until the mixture is thick. Add a little of the boiling milk, whisking constantly. Return to the remaining milk in the pan and cook, stirring, until the custard thickens enough to coat the back of a spoon.

4 Drain the gelatine and melt it in the hot custard, then stir in the passionfruit pulp. Leave to cool. Fold in the whipped cream.

5 Place 1 sponge round in the bottom of a 23-cm (9-inch) springform tin. Make the syrup, and moisten the sponge (see below).

6 Cover the sponge with half the mousse. Set the other sponge layer on top and add the remaining mousse. Smooth over the surface, and chill in the refrigerator until set .

7 Scatter passionfruit seeds over the surface and glaze with cooled apricot jam. Carefully remove the side of the springform tin.

8 Serve the dessert cut into slices, with any remaining syrup spooned around the plate. Decorate with passionfruit wedges and mint.

Making Sugar Syrup and Moistening Sponge

Sponges brushed with syrup are moist and more palatable than if left plain. When the syrup is flavoured, it enhances the overall taste of the dessert. It is important not to add too much syrup or the cake layers will fall apart when they are cut.

1 Put the sugar and water in a saucepan and bring to a boil, stirring to dissolve the sugar.

2 Remove the saucepan from the heat, and stir the passionfruit juice, if using, into the sugar syrup.

3 Use a pastry brush to evenly moisten the sponge in the tin. Keep the remaining syrup.

Le Monaco

Cointreau and Praline Gateau

INGREDIENTS

Serves 8

150 g (5 oz) caster sugar
150 g (5 oz) ground almonds
4 eggs
45 g (1½ oz) flour
30 g (1 oz) butter, melted
4 egg whites

For the praline mousseline

100 g (3½ oz) sugar
75 g (2½ oz) whole almonds
120 ml (4 fl oz) milk
2 egg yolks
1 tsp flour
1 tsp cornflour
3 leaves of gelatine, soaked in cold water
500 ml (16 fl oz) double cream, whipped

For the Cointreau bavarois

500 ml (16 fl oz) milk
125 g (4 oz) sugar
150 g (5 oz) egg yolks
7 leaves of gelatine, soaked in cold water
4 tbsp Cointreau
400 ml (14 fl oz) double cream, whipped

For the decoration

100 g (3½ oz) sugar
100 g (3½ oz) mixed hazelnuts and almonds
1 apple, cut into chevrons (as illustrated above)

PREPARATION

1 Whisk together half of the sugar, the ground almonds, and the eggs until thick. Add the flour and melted butter.

2 Whisk the egg whites and the remaining sugar until stiff. Fold into the almond mixture, turn into a buttered 23-cm (9-inch) cake tin, and bake in a preheated oven at 220°C (425° F, Gas 7) for 7 minutes, or just until firm to the touch. Let cool for 5 minutes, and then remove from the tin.

3 Make the praline mousseline: melt 75 g (2½ oz) of the sugar in a saucepan, add the almonds, and cook to a light caramel. Pour on to an oiled baking tray and leave the praline to set.

4 Put the milk in a saucepan and bring to a boil. In a bowl, whisk the egg yolks with the remaining sugar until thick. Add the flour and cornflour and whisk to mix. Mix in a little of the boiling milk, whisking constantly. Return to the remaining milk in the pan and bring to a boil, whisking all the time. Remove from the heat, and leave to cool.

5 When the praline is set, grind it into a powder in a food processor, and stir it into the pastry cream.

6 Drain the gelatine and melt it in a small saucepan. Stir it into the pastry cream, then fold in the whipped cream. Set the mousseline aside.

7 Make the Cointreau bavarois: put the milk in a pan and bring to a boil. In a bowl, whisk the egg yolks and sugar until thick. Mix in a little of the boiling milk, whisking constantly. Return to the remaining milk in the pan and cook, stirring, until thick enough to coat the back of a spoon. Drain the gelatine and melt it in the hot custard. Cool, then add the Cointreau, and fold in the cream.

8 Cut the sponge horizontally into 2 layers. Put 1 layer in a 23-cm (9-inch) springform tin. Cover with the mousseline. Set the second sponge layer on top, and add the Cointreau bavarois. Smooth over the surface. Cover, and chill until set.

9 Meanwhile, prepare the decoration: melt the sugar in a heavy-based saucepan, add the nuts, and cook to a light caramel. Remove the nuts with a fork and let them set on an oiled surface.

10 To serve, remove the sides of the tin, and decorate the gâteau with caramelized nuts and apple chevrons.

Bitter-Sweet Success

This recipe, originally from the tiny principality of Monaco, is inspired by the traditional elegance of French cooking. It is flavoured with Cointreau, the bitter-sweet orange-flavoured liqueur that has been made by the Cointreau family in Angers, in the Loire valley in France, since 1849.

Bavarois au Gingembre

Ginger Bavarian Cream

INGREDIENTS

Serves 8

750 ml (1 1/4 pints) ginger ale
2 tbsp ginger marmalade or jam, sieved
3 egg yolks
50 g (1 3/4 oz) caster sugar
3 leaves of gelatine, soaked in cold water
400 ml (14 fl oz) double cream, whipped
250 g (8 oz) redcurrant jelly
1 tbsp ginger liqueur (optional)
3 leaves of gelatine, soaked in cold water

For the Genoese sponge

3 eggs
90 g (3 oz) sugar
90 g (3 oz) flour, sifted

For the ginger syrup

300 g (10 oz) sugar
600 ml (1 pint) water
3 tbsp diced root ginger

PREPARATION

1 Make the Genoese sponge: put the eggs and sugar in a bowl set over a pan of simmering water, and whisk until the mixture is thick, and makes a ribbon trail when the whisk is lifted. Remove the bowl from the pan of hot water, and continue whisking until the mixture is cold.

2 Fold the flour into the egg mixture, then pour on to a large baking tray lined with non-stick paper. Smooth over the surface, and bake in a preheated oven at 180°C (350°F, Gas 4) for 10 minutes, or just until firm to the touch. Let cool.

3 Make the ginger syrup: mix the sugar and water in a saucepan and bring to a boil, stirring to dissolve the sugar. Add the diced ginger and simmer for 1 1/2 hours, or until the ginger has candied. Strain, reserving both the syrup and the ginger.

4 Boil the ginger ale to reduce it by half. Add the ginger marmalade and most of the ginger syrup. Reserve the remaining ginger syrup.

5 In a bowl, whisk the egg yolks with the sugar until thick. Add the ginger mixture, and set the bowl in a *bain marie* (or use a double boiler). Cook, stirring, until the ginger custard is thick enough to coat the back of a wooden spoon.

6 Drain 3 leaves of gelatine, and melt them in the hot ginger custard. Leave to cool. Fold the whipped cream into the custard together with three-quarters of the candied ginger. Set aside.

7 When the sponge is cold, cut two 10-cm (4-inch) strips. Warm the redcurrant jelly just until melted, and spread it over one of the cake strips. Set the other strip on top. Cut the sandwich into fingers or *bâtonnets* that are 6 mm (1/4 inch) thick. Stand the bâtonnets upright around the side of a 25-cm (10-inch) springform tin to line it neatly; the lines of jelly should face outwards.

8 Cut 2 rounds from the remaining sponge to fit inside the lined springform tin. Moisten the rounds of sponge with a little ginger syrup mixed together with ginger liqueur (if using). Put one of the rounds in the bottom of the tin, fitting it neatly inside the wall of bâtonnets.

9 Fill the mould with the ginger custard. Set the second sponge round on top and press down gently. Chill until set.

10 Bring the remaining ginger syrup to a boil, drain the 3 leaves of gelatine, and melt them in the syrup. Stir in the remaining candied ginger. Leave to cool slightly, then use to glaze the bavarois by pouring it on top and smoothing over the surface. Chill in the refrigerator until set. Remove the sides of the springform tin to serve.

Eastern Flavour

Ginger is a perennial herbaceous plant, originally found in Asia. Its strongly scented underground stems, or rhizomes, are widely used in cooking throughout Asia, and candied root ginger is a popular confection.

In Western cuisines, ginger is primarily used in desserts, although the increasing popularity of oriental dishes means that it is becoming more widely used.

Bavarois, or Bavarian cream, is a cold egg custard to which whipped cream and melted gelatine are added. The aromatic flavour of ginger gives this dessert its special feature.

PAVE DU ROY

CHOCOLATE AND COINTREAU GATEAU

MAKING CHOCOLATE PLAQUETTES

Chocolate decorations can make desserts look stylish and really stunning. A variety of shapes can be made using the same technique, but plaquettes (rectangles) are usually the easiest. Once you have mastered the art, chocolate ovals or rounds can be made in the same way, using a pastry or aspic cutter.

1 Melt the chocolate in a bain marie, stirring with a wooden spoon until it is very smooth. Cool slightly.

2 Brush a 5-cm (2-inch) strip of non-stick paper with melted chocolate. Cool just until set.

3 Carefully cut the chocolate into plaquettes, then peel the shapes away from the paper.

INGREDIENTS

Serves 8
75 g (2 1/2 oz) sugar
100 ml (3 1/2 fl oz) water
2 tbsp Cointreau
30 g (1 oz) candied orange peel
350 g (12 oz) couverture chocolate
frosted rose petals, for the decoration
chocolate mousse (see below)

For the chocolate Genoa cake
150 g (5 oz) marzipan
45 g (1 1/2 oz) icing sugar
5 eggs, separated
30 g (1 oz) cocoa powder
30 g (1 oz) flour
30 g (1 oz) potato flour
1 tbsp caster sugar

PREPARATION

1 Make the Genoa cake: mix together the marzipan and icing sugar, then add the egg yolks. Sift together the cocoa, flour, and potato flour. Add to the marzipan mixture. Whisk the egg whites with the caster sugar to a stiff meringue, then fold into the mixture.

2 Turn the mixture into a buttered 20-cm (8-inch) square cake tin, which has been lined with non-stick paper. Bake in a preheated oven at 170°C (325°F, Gas 3) for 35 minutes. Cool.

3 Mix the sugar and water in a saucepan and bring to a boil, stirring to dissolve the sugar. Remove from the heat, cool, and add the Cointreau.

4 Chop the candied orange peel in a food processor and soften with a little of the syrup.

5 Cut the cake horizontally into 3 equal layers. Moisten these with the Cointreau syrup.

6 Assemble the gâteau: start with a layer of cake, sprinkle with candied orange peel, and cover with chocolate mousse. Repeat with another layer of cake, candied orange peel, and mousse, and top the gâteau with the final layer of cake. Cover the top and sides of the gâteau with chocolate mousse and leave to set. If possible, leave the gâteau in the refrigerator overnight before serving, to allow the flavours to develop.

7 Using the couverture chocolate, make the chocolate plaquettes (see page 118).

8 Just before serving, press the plaquettes around the side of the cake. Alternatively, cut the cake into individual portions and decorate with the chocolate plaquettes, as illustrated. Decorate the cake with rose petals that have been frosted (dipped in beaten egg white, then dipped in caster sugar, and left to set).

CHOCOLATE MOUSSE

This mousse can be made separately and served as a dessert on its own, or it can be incorporated into a chocolate gâteau, as above. If it is served on its own, stir in a little Cointreau to make it extra special.

Serves 8
- *125 g (4 oz) plain chocolate, broken into pieces*
- *60 g (2 oz) butter*
- *2 egg yolks* ♦ *4 egg whites*
- *45 g (1 1/2 oz) sugar*

Melt the chocolate in a bowl in a *bain marie*. Remove from the hot water and stir in the butter until it has melted, then mix in the egg yolks. Whisk the egg whites with the sugar to a stiff meringue, then fold into the chocolate mixture. Make sure the meringue is completely folded into the chocolate mixture, but do not overwork, or the mousse will lose volume.

"TASTE DOES NOT COME BY CHANCE: IT IS A LONG LABORIOUS TASK TO ACQUIRE IT."
Sir Joshua Reynolds (1723-1792)

Feuille d'Automne

Chocolate Meringue Gateau

INGREDIENTS

Serves 6–8

For the almond meringue
100 g (3 1/2 oz) ground almonds
100 g (3 1/2 oz) icing sugar, sifted
3 1/2 tbsp milk
7 egg whites
350 g (12 oz) caster sugar

For the chocolate mousse
150 g (5 oz) plain chocolate, broken into pieces
250 g (8 oz) butter
4 eggs, separated
45 g (1 1/2 oz) caster sugar

For the decoration
500 g (1 lb) couverture chocolate
5 tbsp vegetable oil

PREPARATION

1 Make the almond meringue: mix together the almonds, icing sugar, and milk. Whisk the egg whites with the caster sugar to a stiff meringue, then gently fold into the almond mixture.

2 Put the mixture in a piping bag fitted with a plain nozzle. Pipe three 23-cm (9-inch) rounds on baking trays lined with non-stick paper. Cook in a preheated oven at 130°C (250°F, Gas 1/2) for 1 1/2 hours. Leave to cool.

3 Make the mousse: melt the chocolate in a bowl set in a *bain marie* (or use a double boiler). Remove from the hot water. Add the butter and stir until melted, then mix in the egg yolks. Whisk the egg whites with the sugar to a stiff meringue and fold into the mixture. Set aside in a cool place.

4 Set one of the meringue rounds in the bottom of a 25-cm (10-inch) springform tin. Add enough chocolate mousse to half fill the tin. Set another meringue round on top and cover with half the remaining mousse. Place the third meringue round on the top and cover with the remaining mousse. Smooth over the top and mask the side of the gâteau.

5 Prepare the decoration: melt the couverture chocolate in a bowl set in a bain marie, then stir in the oil. Pour the chocolate on to a marble surface or a cold baking tray. Smooth out evenly, and leave to chill slightly.

6 Scrape the chocolate into "cigarettes" or small fans with a palette knife.

7 Remove the side of the tin. Decorate the top and sides of the gâteau with chocolate "cigarettes" or small fans.

Tartelettes Chaudes au Chocolat

Hot Chocolate Tartlets with Pears and Pistachio Sauce

INGREDIENTS

Serves 10
175 g (6 oz) couverture chocolate
150 g (5 oz) butter, softened
30 g (1 oz) cocoa powder
6 eggs, separated
200 g (7 oz) caster sugar
10 pears, poached in a sugar syrup, to serve
a few chopped pistachios, to decorate

For the pistachio custard
250 ml (8 fl oz) milk
1 vanilla pod, split
3 egg yolks
45 g (1 1/2 oz) caster sugar
2 tbsp single cream
1 tbsp pistachio paste, or pistachios puréed in a food processor

PREPARATION

1 Butter the insides of 10 tartlet tins, 7·5 cm (3 inches) in diameter and 4 cm (1 1/2 inches) deep, then coat with flour.
2 Make the chocolate tartlets: break the chocolate into pieces, and melt in a bowl set in a *bain marie*. Remove from the hot water, and add the butter and cocoa powder. Stir until smooth.
3 Whisk the egg yolks with 125 g (4 oz) of the sugar until thick. Add the chocolate mixture and mix evenly. Whisk the egg whites with the remaining sugar to a stiff meringue, and fold into the chocolate mixture.
4 Divide half of the chocolate mixture among the prepared tins; only filling them halfway. Bake in a preheated oven at 170°C (325°F, Gas 3) for 10 minutes. Leave to cool.
5 Make the pistachio custard: put the milk in a saucepan with the vanilla pod and bring to a boil. Remove from the heat, cover, and leave to infuse for 15 minutes.
6 Reheat the milk. In a bowl, whisk the egg yolks with the sugar until thick. Pour in a little of the hot milk, whisking constantly. Return to the milk in the pan, and cook gently, stirring, until thick enough to coat the back of a spoon. Strain into a bowl and stir in the cream and pistachio paste. Cover the surface with a piece of dampened non-stick paper and set aside to cool.
7 Add the remaining chocolate mixture to the tins, filling them completely. Bake for a further 15 minutes, or until set. Remove from the tins.
8 Meanwhile, drain the pears and slice them. Arrange around the edge of each plate, slightly overlapping the slices.
9 Make pools of pistachio custard in the centre of individual plates. Set a hot chocolate tart on top. Serve the tarts sprinkled with the chopped pistachios.

Creme Brulee au Chocolat

Chocolate Cream Pots with a Caramel Topping

INGREDIENTS

Serves 10

250 ml (8 fl oz) milk
3 vanilla pods, split
150 g (5 oz) couverture chocolate or plain chocolate, broken into pieces
10 egg yolks
150 g (5 oz) caster sugar
750 ml (1 1/4 pints) double cream
175 g (6 oz) soft brown sugar, to serve

PREPARATION

1 Put the milk in a saucepan with the vanilla pods and bring to a boil. Remove from the heat, cover, and leave to infuse for 15 minutes.
2 Put the chocolate in a bowl. Reheat the milk and strain over the chocolate. Stir until smooth.
3 In a separate bowl, whisk the egg yolks with the sugar until thick. Add the chocolate mixture and stir until evenly blended. Stir in the cream.
4 Ladle the chocolate mixture into small ramekins. Arrange the ramekins in a *bain marie,* and pour in enough cold water to come halfway up the sides of the ramekins.
5 Set the bain marie in a preheated oven at 130°C (250°F, Gas 1/2) and bake for 50 minutes or until set. Let cool before caramelizing the tops.
6 Sprinkle the brown sugar over the ramekins, to form a thin even layer. Place them under a hot grill, as close to the heat as possible, until the sugar melts and caramelizes. Let cool a few minutes before serving, so the caramel becomes crisp.

Chocolate

Cocoa beans were first used by the Aztecs in a drink called "chocolatl". When the drink was first introduced into Europe it was not well-received. However, when it was said to have aphrodisiacal qualities, it quickly grew in popularity.

There are many different varieties of chocolate: bitter, couverture, plain, milk, and white.

Couverture chocolate contains no ingredients other than cocoa butter and cocoa solids. Hence, it has a very rich chocolate flavour and a creamy texture; it is perfect for use in cooking.

PUITS D'AMOUR

PASTRY HEARTS WITH RICH VANILLA CREAM

COMPLETING PASTRY HEARTS

Decoration is a subjective art; here is just one example of how to make a pastry case. Shaping pastry into hearts emphasizes the association with love in the recipe's title. More traditional is the Saint Honoré assemblage: choux pastry is piped in a ring, with balls of pastry placed at intervals on top.

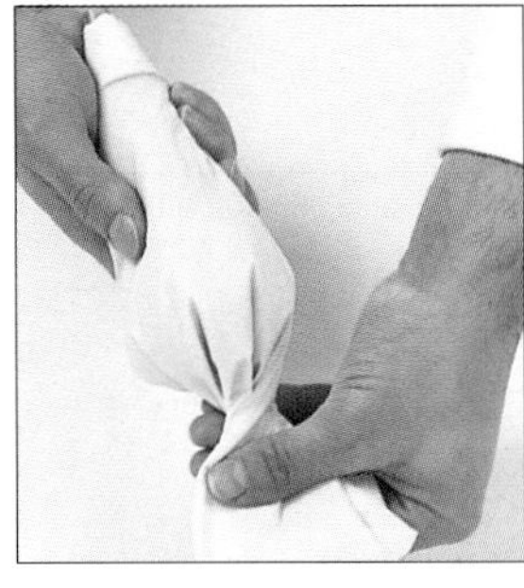

1 Spoon the choux pastry into a piping bag and twist the end to remove any air pockets.

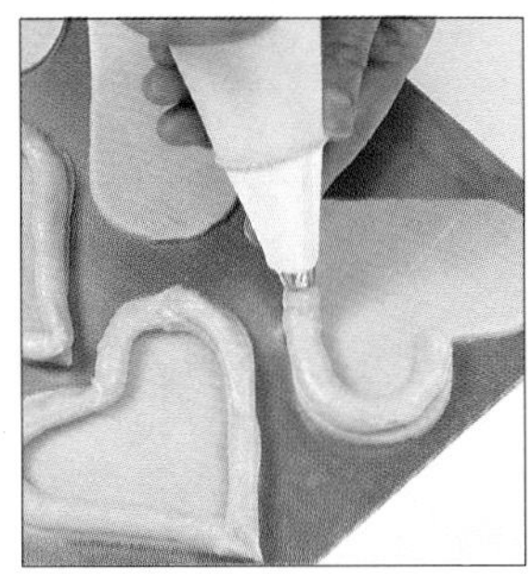

2 Pipe an even border of choux pastry around the edge of each of the pâte brisée hearts.

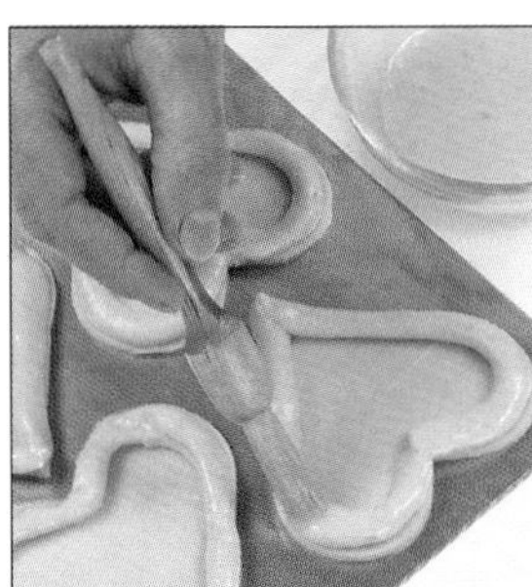

3 Using a pastry brush, glaze the edges of the choux pastry hearts evenly with beaten egg.

INGREDIENTS

Serves 12
125 g (4 oz) caster sugar
200 g (7 oz) cape gooseberries
a few mint leaves
redcurrants, for the decoration
a little icing sugar

For the pâte brisée
300 g (10 oz) flour
150 g (5 oz) butter
1 tsp salt
15 g (1/2 oz) caster sugar
1 1/2 eggs, beaten to mix
25 ml (1 1/2 tbsp) water

For the choux pastry
250 ml (8 fl oz) water
1 tsp salt
1 tsp sugar
100 g (3 1/2 oz) butter
150 g (5 oz) flour
4 eggs, plus 1 beaten egg, for glazing

For the crème chiboust
175 g (6 oz) sugar
5 1/2 tbsp water
3 eggs, separated
250 ml (8 fl oz) milk
1 tsp vanilla essence
60 g (2 oz) caster sugar
15 g (1/2 oz) flour
15 g (1/2 oz) cornflour
2 leaves of gelatine, soaked in cold water

CAPE GOOSEBERRIES

These exotic little yellow berries, sometimes known as physalis, not only make an attractive decoration when dipped in caramel (or melted chocolate), but they also taste delicious. When ripe, their spicy, tart flavour can add a piquant twist to desserts. The berry is covered with papery leaves that can be gently peeled back to reveal the shiny fruit.

PREPARATION

1 Make the pâte brisée (see page 152). Roll out the dough on a lightly floured surface and cut into 12 heart shapes, each about 7·5 cm (3 inches) across. Place on a baking tray. Set aside.

2 Make the choux pastry (see page 152).

3 Complete the pastry hearts (see page 122).

4 Bake the pastry hearts in a preheated oven at 170°C (325°F, Gas 3) for about 20 minutes, or until lightly browned. Leave to cool.

5 Make the crème chiboust: combine the sugar and water in a saucepan and slowly bring to a boil, stirring to dissolve the sugar. Boil to 118°C (245°F) on a sugar thermometer, without stirring. Meanwhile, whisk the egg whites to soft peaks. Add the sugar syrup to the egg whites in a steady stream, whisking constantly. Continue whisking until the meringue is stiff. Set aside.

6 In another saucepan, bring the milk and vanilla to a boil. In a bowl, whisk the egg yolks and caster sugar until thick. Add the flour and cornflour, and stir to mix. Pour in a little of the boiling milk, whisking constantly. Return this mixture to the milk in the pan, and cook, stirring, until thick. Remove from the heat.

7 Drain the gelatine and melt it in the hot custard. Leave to cool, then fold in the meringue. Spoon the crème chiboust into the pastry hearts and chill until it has set.

8 Meanwhile, melt half the caster sugar in a heavy pan until a golden caramel. Remove the pan from the heat and dip the cape gooseberries into the caramel. Let them set on an oiled surface.

9 Sprinkle the tops of the pastry hearts with the remaining caster sugar and place under a hot grill until the sugar melts and caramelizes. Decorate with the cape gooseberries, mint leaves, and redcurrants. Dust with icing sugar.

Baton aux Fruits Puree de Cassis

Choux Log filled with Cream and Fruits in Cassis

INGREDIENTS

Serves 8-12

3 oranges, peeled and segmented (see page 149)
200 g (7 oz) strawberries, halved or quartered
30 g (1 oz) blackcurrants
2 kiwi fruit, peeled and sliced
20 cherries, stoned
3 tbsp crème de cassis (blackcurrant liqueur)

For the choux pastry
500 ml (16 fl oz) water
125 g (4 oz) butter
a pinch of salt
30 g (1 oz) sugar
250 g (8 oz) flour
8 eggs
1 beaten egg, for glazing

For the Chantilly cream
500 ml (16 fl oz) double cream
125 g (4 oz) caster sugar
a few drops of vanilla essence

For the decoration
200 g (7 oz) apricot jam, melted and sieved, to glaze
125 g (4 oz) toasted flaked almonds
a few mint leaves (optional)

PREPARATION

1 Make the choux pastry (see page 152).
2 Put the choux into a piping bag fitted with a large plain nozzle. Pipe three 25-cm (10-inch) long sausage shapes, side-by-side, on a buttered baking tray. Pipe 2 more on top, along the joins of the first 3 sausage shapes. Glaze with beaten egg, and bake in a preheated oven at 220°C (425°F, Gas 7) for 12 minutes.
3 Reduce the temperature to 180°C (350°F, Gas 4) and bake for a further 15 minutes.
4 Meanwhile, mix together the prepared fruit and crème de cassis. Set aside to macerate.
5 Make the Chantilly cream: whip the cream with the sugar and vanilla until soft peaks form.
6 When the choux log is baked, carefully cut it horizontally in half, and set the top aside. Fill the bottom half with the Chantilly cream and the macerated fruit. Replace the top half, brush it with melted apricot jam, and sprinkle with toasted almonds. Decorate the choux log with mint leaves, if you like.

Profiteroles Glacees au Chocolat

Profiteroles with Coffee Ice Cream and Chocolate Sauce

INGREDIENTS

Serves 6

For the choux pastry
120 ml (4 fl oz) milk
120 ml (4 fl oz) water
100 g (3½ oz) butter
a pinch each of salt and sugar
150 g (5 oz) flour
4-5 eggs
1 beaten egg, for glazing

For the coffee ice cream
100 g (3½ oz) coffee beans, coarsely ground
1 vanilla pod, split
500 ml (16 fl oz) milk
6 egg yolks
125 g (4 oz) caster sugar
4 tbsp double cream

For the chocolate sauce
100 g (3½ oz) sugar
250 ml (8 fl oz) water
250 g (8 oz) couverture chocolate, broken into pieces
30 g (1 oz) butter

For the Chantilly cream
200 ml (7 fl oz) double cream
30 g (1 oz) caster sugar
a few drops of vanilla essence

PREPARATION

1 Make the ice cream: put the coffee beans, vanilla pod, and milk in a saucepan and bring to a boil. Cover, and leave for 1 hour. Strain and reheat.
2 In a bowl, beat the egg yolks and sugar until thick. Add a little flavoured milk and the cream. Return the mixture to the milk in the pan and cook, stirring, until thick enough to coat the back of a spoon. Cool, then freeze in an ice-cream machine.
3 Make the choux pastry (see page 152). Spoon the choux pastry into a piping bag fitted with a plain nozzle. Pipe 1-cm (3/8-inch) diameter buns on buttered baking trays. Brush with egg glaze and bake in a preheated oven at 180°C (350°F, Gas 4) for about 20 minutes. Cool on a wire rack.
4 Make the chocolate sauce: dissolve the sugar in the water. Stir in the chocolate and butter until smooth.
5 Make the Chantilly cream: whip the cream with the sugar and vanilla until soft peaks form.
6 Halve the profiteroles and fill with ice cream. Serve with chocolate sauce and Chantilly cream.

PARIS-BREST

CHOUX PASTRY CROWN

INGREDIENTS

Serves 8

For the choux pastry
120 ml (4 fl oz) milk
120 ml (4 fl oz) water
125 g (4 oz) butter
1 tsp salt
15 g (1/2 oz) caster sugar
150 g (5 oz) flour
4 eggs, plus 1 beaten egg, for glazing
30 g (1 oz) flaked almonds, for the decoration

For the pastry cream
1 litre (1 3/4 pints) milk
a few drops of vanilla essence
10 egg yolks
250 g (8 oz) caster sugar
60 g (2 oz) flour
60 g (2 oz) cornflour
250 g (8 oz) butter

For the praline
100 g (3 1/2 oz) sugar
75 g (2 1/2 oz) whole almonds
a little icing sugar (optional)

PREPARATION

1 Make the choux pastry (see page 152).
2 Put the dough into a piping bag fitted with a 2·5-cm (1-inch) nozzle. Pipe a 23-cm (9-inch) ring of dough on a buttered baking tray. Pipe another ring directly on top of the first, then pipe a third ring on top of that. Brush with egg glaze and sprinkle some flaked almonds on top. With remaining dough, pipe some small éclairs on the baking tray and brush with egg glaze. Bake in a preheated oven at 180°C (350°F, Gas 4) for 20-25 minutes, or until golden brown. Let cool.
3 Make the pastry cream: put the milk and vanilla in a saucepan and bring to a boil. Beat egg yolks and sugar until thick. Add the flour and cornflour, and stir to mix. Add a little of the boiling milk, whisking constantly. Return the mixture to the milk remaining in the pan and cook gently, stirring, until thickened.
4 Add one-third of the butter and stir until melted. Pour the pastry cream into a shallow dish and cover the surface with dampened non-stick paper. Leave to cool.
5 Make the praline: melt the sugar in a saucepan, add the almonds, and cook to a light caramel. Pour on to an oiled surface and leave to cool and set. When set, grind to a powder in a food processor.
6 When the pastry cream is cold, whisk in the remaining softened butter. Mix in the praline powder. Put the praline cream into a piping bag fitted with a star nozzle.
7 Carefully cut the pastry ring horizontally in half, and set the top aside. Pipe some praline cream into the bottom half to fill the hollow, then replace the top. Arrange the éclairs like spokes of a wheel in the centre and pipe the remaining praline cream between the éclairs. Dust the dessert with a little icing sugar, if you like.

PASTRY WHEELS

The French are enthusiastic cyclists, and the gruelling annual cycle race between Paris and Brest, on the French northern Atlantic coast, is a highlight of the sporting year. In 1891, an enterprising pastry cook, whose shop bordered the race circuit, created a large, wheel-shaped pastry filled with praline-flavoured cream and scattered with toasted almonds: the Paris-Brest quickly became a classic. A variation, Saint-Honoré, filled with Chantilly cream, celebrates the equally famous Paris-Nice race.

Coupe aux Trois Glacees

Vanilla, Strawberry, and Pistachio Ice Cream in Tulip Cups

Vanilla custard, or crème anglaise *in French, is by far the most versatile of all dessert sauces. This mixture of milk, egg yolks, and vanilla forms the ice-cream base. Flavouring can be added for variety; here, strawberry and pistachio complement the vanilla.*

INGREDIENTS

Serves 4
500 ml (16 fl oz) milk
2 tsp vanilla essence
12 egg yolks
250 g (8 oz) sugar
500 ml (16 fl oz) double cream

For the strawberry ice cream
150 g (5 oz) strawberries, puréed and sieved
100 g (3½ oz) strawberries, diced

For the pistachio ice cream
75 g (2½ oz) pistachio paste, or pistachios puréed in a food processor
45 g (1½ oz) pistachio nuts, coarsely chopped
a few drops of green food colouring (optional)

For the decoration
100 g (3½ oz) chocolate, broken into pieces
250 g (8 oz) fresh whole strawberries
4 tulip cups (see page 127), to serve
a few mint leaves

PREPARATION

1 Make a vanilla custard (see below). Remove from the heat, stir in the cream, and let cool. Divide the custard into 3 equal parts. Freeze one-third for the vanilla ice cream in an ice-cream machine until set.

2 For the strawberry ice cream, add the strawberry purée and the chopped strawberries to another third of the custard. Freeze as for the vanilla ice cream.

3 For the pistachio ice cream, add the pistachio paste and the coarsely ground pistachio nuts to the remaining custard. Stir in the food colouring, if you like. Freeze as for the vanilla ice cream.

4 Meanwhile, prepare the decoration: melt the chocolate in a bowl in a *bain marie* (or double boiler), stirring until smooth. Remove from the heat, dip in the strawberries, and leave to set on non-stick paper.

5 Set tulip cups on individual plates. Put 1 scoop of each ice cream into each cup. Decorate with the chocolate-dipped strawberries and the mint.

Making Vanilla Custard

It is important not to boil custard once the eggs have been added, as it might curdle. Stirring the mixture will prevent it from burning. Vanilla is the most common flavouring, but coffee, chocolate, and pistachio flavours are all equally delicious.

1 Boil the milk and vanilla, and set aside. Whisk the egg yolks and sugar until thick and pale.

2 Pour half the hot milk over the egg mixture and whisk until combined. Return to pan.

3 Gently cook until thickened, stirring. It is ready when your finger leaves a trail on a spoon.

Tulip Cups

- 60 g (2 oz) butter, softened • 90 g (3 oz) icing sugar
- 2 egg whites, lightly beaten
- 75 g (2½ oz) flour, sifted
- 1 tsp vanilla essence
- 60 g (2 oz) flaked almonds (optional)

Beat the butter until creamy. Add the icing sugar, egg whites, vanilla, and flour, and whisk just until smooth. Let the mixture stand for 30 minutes. Generously butter 4 brioche moulds and a baking tray. Put large spoonfuls of the mixture on to the buttered baking tray. Smooth out the batter into rounds. If you like, press some almonds around the outside of the rounds. Bake in a preheated oven at 200°C (400°F, Gas 6) for 4-5 minutes, or until golden. Use a spatula to remove the rounds and quickly press into the brioche moulds, placing another mould inside. Let cool for 30 seconds, then unmould and let cool completely.

Sorbet au Vouvray et Poires Caramelisees

White Wine Sorbet with Spiced Pears in Caramel

INGREDIENTS

Serves 12

For the Vouvray sorbet
250 g (8 oz) sugar
500 ml (16 fl oz) water
1 bottle dry or semi-dry Vouvray wine
4 tbsp Cognac
juice of 2 lemons or 2 oranges
1 tbsp freshly grated root ginger

For the pears in caramel
6 large or 12 small pears, peeled and cored
juice of 3 lemons
100 g (3 1/2 oz) honey
2 tbsp sugar
1 tbsp mixed ground spices, such as cinnamon, ginger anise, coriander, and mace (optional)

For the decoration
fresh mint leaves
petits fours (see page 130)

PREPARATION

1 Make the sorbet: combine the sugar and water in a pan and slowly bring to a boil, stirring to dissolve the sugar. Add all of the remaining ingredients. Remove from the heat and let cool. Freeze the mixture in an ice-cream machine until set.

2 Meanwhile, cut a thin slice off the bottom of each pear, so that they stand upright. Coat the pears with lemon juice to prevent discoloration.

3 Put the pears in a baking dish with the honey, sugar, spices, and remaining lemon juice. Bake in a preheated oven at 220°C (425°F, Gas 7) for 10 minutes, or until the pears are tender. Baste the pears occasionally.

4 Remove the pears with a slotted spoon and keep warm. Reduce the liquid to make a sauce.

5 Set warm pears in the centre of individual plates and spoon a little sauce around them. Decorate with the mint leaves and petits fours, if you like, and serve with the sorbet.

Sorbet

The earliest forms of iced desserts originated in China. Traders introduced them into Persia and Arabia, and then into Italy. Le Cordon Bleu chefs have created this light, sparkling Sorbet au Vouvray for the health-conscious gourmand. Based on sorbet rather than the usual ice cream, it contains neither egg yolks nor cream. In small portions, it can be served between the first and main courses of a formal dinner, to cleanse the palate.

Glace aux Truffes

Truffle Ice Cream

INGREDIENTS

Serves 8
4 small Perigord truffles (fungi)
1 litre (1 3/4 pints) milk
1 vanilla pod, split
10 egg yolks
275 g (9 oz) caster sugar
1/2 tbsp port

PREPARATION

1 Put the truffles, milk, and vanilla pod in a saucepan and bring to a boil. Remove from the heat, cover the pan, and set aside to infuse for 15 minutes. Strain, reserving both the truffles and the flavoured milk.

2 Beat the egg yolks and sugar until thick. Add a little of the flavoured milk; whisking constantly. Return the mixture to the milk remaining in the pan, and cook gently, stirring, until the custard is thick enough to coat the back of a wooden spoon. Remove from the heat and let cool.

3 Chop the truffles and add them to the custard with the port.

4 Freeze in an ice-cream machine until set. Serve in small scoops.

Milly La Foret

Chocolate Sorbet with Chocolate Sauce

INGREDIENTS

Serves 8–10

For the chocolate sorbet
900 ml (1 1/2 pints) water
200 g (7 oz) sugar
100 g (3 1/2 oz) glucose
150 g (5 oz) cocoa powder
100 g (3 1/2 oz) plain chocolate, broken into pieces

For the chocolate sauce
100 ml (3 1/2 fl oz) water
45 g (1 1/2 oz) sugar (optional)
100 g (3 1/2 oz) cocoa powder
100 ml (3 1/2 fl oz) single cream
100 g (3 1/2 oz) plain chocolate, broken into pieces

For the decoration
slivered almonds, toasted
fresh mint leaves

PREPARATION

1 Make the sorbet: combine 750 ml (1 1/4 pints) water, 100 g (3 1/2 oz) sugar, and the glucose in a saucepan and slowly bring to a boil, stirring to dissolve the sugar.
2 In another pan, bring the remaining water and sugar to a boil, stirring occasionally.
3 Mix the sugar syrups together and gradually stir in the cocoa powder.
4 Melt the chocolate, then pass through a fine sieve. Add the melted chocolate to the cocoa mixture and blend well. Let cool, then freeze in an ice-cream machine until set.
5 Make the chocolate sauce: bring the water to a boil, with the sugar, if you like. Gradually add the cocoa powder, stirring constantly. Stir in the cream. Melt the chocolate in a *bain marie* (or a double boiler) and stir it into the sauce.
6 Put scoops of sorbet into dessert glasses, spoon over the sauce, and sprinkle with toasted almonds. Decorate with mint leaves.

A Fashionable Feast

Le Cordon Bleu chefs devised this chocolate sorbet for Sonia Rykiel, who has inspired French fashion and home decoration with her creations. A celebration dinner was held at Milly La Forêt on her behalf, and the dessert was named in honour of this occasion.

Truffes Glacees a la Cannelle

Frozen Cinnamon and Chocolate Truffles

INGREDIENTS

Serves 8
cocoa powder, sifted

For the cinnamon ice cream
500 ml (16 fl oz) milk
2 cinnamon sticks
6 egg yolks
100 g (3 1/2 oz) caster sugar

For the ganache
250 ml (8 fl oz) single cream
45 g (1 1/2 oz) caster sugar
250 g (8 oz) plain chocolate, chopped

PREPARATION

1 Make the ice cream: put the milk and cinnamon sticks in a saucepan and bring to a boil. Remove from the heat, cover the pan, and set aside to infuse for about 15 minutes.
2 In a bowl, beat the egg yolks and sugar until thick. Pour in a little of the hot milk, whisking constantly. Return the mixture to the remaining milk in the pan and cook gently, stirring constantly, until the custard is thick enough to coat the back of a wooden spoon. Strain the custard into a bowl, and leave to cool completely.
3 Set aside a little of the custard to serve as a sauce. Freeze the remaining custard in an ice-cream machine until set.
4 Using an ice-cream scoop or spoons, make balls of ice cream about 6 cm (2 1/2 inches) in diameter. Arrange them in a single layer on a baking tray and freeze until very firm.
5 Make the ganache: heat the cream with the sugar, stirring to dissolve. Pour the hot cream over the chopped chocolate and stir until melted and smooth. Cool just until slightly warm.
6 Dip the ice-cream balls in the liquid ganache to coat all over, then roll them in cocoa powder.
7 Pour pools of the reserved cinnamon custard on to the centre of individual plates. Put 2 or 3 truffles on top and serve immediately.

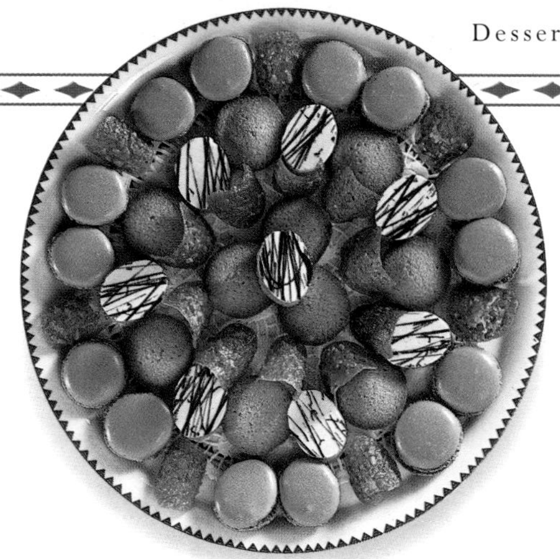

Financier Pistache

Pistachio Sponge Cakes

INGREDIENTS

Makes about 100

125 g (4 oz) ground almonds
350 g (12 oz) icing sugar
125 g (4 oz) flour
250 g (8 oz) egg whites, whisked until stiff
250 g (8 oz) butter, melted until brown, and sieved
30 g (1 oz) pistachio paste

PREPARATION

1 Butter and chill some small round moulds.
2 Gently mix all the ingredients together and fill as many moulds as the mixture allows.
3 Bake in a preheated oven at 200°C (400°F, Gas 6) for 10 minutes. Let cool.

Tuiles au The

Thin Tea Biscuits

INGREDIENTS

Makes about 50

20 g (2/3 oz) tea, infused in 4 tbsp boiling water
200 g (7 oz) icing sugar
60 g (2 oz) flour
100 g (3 1/2 oz) chopped almonds
125 g (4 oz) butter, melted until brown, and sieved

PREPARATION

1 Mix all the ingredients and let stand for 1 hour.
2 Place small spoonfuls of the mixture on a buttered baking tray. Flatten and bake in a preheated oven at 180°C (350°F, Gas 4) for 5 minutes, until golden. Remove the tuiles and rest on an oiled rolling pin to set their shape.

Macarons Cafe

Coffee Macaroons

INGREDIENTS

Makes about 60

125 g (4 oz) ground almonds
300 g (10 oz) icing sugar
150 g (5 oz) egg whites, whisked until stiff
15 g (1/2 oz) caster sugar
1 tsp coffee extract

For the ganache

3 1/2 tbsp double cream
45 g (1 1/2 oz) plain chocolate, chopped

PREPARATION

1 Make the *ganache*: boil the cream, pour over the chocolate, and stir until smooth.
2 Gently mix all the other ingredients together and pipe the mixture into small, even rounds on a buttered baking tray. Bake in a preheated oven at 170°C (325°F, Gas 3) for 15 minutes. Let cool.
3 Sandwich the macaroons together with ganache.

Duchesse Cannelle

Cinnamon Ovals

INGREDIENTS

Makes about 20

175 g (6 oz) ground almonds
175 g (6 oz) icing sugar
45 g (1 1/2 oz) flour, sifted
175 g (6 oz) egg whites, whisked until stiff
90 g (3 oz) butter, melted
1 tbsp ground cinnamon
30 g (1 oz) plain chocolate, melted
1 tbsp praline paste
chocolate ovals (see page 118), for the decoration

PREPARATION

1 Mix the ground almonds, sugar, flour, egg whites, melted butter, and cinnamon together.
2 Pipe the mixture in oval shapes about 2 cm (3/4 inch) long on a buttered baking tray. Bake in a preheated oven at 170°C (325°F, Gas 3) for 10-12 minutes. Let cool.
3 Mix the chocolate and praline together and use to sandwich the petits fours together in threes. Top with chocolate ovals.

TECHNIQUES

A collection of basic culinary techniques needs to be learned in order to master the art of French cooking. On the following pages, the chef-instructors from Le Cordon Bleu demonstrate these techniques in an easy-to-follow, step-by-step format.

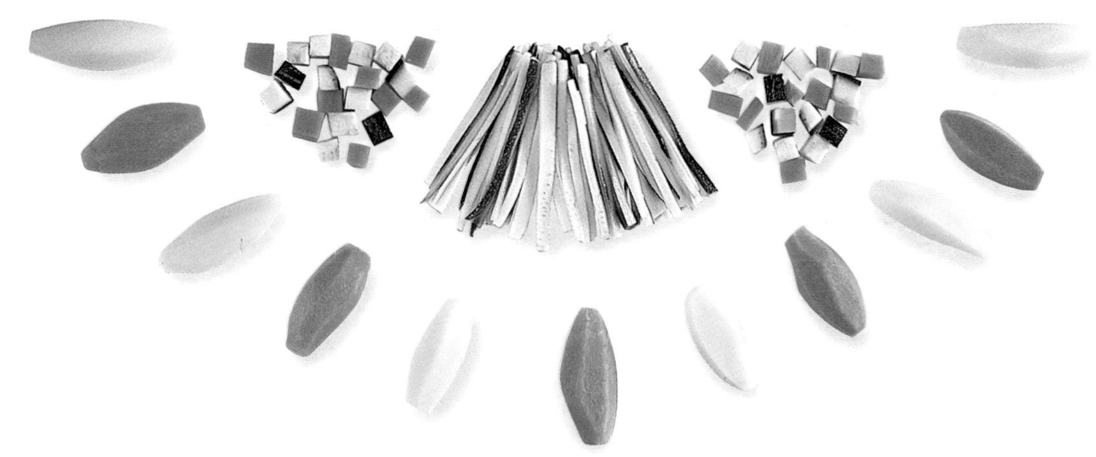

Vegetable Techniques

Vegetables cut neatly into slices, dice, mirepoix, or julienne, not only cook evenly, they also look attractive when served. For best results when slicing, dicing, and chopping vegetables, use a very sharp large chef's knife, as illustrated here.

Slicing Onions

Onions are sliced in varying thicknesses depending on their intended use. They can be sliced whole into thick rings, or halved and very thinly sliced as shown here, to top a salad or for using in the classic French Onion Soup (see page 29).

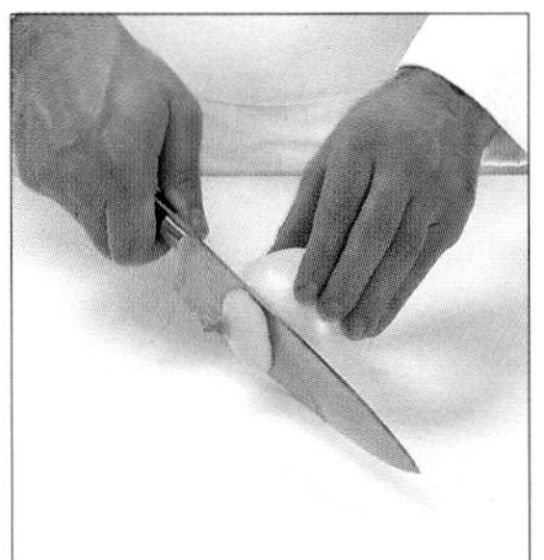

1 Peel the onion and trim the stem end. Trim off any roots, leaving a little of the root end attached.

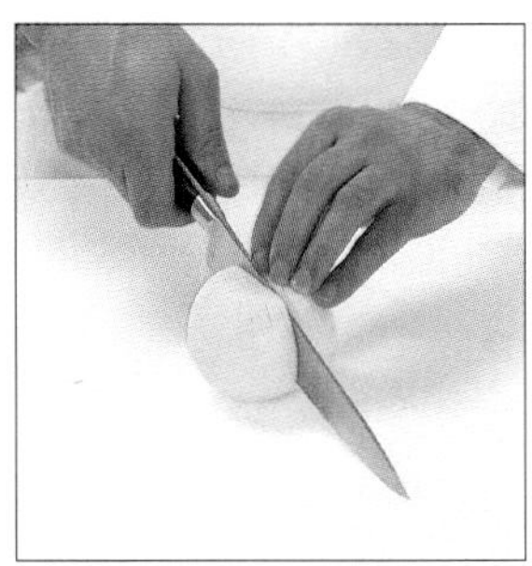

2 Cut onion lengthwise in half, and lay each onion half cut-side down on a chopping board.

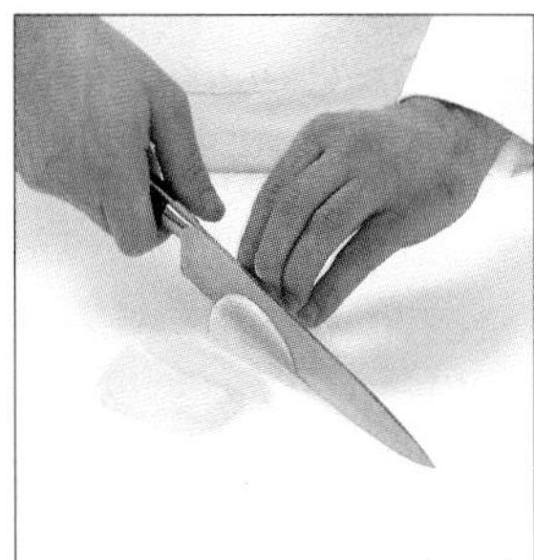

3 Hold the root end and slice each onion half crosswise until you reach the root end.

Dicing Onions and Shallots

Onions are cut into dice for use in the foundation of stews, casseroles, and soups. The size of the dice depends on the recipe, and can vary from small to large. Peel, trim, and halve the onion before dicing. Shallots, separated into two sections if necessary, are diced in exactly the same way as onions.

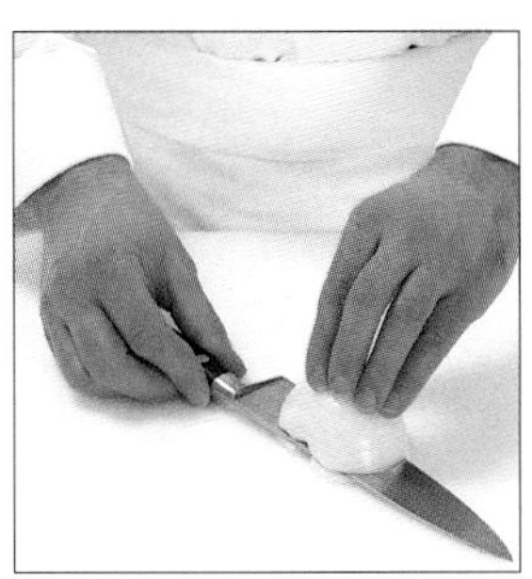

1 Place onion half cut-side down and make several horizontal cuts from the stem towards the root (but not through it).

2 Similarly, make several lengthwise vertical cuts in the onion, without cutting through the vegetable's root end.

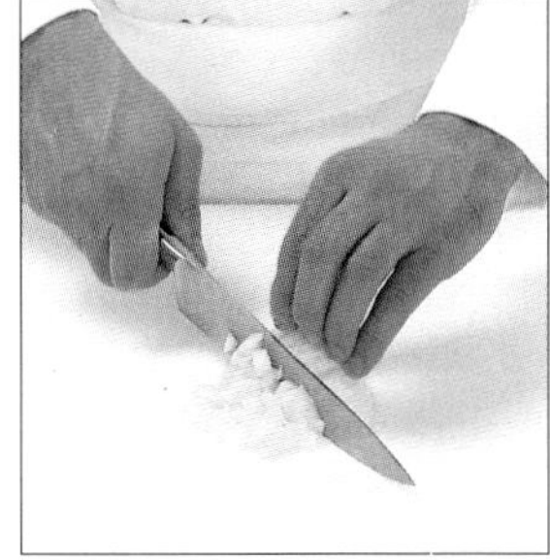

3 Finally, chop the onion crosswise into dice. For finer pieces, continue chopping, using a rocking motion with the knife.

Peeling and Chopping Garlic

There are two methods for chopping garlic, the first using a knife and the second using a garlic press. If using a garlic press, the garlic will be crushed finer and will not have any fibres, but a lot of the garlic will be wasted. It is better, therefore, to chop garlic by hand.

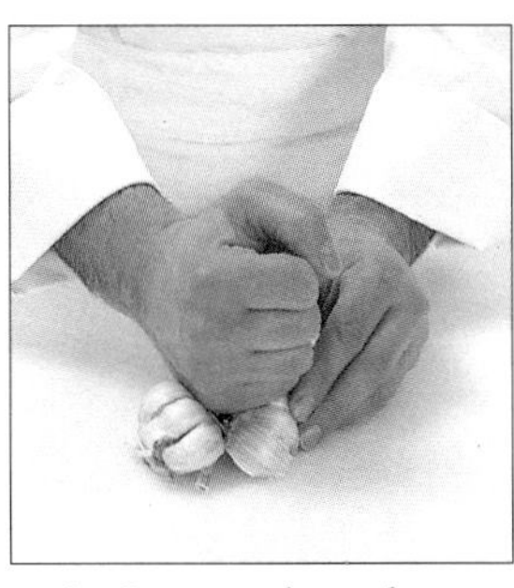

1 Separate the garlic cloves by pounding the whole head of garlic with your fist.

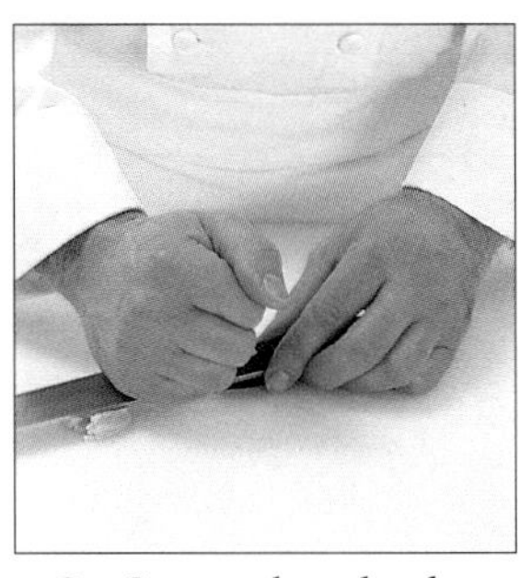

2 Press each garlic clove with the flat side of a chef's knife. This will crush the clove to loosen the skin.

3 Peel the clove and discard the skin. Chop the garlic to desired fineness using a rocking motion.

Coring, Seeding, and Dicing Peppers

Peppers are always cored and seeded before they are used. Whether they are left whole, sliced, or diced depends on each individual recipe. Peppers can also be peeled before they are prepared: roast peppers under a hot grill until their skins blacken, leave to cool slightly, then peel off their skins.

1 Cut round to remove the core of the pepper. Halve the pepper lengthwise. Scrape away the seeds and cut out the white ribs.

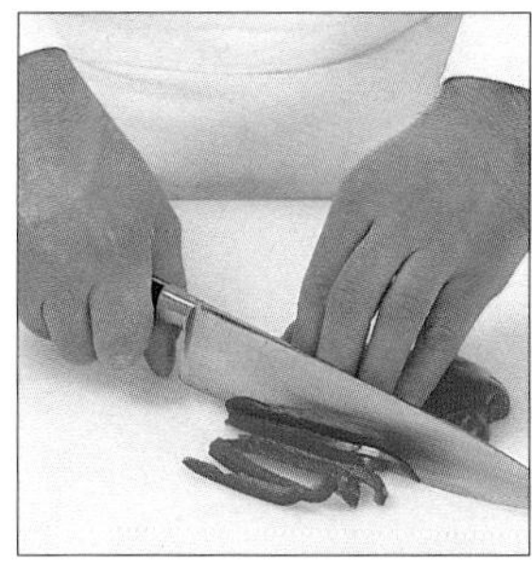

2 Lay each pepper half cut-side down on a chopping board, press firmly, and slice the pepper half lengthwise into strips.

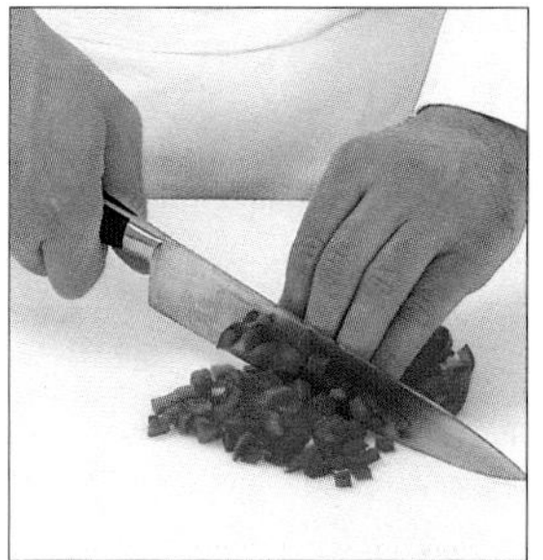

3 Cut the pepper strips crosswise into dice. Continue chopping if finer dice are required.

Making a Mirepoix

A mirepoix is a rough dice of mixed vegetables with equal amounts of carrot, onion, celery, and leek. It is used as the basic flavouring for stocks and consommés, and is added to meat dishes to enhance the flavour of the cooking juices. It takes its name from the 18th-century Duc de Lévis-Mirepoix, who created it.

1 Cut a carrot into 5-cm (2-inch) pieces. Square pieces off, and cut lengthwise, thick for large dice, thin for small dice.

2 Stack the slices and cut them lengthwise again into strips of uniform thickness. These strips are known as bâtonnets.

3 Gather the strips into a pile and cut them crosswise into dice. Repeat technique with onion *(see page 132)* *and celery.*

Vegetable Julienne

Matchstick-thin strips of vegetable are called *julienne* in French. A medley of different julienne, such as leeks, carrots, and courgettes, is especially striking as a garnish or accompaniment. If courgettes are partially peeled before being cut, the julienne will look more effective.

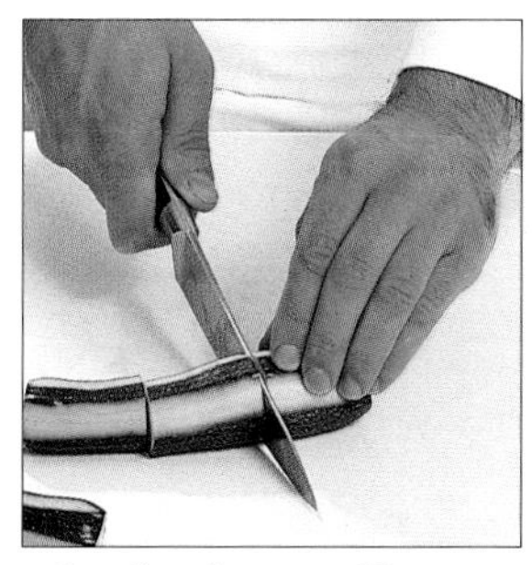

1 Cut the vegetable crosswise into even pieces. Make sure the vegetable sits flat.

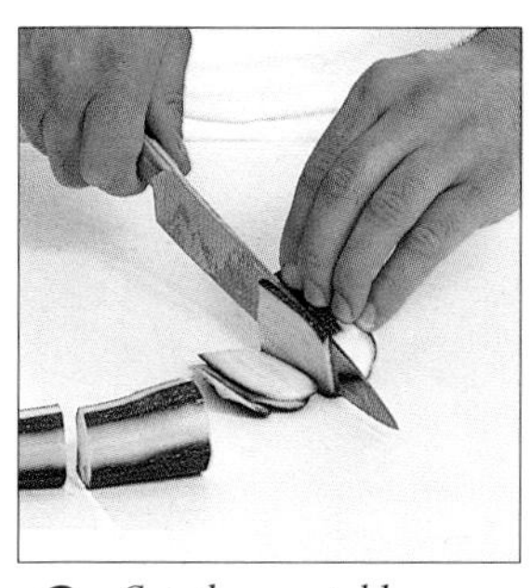

2 Cut the vegetable pieces lengthwise into very thin slices, guiding the knife with bent fingers.

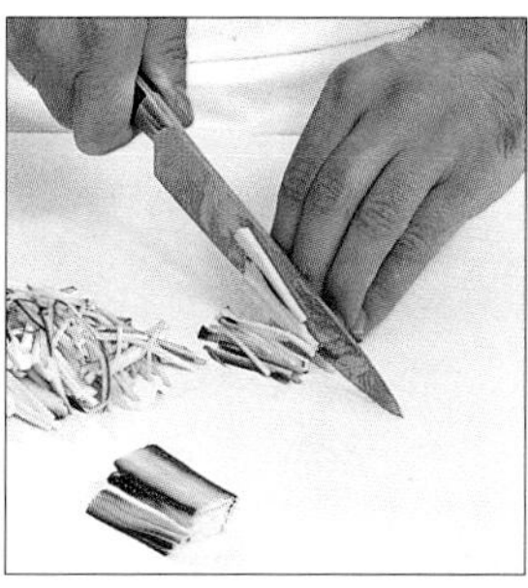

3 Stack the slices and cut lengthwise again into very fine strips, keeping the tip of the knife on the board.

Cleaning and Slicing Mushrooms

Choose firm but moist mushrooms with no wet patches. Common cultivated mushrooms should be gently wiped clean with damp paper towels, instead of being washed, because they can easily become soggy and waterlogged.

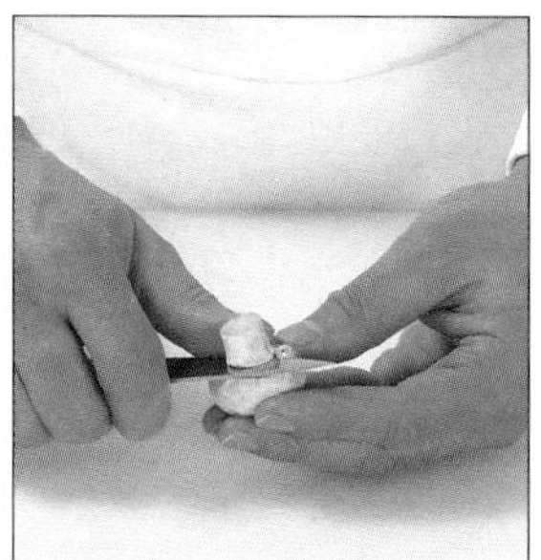

1 Trim the mushroom stems even with the caps; reserve the trimmings for stock, soup, or stuffings.

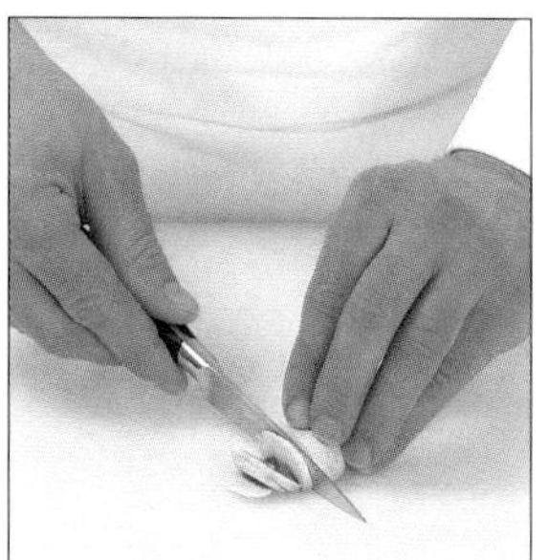

2 Hold each mushroom stem-side down and cut vertically into even slices from top to stem.

Before using, wild mushrooms should be picked over and brushed or washed, depending on how dirty they are.

Turning Mushrooms

Turned mushrooms are an elegant garnish for any dish. Preparing them requires a good sharp knife and a little practice. The key is being able to turn the mushroom as you are turning the knife. The star shape on the top of the mushroom is an optional extra that adds to the decorative effect.

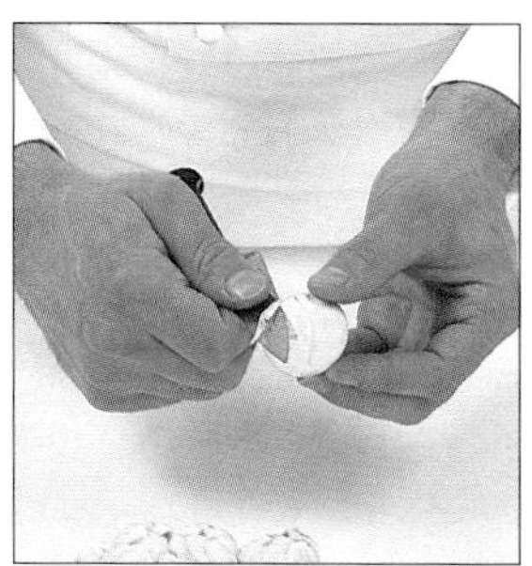

1 Trim the stem. Hold a paring knife at a slight angle to the mushroom, and cut a channel from the centre of its cap to the edge.

2 Continue to make channels until the entire surface of the mushroom has been turned. Cut a level surface on the top of the mushroom.

3 Use the point of the knife to press a 5-or 6-point star shape around the centre of the mushroom cap. Rub with lemon juice to prevent discoloration.

Turning Artichokes

Artichokes can be cooked whole or, as in this technique, "turned" to expose the tender heart that is hidden within the artichoke. Use an up-and-down sawing motion with your knife, slowly turning the artichoke to cut away all of the leaves.

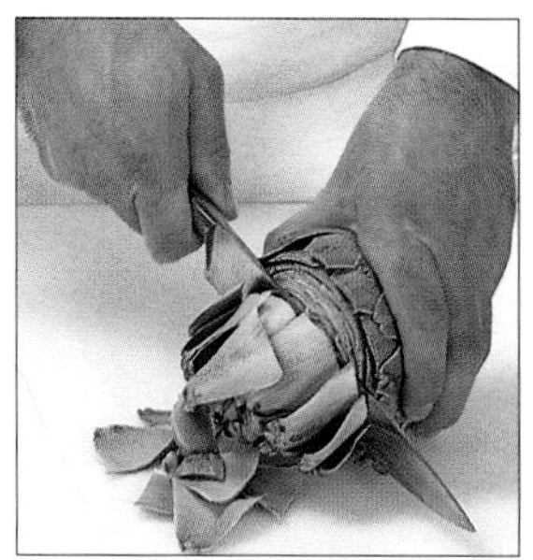

1 Break off the artichoke stem at its base to remove all of its fibres. Place the artichoke on its side and cut off the top of the artichoke leaves, making sure you do not cut off any of the heart.

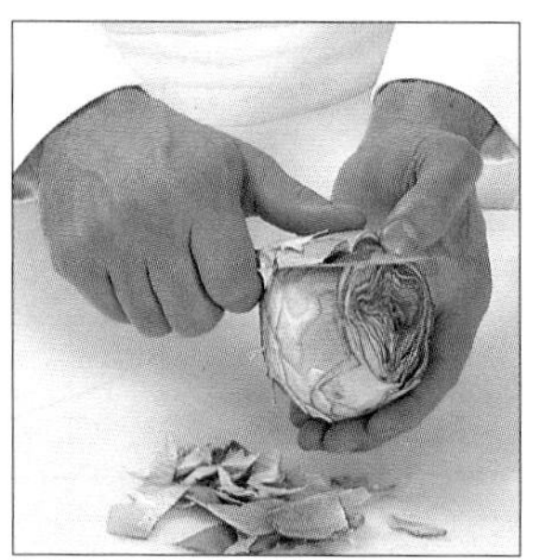

2 Cut off all the outer artichoke leaves, turning as you go. Cut off the soft cone of leaves in the centre of the artichoke, leaving only the choke behind. Trim any dark green areas left on the bottom.

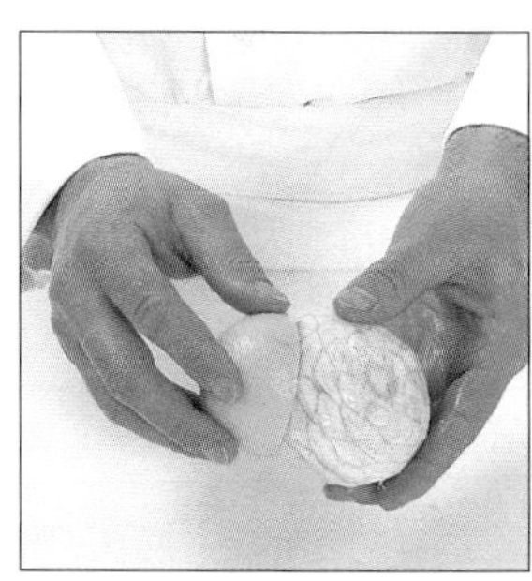

3 Immediately rub a lemon half all over the artichoke, to prevent discoloration. Cook it in boiling water for 15-20 minutes. Remove the choke, leaving only the tender heart exposed.

Vegetables Parisienne

This is a way of preparing vegetables for garnish that originally applied just to potatoes, but other ingredients, such as courgettes, cucumbers, and melons, can also be cut into *parisienne*.

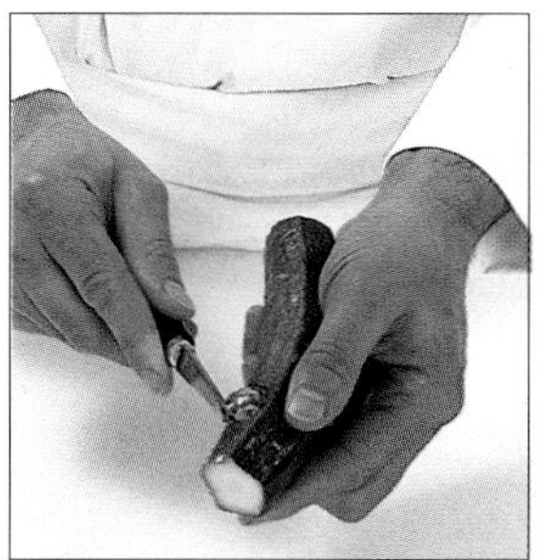

1 Insert a medium-sized melon baller into the vegetable flesh and carefully scoop into a ball.

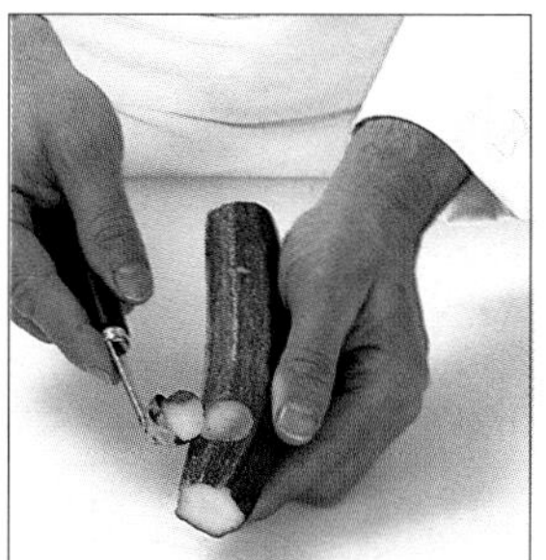

2 When the ball has been completed, carefully remove the melon baller and tap the ball out into a bowl.

Turning Tubular and Round Vegetables

Turned vegetables are the hallmark of classic French cuisine. Traditionally they have seven sides, but this is not absolutely essential as long as each vegetable has a neat barrel or olive shape, and they are all uniform in size. Courgettes, turnips, cucumbers, celeriac, and potatoes are all turned in the same way.

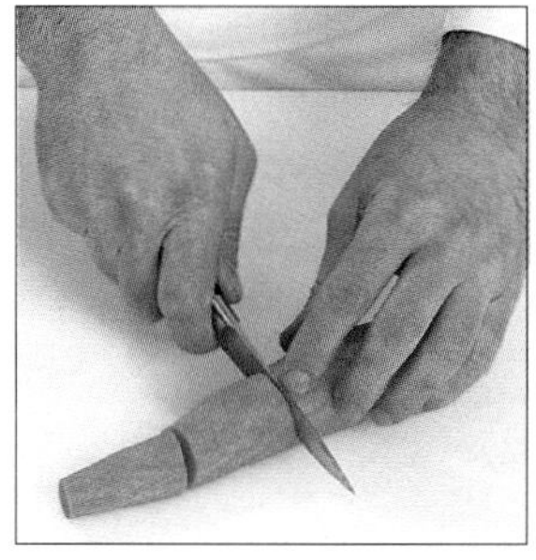

1 When turning tubular vegetables, such as carrots or courgettes, start by cutting them into 5-cm (2-inch) lengths.

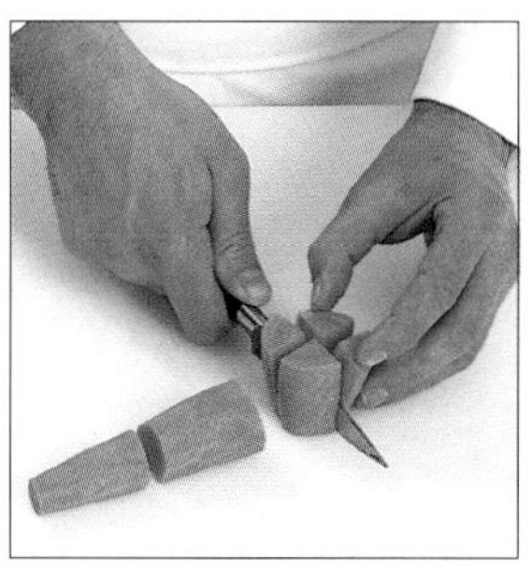

2 Set each vegetable length cut-side down on a chopping board. Cut each piece lengthwise in half or into quarters if too thick.

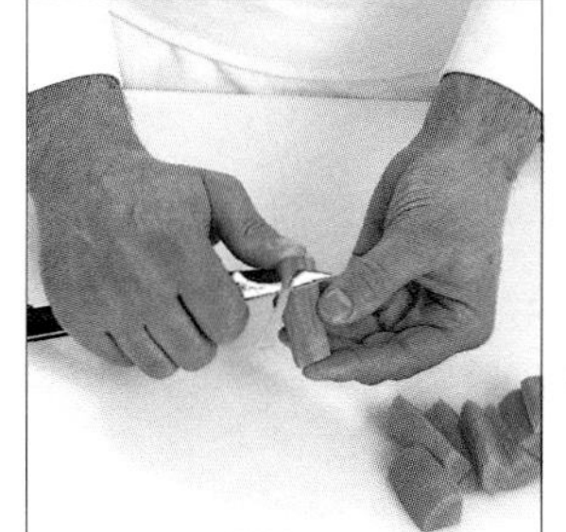

3 Trim off all the sharp edges and pare down from top to bottom in a quick curving movement.

4 Continue shaping each length into a barrel by turning it slightly after each cut.

Tomatoes Concassees

Peeled, seeded, and chopped tomatoes, or tomatoes *concassées,* are used as the foundation of many sauces, stews, and soups. They can also be used as a finishing garnish. It is important to choose firm ripe tomatoes – if they are too soft they will go mushy when peeled.

Once the tomatoes have been peeled and chopped they must be used fairly quickly or they will begin to lose some of their texture and flavour.

Tomatoes concassées can also refer to strips of tomato.

1 Core tomatoes with a small knife, then turn over and score a cross on the base.

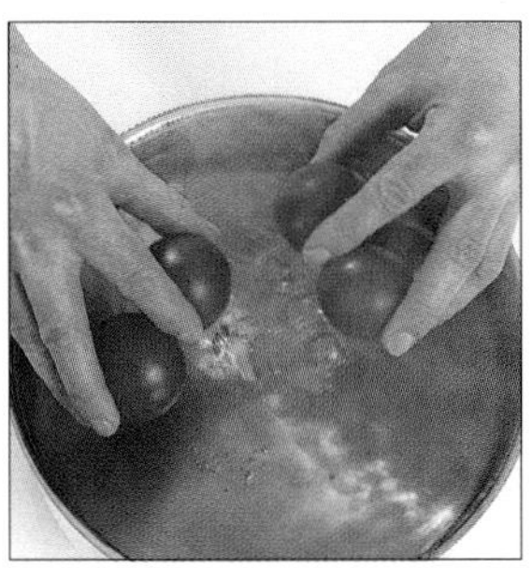

2 Drop the tomatoes into boiling water for 10-30 seconds, until the skin begins to peel away.

3 Remove the tomatoes with a slotted spoon and plunge into cold water to stop them cooking.

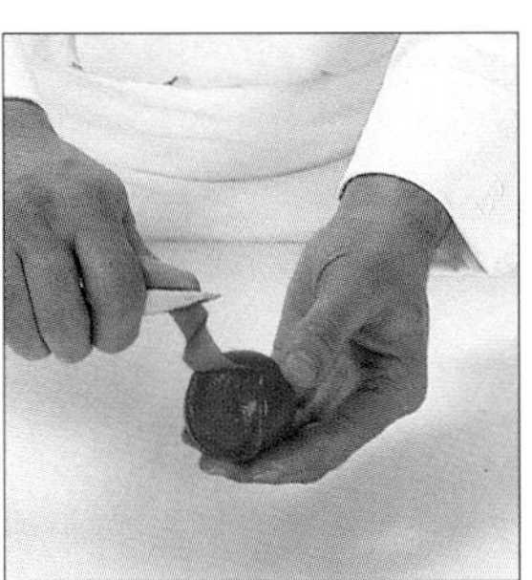

4 Peel the tomatoes when cool, cut crosswise in half, and squeeze over a sieve to remove any seeds.

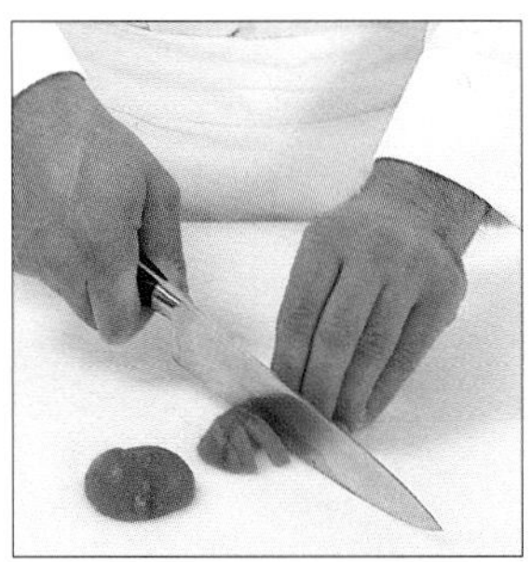

5 Set each tomato half cut-side down on a chopping board and slice into strips.

6 Chop the tomato strips crosswise into dice, carefully guiding the knife with bent fingers.

Chopping Fresh Herbs

Fresh herbs can be chopped using a chef's knife, or a *mezzaluna*, a two-handled, curved knife. If chopping large quantities of fresh herbs, use a food processor, making sure not to overwork them.

1 Strip the leaves or sprigs from herb stems and pile them together on a chopping board.

2 Chop the herbs to the desired fineness, using a rocking motion with the knife.

Bouquet Garni

A bouquet garni is a bundle of aromatic herbs, such as bay leaf, parsley, rosemary, and thyme, sometimes wrapped in leek, tied together with string. It is always removed at the end of cooking.

Fish and Shellfish Techniques

There are many intricate techniques involved in preparing seafood, but they are well worth mastering to avoid waste. An oyster knife and a filleting knife are good investments for the committed seafood cook.

Shucking Oysters and Clams

Oysters and clams can be prepared by steaming, frying, or poaching, and they are often served raw on the half shell. Shucking oysters and clams will take some practice; before you start, rinse any mud and seaweed from the shells, but there is no need to scrub or soak them.

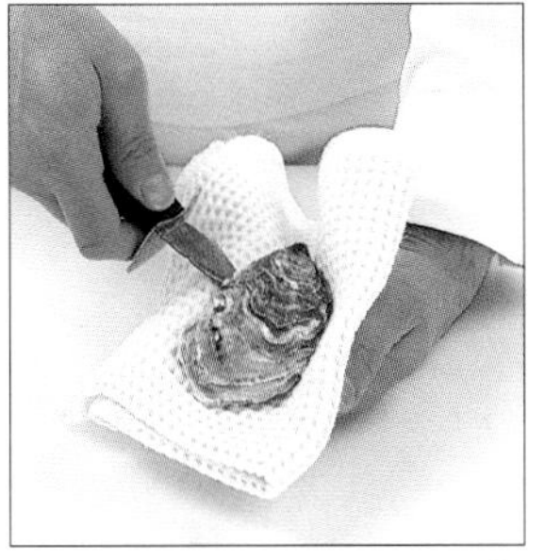

1 Hold the rounded shell of the oyster in a cloth. Insert the point of an oyster knife next to the shell hinge. Twist the knife to force the shell open.

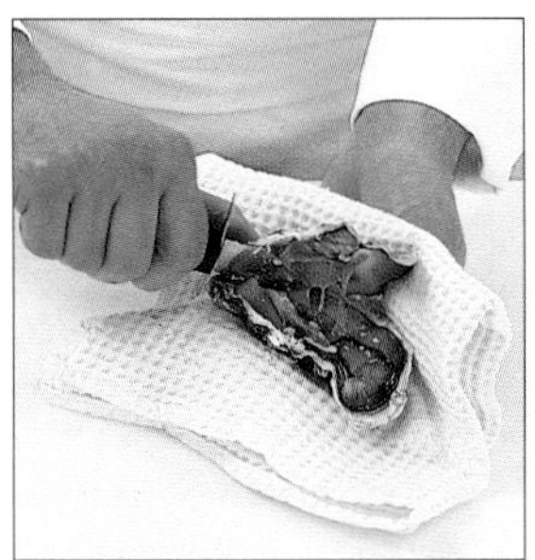

2 Slide the knife along the inside of the top shell to release the small muscle attaching the oyster to the shell. Carefully remove the top shell.

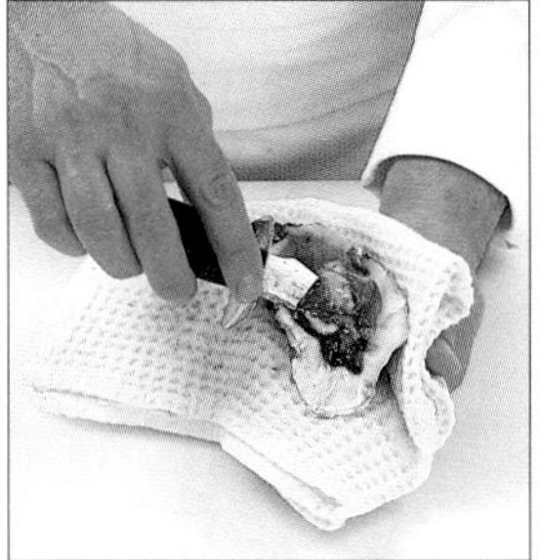

3 Loosen the meat from the bottom shell, leaving the oyster in its juices in the shell. Remove any shell that has fallen into the oyster.

Peeling and Deveining Prawns and Langoustines

Raw prawns and langoustines are peeled and deveined in the same way. It is important to remove the intestinal vein because it becomes gritty when it is cooked.

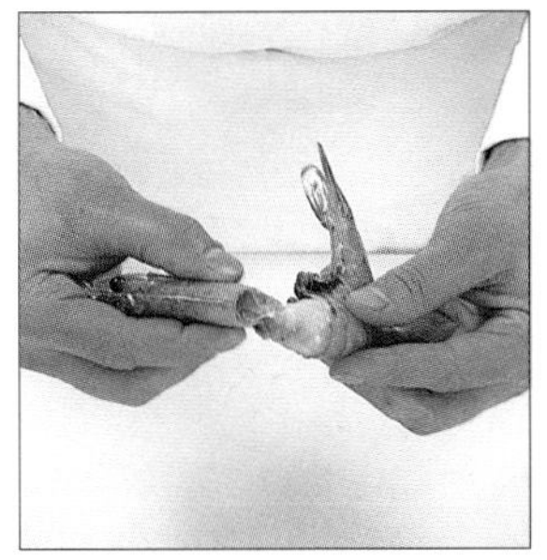

1 Remove the head from the prawn. Carefully peel off the prawn shell and tail section, if you like.

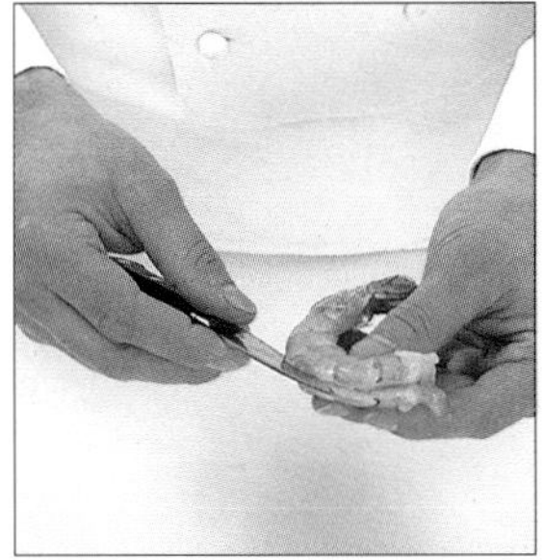

2 Make a shallow cut lengthwise along the back of the prawn, using a small sharp knife.

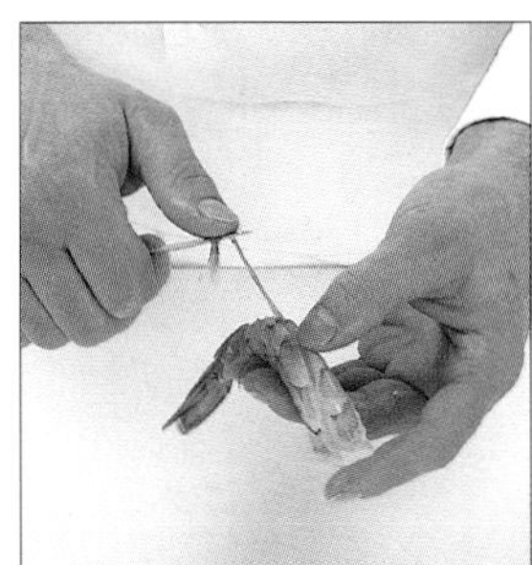

3 Carefully pull out the intestinal vein, preferably in one movement. Rinse prawn after deveining.

Skinning and Filleting a Flat Fish

Some flat fish, such as sole and plaice, can be skinned before they are filleted. Others, such as turbot and brill, have to be filleted first and then skinned; in these cases, fillet the fish as illustrated in steps 3-6, then place the fillet skin-side down on the chopping board. Make a small cut at the tail end to separate the skin from the flesh. Grasping the tail, slide the blade between the skin and the flesh, until the whole fillet is removed.

1 With the tip of a filleting knife, slit the skin near the tail end of the fish to loosen it. Turn the fish over and slit the skin on the other side.

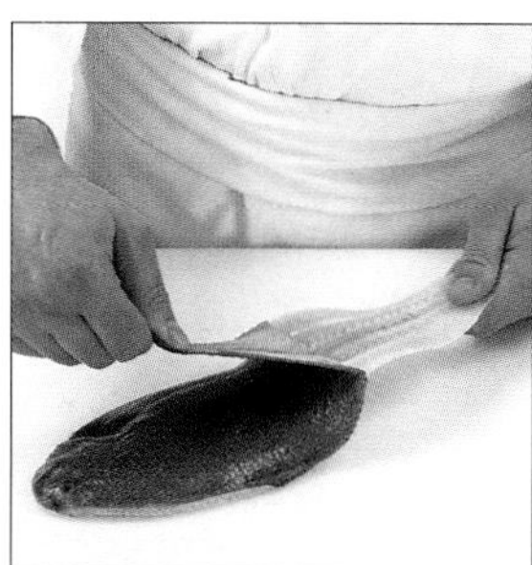

2 Firmly gripping the tail end of the fish, strip the skin away from the flesh on both sides of the flat fish. A little salt may help you grip the skin.

3 Using a filleting knife, begin to remove the fillets. Cut the fish from behind its head and make a slit following the natural line of the spine.

4 Keeping the filleting knife flat, slide the blade in a smooth motion between the flesh and bones, starting from the head of the fish and finishing at the tail.

5 Cut the fillet from the fish and remove the small row of bones attached along the edge, and any dark membranes or bones that may also be attached.

6 Cut the adjacent fillet from the fish in the same way. Turn the fish over and repeat steps 3-5 for the other 2 fillets. The bones can be used for stock, if you like.

Boning a Round Fish for Stuffing

Round fish, such as bass, mackerel, mullet, and trout are often boned from the back. When boned in this way, the flesh of the fish is kept intact for stuffing. The fish should be prepared (see Preparing a Round Fish, page 139) before it is boned.

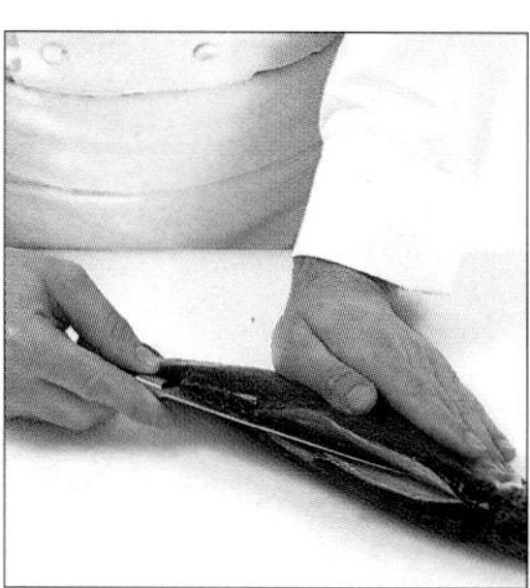

1 Working from the head of the fish, cut along the backbone to the tail end, with a filleting knife. Do not cut completely through the fish.

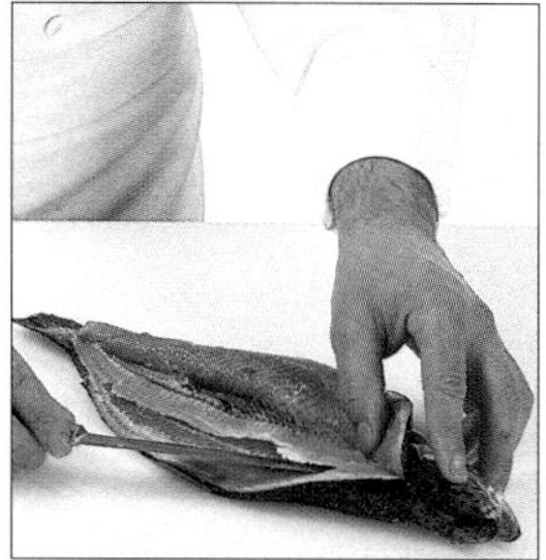

2 Using the tip of the knife, loosen the flesh away from either side of the bone, again taking care not to cut completely through the fish.

3 Snip the backbone from the tail and head using scissors. Remove the bone with the stomach contents. Use tweezers to remove any small bones.

Preparing a Round Fish and Cutting it into Steaks

When preparing any round fish, the fins, scales, gills, and stomach contents should all be removed. Fish steaks can be cut from a variety of large fish. A 2-cm (3/4-inch) thick steak is ideal for grilling, frying, poaching, or baking. The tail meat can be filleted, and either used to make a fish mousse, or it can be cooked in the same way as the steaks.

1 Using a pair of kitchen scissors, cut away the fins on either side of the tail. Then cut the fins from the belly and from along the back of the fish.

2 Scale the fish, running the back of a chef's knife from tail to head. Alternatively, use a fish scaler. Rinse the fish under cold running water.

3 Cut the fish across into even steaks. Continue along the fish until the tail is too small to make a steak.

Gutting, Filleting, and Skinning a Round Fish

Small fish can be gutted through the gills, but the stomach contents of larger fish, such as the salmon illustrated here, have to be removed through the stomach. Perfecting the art of filleting round fish as described in steps 2-3 ensures that the minimum amount of flesh is wasted.

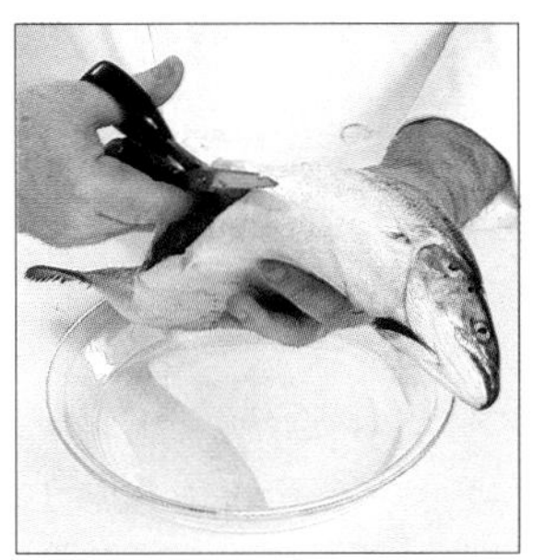

1 Trim and scale the fish (steps 1-2, above). Cut along the underside of the fish. Loosen the stomach contents and pull them out.

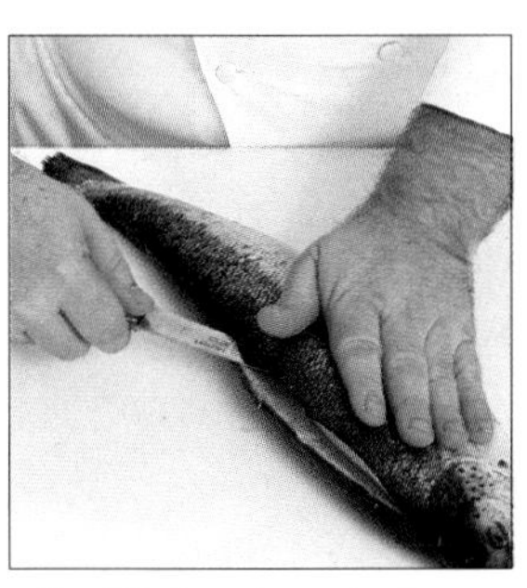

2 With a sharp knife, cut along the backbone of the fish, from behind the head right down to the tail. Keep the knife level with the backbone and slide the knife along the bones. Cut the fillet from the fish.

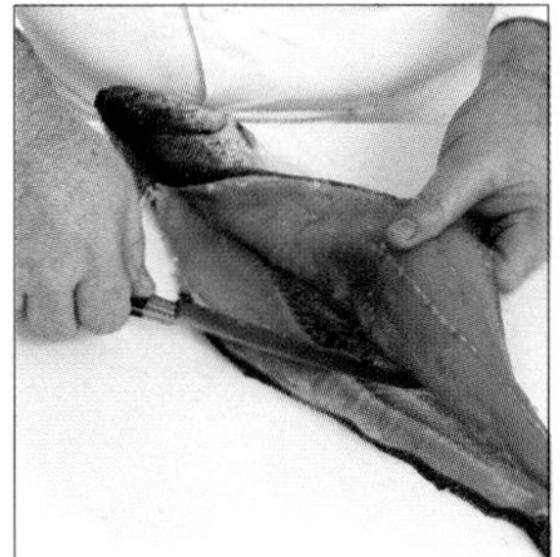

3 Turn the fish over and remove the second fillet in the same way.

4 Grasp the tail end of the fish and slide the blade against the flesh (cutting as close as possible) to remove the skin. Repeat for the other fillet.

Poultry and Game Techniques

Poultry is the generic term for any bird, such as chicken, duck, and turkey, that has been reared for the kitchen. The following techniques relate to these birds, but they can be used on wild game birds as well. Rabbit is a member of the "furred" game family.

Trussing Poultry

Trussing serves several purposes: it closes the cavity of a bird, and holds the bird and its juices together during cooking. It also helps keep the bird in good shape, which in turn makes it easier to carve.

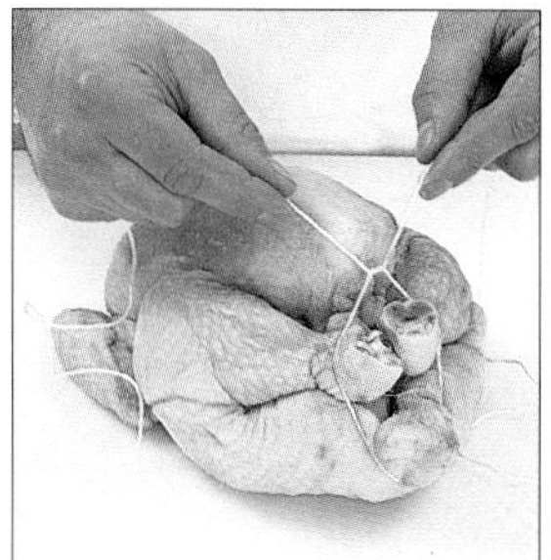

1 Loop string under the tail end and around the legs, and tie to secure over the top of the legs.

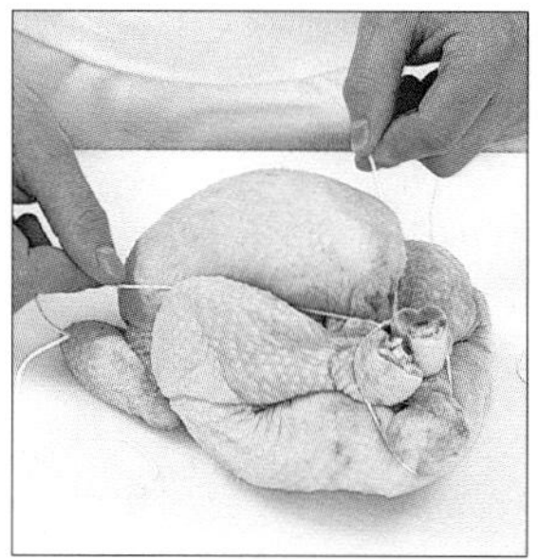

2 Pull the string along and under the legs to pull them tight to the body. Turn the bird over.

3 Bring the string around the wings. Tie the two ends together to secure the bird.

Jointing Poultry into Six or Eight Pieces

Poultry can be jointed into either six or eight pieces, depending on the size of the bird and the intended use. When jointed in this way, the backbone is discarded, and the bird will provide pieces of equal size.

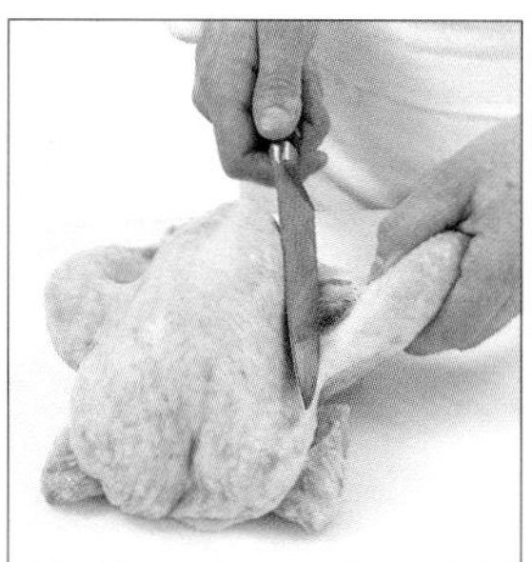

1 Cut the skin between each leg and each breast. Twist legs to break the joints. Remove the legs.

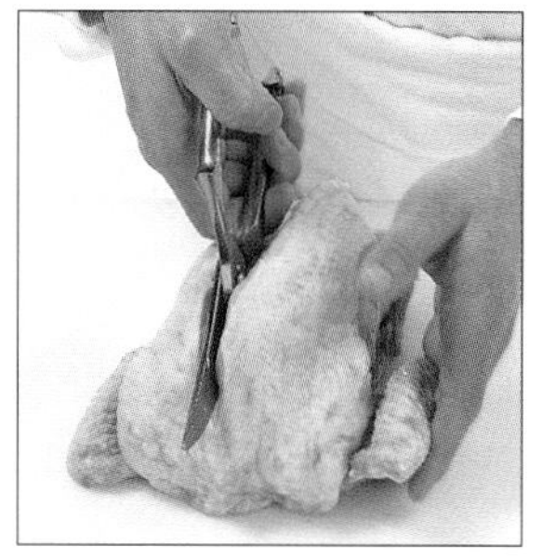

2 Cut along breastbone and through the wishbone with poultry shears, from tail to neck.

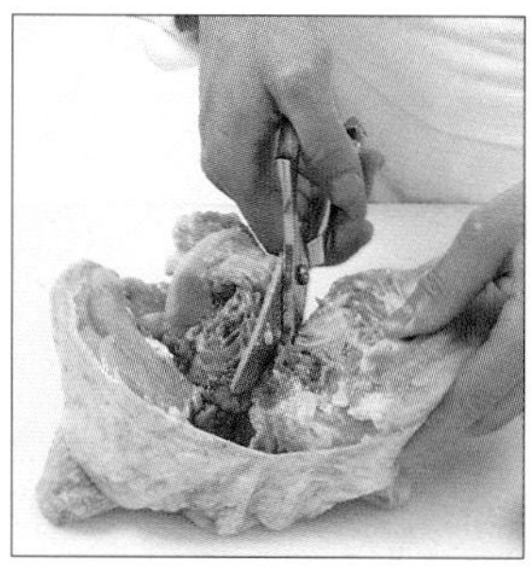

3 Split the bird open and cut out the backbone with poultry shears. Leave the wing joints attached.

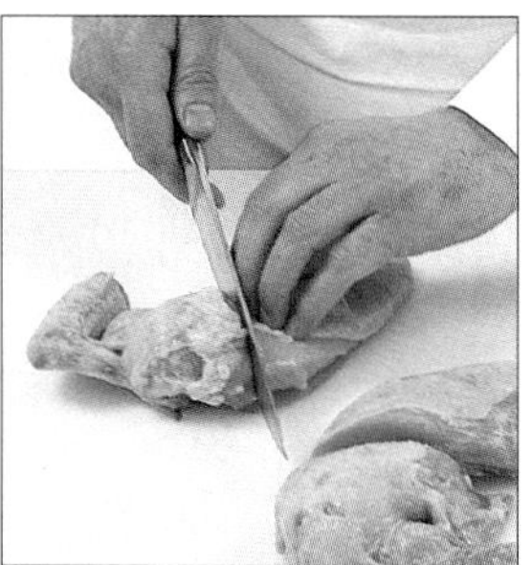

4 For six pieces: cut the breasts in half on the diagonal so that part of the breast is left on the wing.

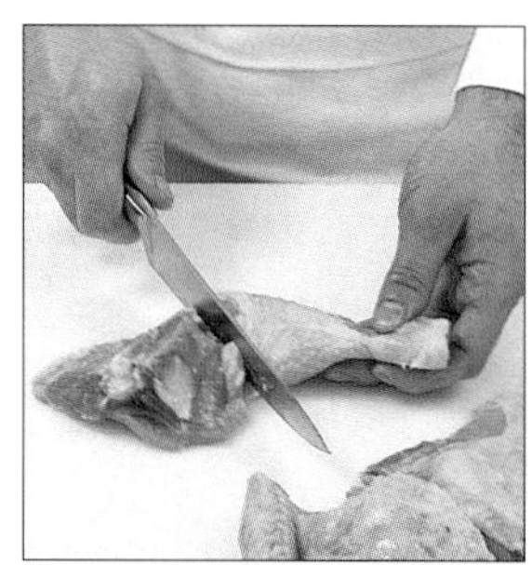

5 For eight pieces: cut the legs in half through the thigh and drumstick joint.

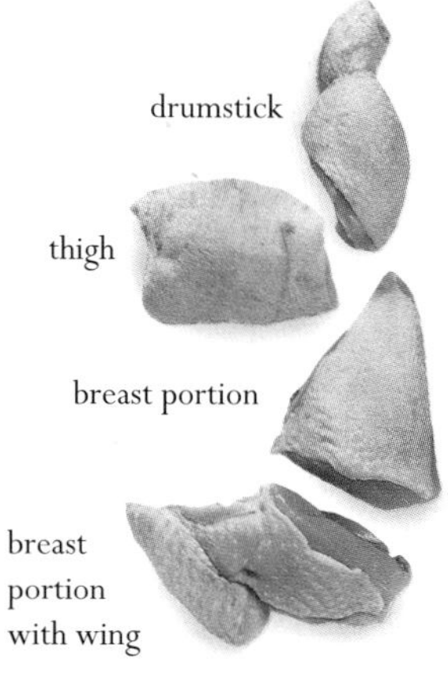

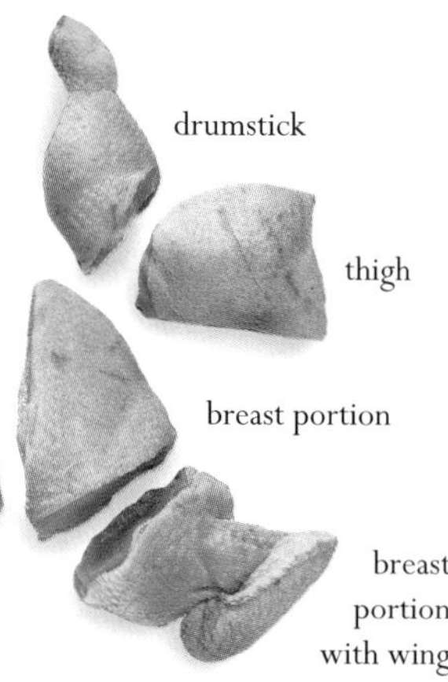

Removing Duck Breasts

Meaty duck breasts are called *magrets* in French. This technique of removing the breasts from the bird ensures that the maximum amount of meat is removed in one piece. Chicken breasts can be removed in a similar way.

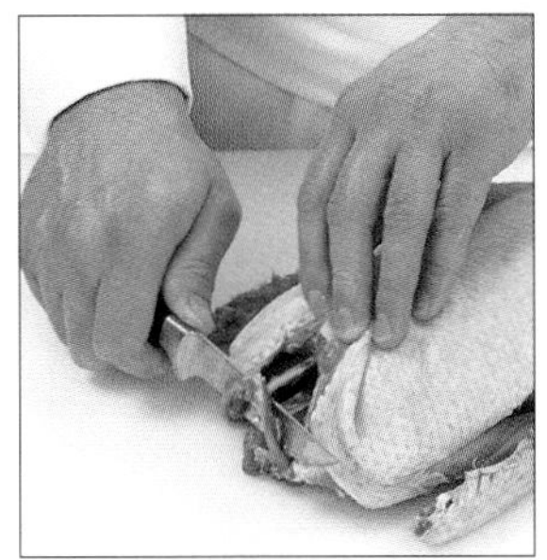

1 Using a boning knife, carefully cut away the wishbone from just inside the neck end of the duck. Discard the wishbone.

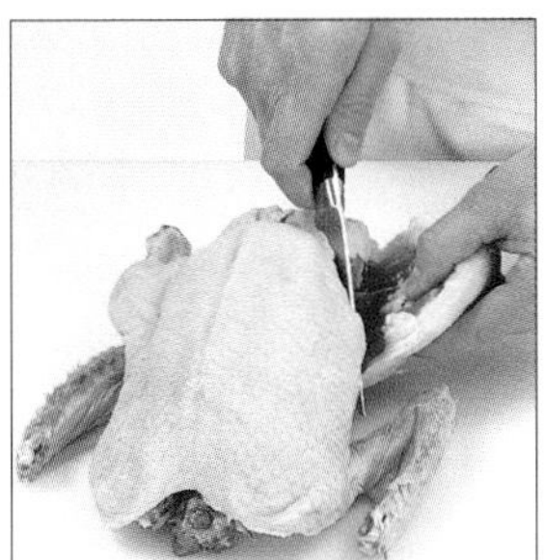

2 Cut between the legs and the breast of the duck, and then twist the legs to break the thigh joints.

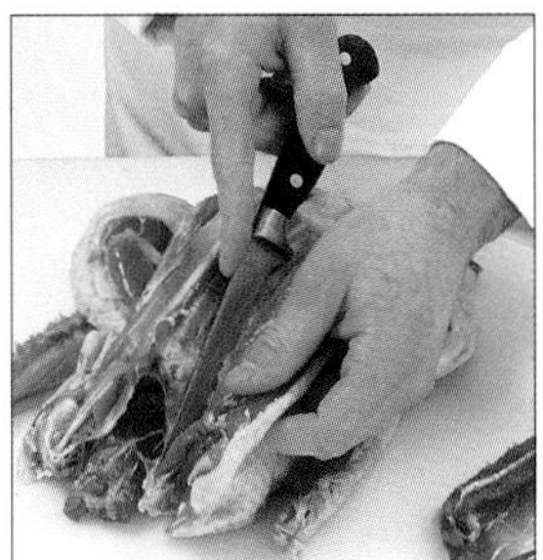

3 Cut along one side of the breastbone, and carefully scrape the breast meat from the ribs. Repeat on the other side.

Boning a Turkey Leg

Removing the bone from the leg of a turkey is a useful technique to learn. A boned leg provides a natural pocket for stuffing, and will make a neat joint for easy carving.

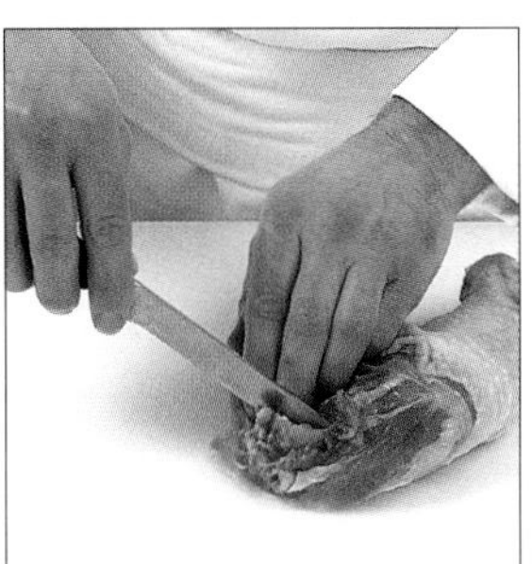

1 Using a boning knife, cut from the top of the leg following the line of the bone. Use short, sharp strokes with the knife, and ease the flesh away from the bone. Try not to cut through too much flesh or skin.

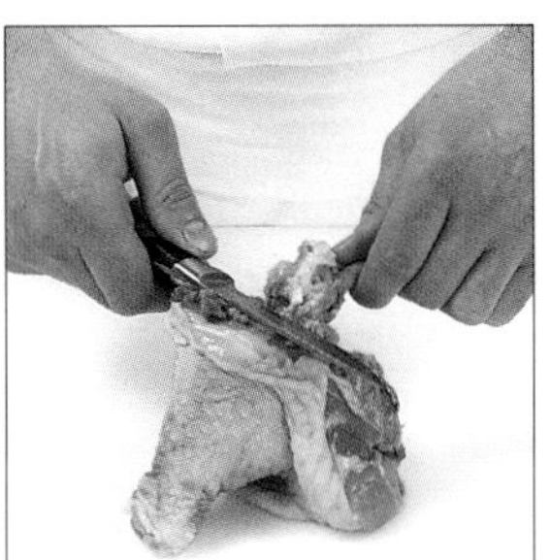

2 Scrape around the joint of the leg with the knife, carefully easing all of the meat free from the bone. Do not work all the way down, but stop about 5 cm (2 inches) away from the end of the leg.

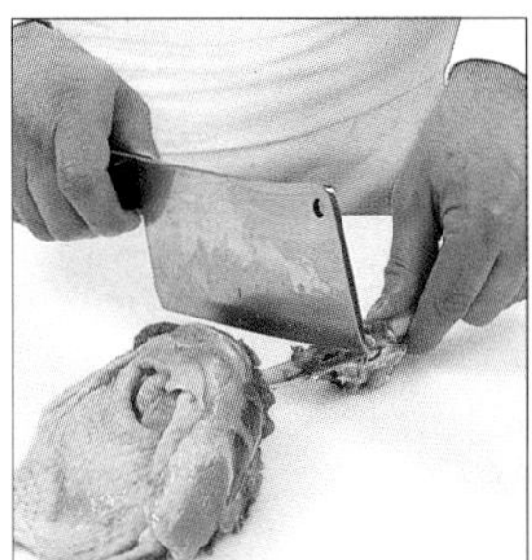

3 Pull all the meat back to expose the bone. Using a cleaver or a chef's knife, cut off the bone, leaving a small portion at the end of the leg. Reshape the leg. The bone can be used to flavour a stock or sauce.

Boning a Rabbit

Rabbit is a very popular meat in France. It is a lean meat that needs to be kept moist during cooking, so it is most often found in stews. Here, the rabbit is completely boned so that the meat can be used in a terrine.

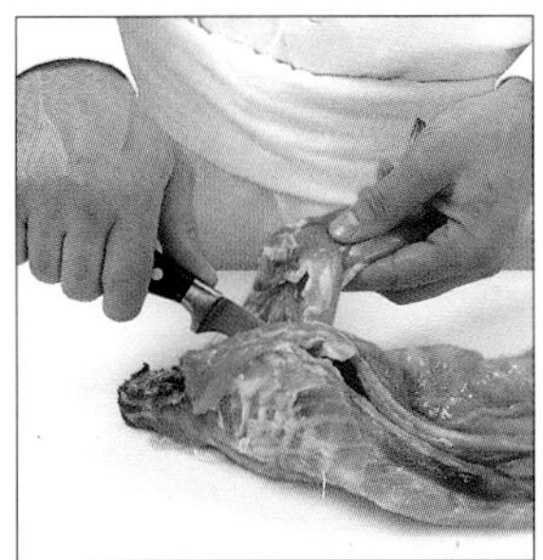

1 Using a boning knife, remove the forelegs from the rabbit: cut between the shoulder and the breastbone, and twist to break the joint. Bone the forelegs by carefully scraping away as much flesh as possible.

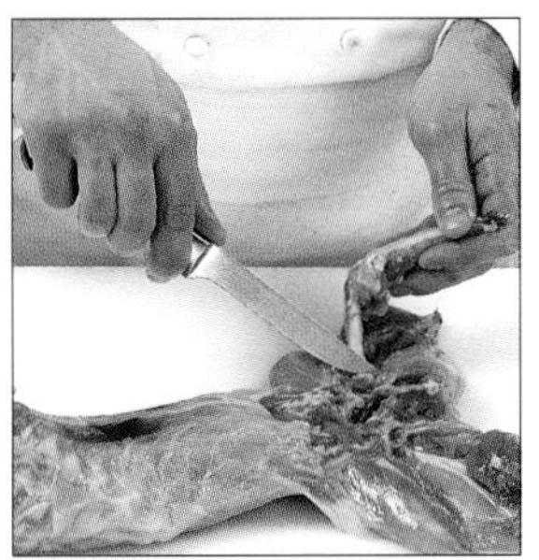

2 Push down on the hind legs of the rabbit to split the pelvic bones. Starting at the hip joint, carefully scrape away the flesh from one leg bone. Cut around to loosen the meat from the backbone. Repeat on the other side.

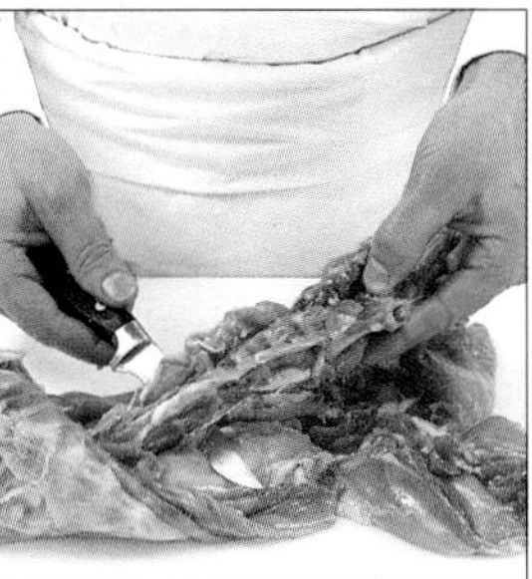

3 Lift off the backbone. Split the breastbone and scrape away the flesh from the rib bones. Continue to scrape away the meat from the remaining bones, until only meat remains. The bones can be used to make stock.

Meat Techniques

These techniques can be carried out by a butcher, but it is useful to know how to do them yourself at home. Choose meat that looks and smells fresh. Avoid meat that looks dry, has a greyish tinge, or is excessively moist.

Trimming Beef Tenderloin and Cutting Tournedos

Beef tenderloin is the most luxurious cut of beef. Trimming the tenderloin requires a sharp knife and a steady hand so that none of the good meat is lost. A small section of meat known as the chain muscle may be attached to the tenderloin; this should be removed because it toughens when cooked. Tournedos are often known as mignon steaks. They are cut from the thick end of the tenderloin.

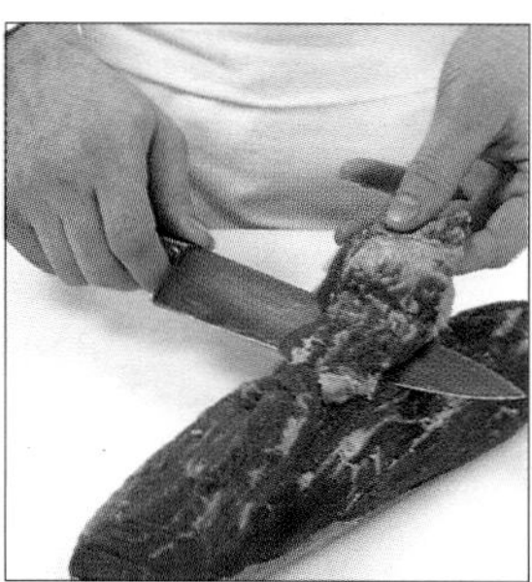

1 With a chef's knife, trim away any excess fat and sinew surrounding the tenderloin. Remove the chain muscle, and use it in a stew, if you like.

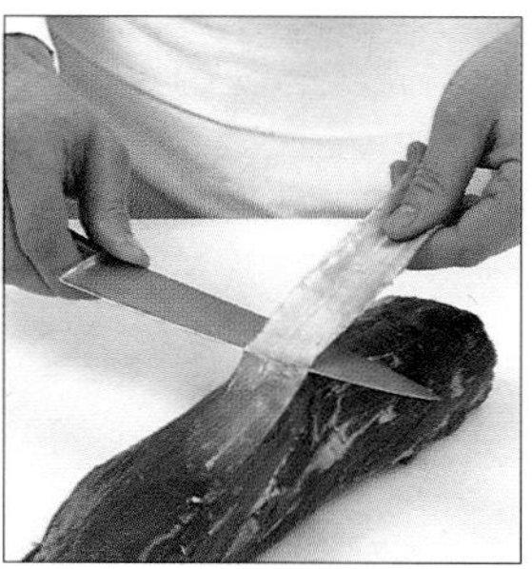

2 Insert knife under any white membrane, or "silverskin", that surrounds the meat. Pull one end of the membrane and slit away from the tenderloin.

3 Cut into tournedos: starting with the thick end of the tenderloin, slice into thick rounds. Secure string around them, to keep their shape while cooking.

Cutting Beef into Cubes

A variety of beef cuts can be used for stewing. Chuck, shoulder, clod, or skirt are the most economical. Other meats, such as veal, pork, lamb, and venison, can be cubed in the same way.

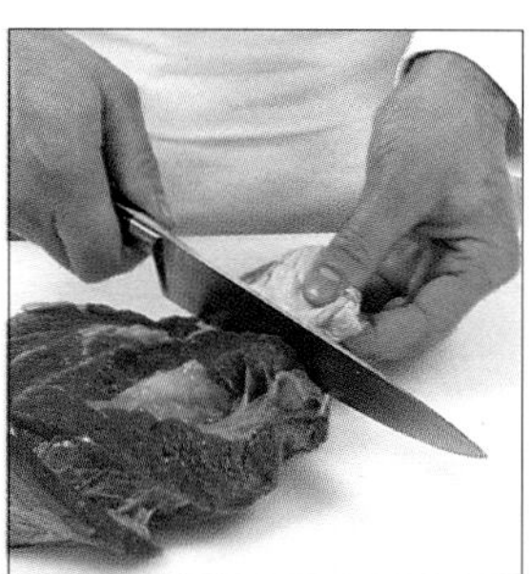

1 Using a chef's knife, trim off any fat or sinew from the meat.

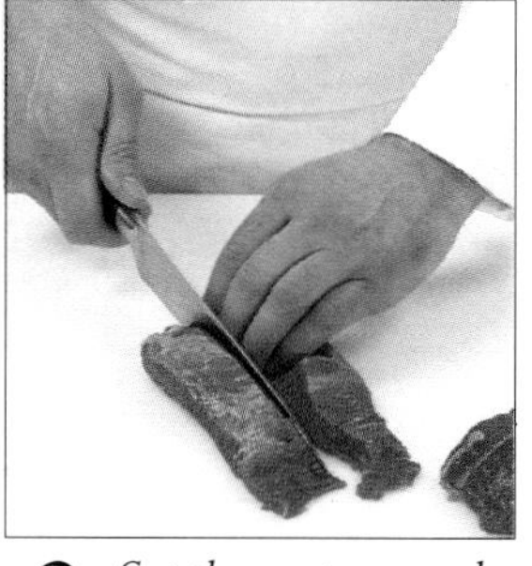

2 Cut the meat across the grain into strips of equal thickness.

3 Cut across each strip of meat to make cubes of equal size.

Pounding Escalopes

Escalopes can be cut from veal, beef, and poultry, and even abalone (see page 58). Pounding tenderizes the meat and also enlarges the escalope; this is useful if the escalope is to be stuffed and rolled.

1 Place meat between non-stick paper and pound with a rolling pin.

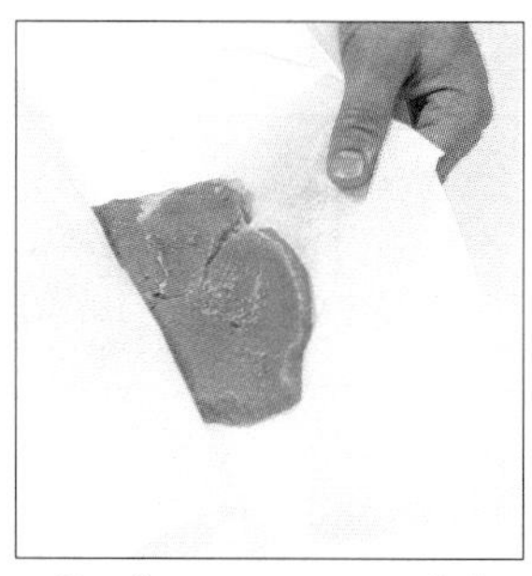

2 Continue to pound the meat until the desired thickness is reached.

Preparing a Best End of Neck of Lamb

Best end of neck of lamb, called *carré d'agneau* in French, is one of the most elegant ways in which to present lamb. The same technique is used when preparing two best ends of neck of lamb for a crown roast. Secure the two prepared racks together with kitchen string and stuff the centre of the crown.

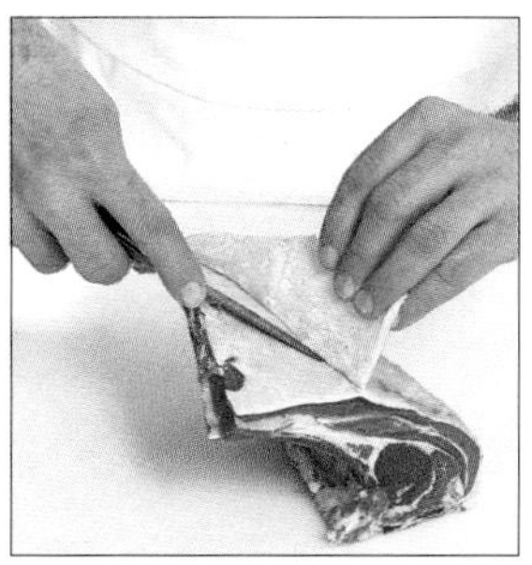

1 Trim away all but 1·25 cm (1/2 inch) of fat from the lamb. Score the remaining layer of fat.

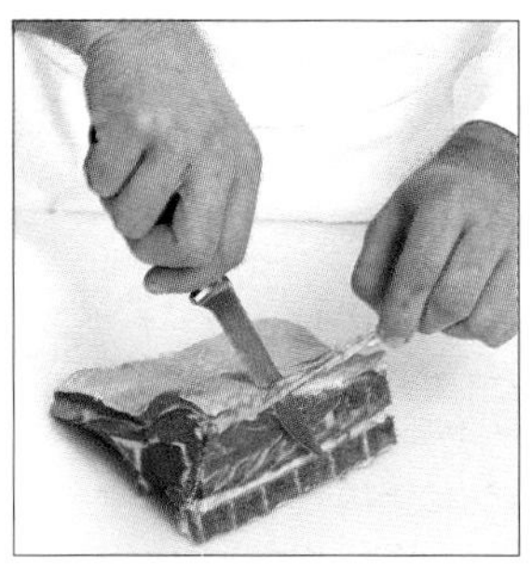

2 Cut away the strip of fat from the lamb which connects the tissue under the chine bone.

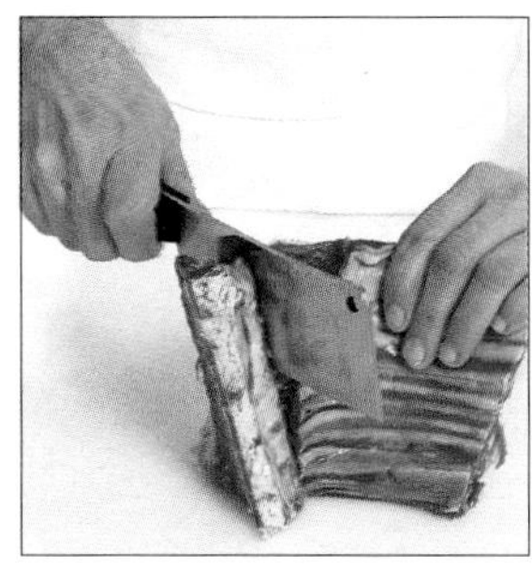

3 Place the lamb on its side and, using a cleaver or chef's knife, remove the chine bone.

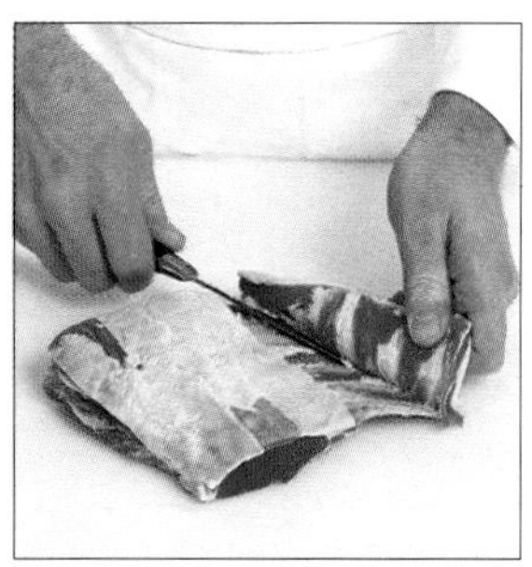

4 Cut along both sides of the ribs about 5 cm (2 inches) from the tips of the bones.

5 Trim away all meat between the ribs. Scrape the bones clean with the back of the knife.

Stock Techniques

Stocks are the foundation of French cuisine, and the key element in most soups, sauces, and stews. They will keep in the refrigerator for up to 2 days, or in the freezer for up to 1 month.

Fish Stock

White fish bones, such as those from plaice, sole, or whiting, are best for fish stock. Avoid oily fish bones, such as those from mackerel or herring. Fish heads can be used, but the eyes and gills should be removed first.

INGREDIENTS

2·5 kg (5 lb) fish bones
5 litres (4 quarts) water
500 ml (16 fl oz) dry white wine
1 large onion, quartered
100 g (3½ oz) mushrooms, roughly chopped
12 black peppercorns
a bouquet garni

PREPARATION

1 Wash the fish bones well. Chop the bones into pieces and put them into a large pan with all the remaining ingredients.
2 Slowly bring to a boil, and simmer for 20 minutes. Skim off any froth from the surface of the simmering stock.
3 Do not allow the stock to simmer for more than 20 minutes or it will be bitter. Strain the stock.

Chicken Stock

Chicken stock is probably the most versatile of all the stocks. When making chicken stock you can use a whole chicken, chicken pieces, or just the carcass of the bird.

INGREDIENTS

1 chicken, weighing about 3 kg (6 lb)
750 g (1½ lb) mirepoix of vegetables (see page 133)
5 litres (4 quarts) water
1 tomato, quartered
3 garlic cloves, crushed
12 black peppercorns
a bouquet garni

PREPARATION

1 Put the chicken in a pan of cold water, and slowly bring to a boil. Drain and rinse the chicken, then return it to the pan. Add the remaining ingredients and bring to a boil.
2 Simmer for about 3 hours. Skim off any froth or fat that floats to the surface during simmering.
3 Remove the chicken from the stock and reserve for another use. Strain the stock.

Beef and Brown Veal Stock

Beef or veal bones are roasted with aromatic vegetables, then gently simmered to make stock. Roasting the bones adds colour and flavour to the stock, which is perfect for all meat-based sauces.

INGREDIENTS

3 kg (6 lb) beef or veal bones
750 g (1½ lb) mirepoix of vegetables (see page 133)
150 g (5 oz) tomatoes concassées (see page 136)
250 ml (8 fl oz) dry white wine
1 tbsp tomato purée
12 black peppercorns
a bouquet garni
5 litres (4 quarts) water

PREPARATION

1 Roast the bones in a hot oven with the mirepoix; this allows all the flavours to be released.
2 Place the roasted bones and mirepoix in a large pan. Add all the remaining ingredients, with enough water to cover.
3 Bring the stock to a boil and skim off any froth that floats to the surface. Lower the heat and simmer the stock for 3½-4 hours; the longer the stock is simmered the richer it will be.
4 Strain the stock through a sieve, and blot the surface with paper towels to remove as much of the excess fat as possible.

White Veal Stock

White veal stock differs from brown veal stock in that the bones are not roasted in the oven. Browning the bones turns the stock a dark colour; for white veal stock it is essential to keep the ingredients as light in colour as possible.

INGREDIENTS

3 kg (6 lb) chopped veal bones
750 g (1½ lb) mirepoix of vegetables (see page 133)
5 litres (4 quarts) water
3 garlic cloves, crushed
12 black peppercorns
a bouquet garni

PREPARATION

1 Put the veal bones in a large pan with enough water to cover, bring to a boil, and simmer for 10 minutes. Drain and rinse the bones.
2 Return the blanched veal bones to the pan, add the remaining ingredients, and bring to a boil. Lower the heat and simmer for 3-4 hours. Skim off any froth or fat that floats to the surface during simmering.
3 Strain the stock through a muslin-lined sieve.

Clarified Chicken Stock

This is used for making clear soups, jellies, and aspic. This recipe is for chicken, but meat stock can be clarified in the same way.

INGREDIENTS

meat from 2 chicken legs
200 g (7 oz) mirepoix of vegetables (see page 133)
3 tomatoes concassées (see page 136)
4 egg whites, lightly beaten
salt and freshly ground pepper
2 litres (3½ pints) chicken stock

PREPARATION

1 Prepare the clarification mixture: mix the meat from the chicken legs with the mirepoix, tomatoes, and the egg whites. Season with salt and pepper.
2 Mix the clarification mixture and the stock in a large pan. Bring the mixture slowly to a boil, stirring constantly. When the egg whites start to solidify into a soft crust on top of the stock, stop stirring. Leave over a gentle heat for 20-25 minutes.
3 Carefully strain the stock through a muslin-lined sieve. Do not press the solids left in the sieve or the impurities will return to the stock.

Meat Jus

A meat *jus* is a gravy that has been made with stock. It is a cross between a stock and a meat glaze in both flavour and richness. Beef, veal, and even chicken can be used to make meat jus.

INGREDIENTS

1 kg (2 lb) chopped beef, veal, or chicken bones
500 g (1 lb) mirepoix of vegetables (see page 133)
2 tbsp vegetable oil
about 2 litres (2 quarts) brown stock

PREPARATION

1 Roast the bones and mirepoix in the oil in a hot oven until well browned. Drain off any excess oil.
2 Deglaze the pan with enough brown stock to cover the bones and allow this to reduce by half. Remove from the heat and pass the meat jus through a sieve.

Meat Glaze

A meat glaze or *demi-glace*, is a congealed, concentrated stock that is added to sauces by the spoonful. Any meat or poultry stock can be reduced to a glaze, but beef is the most popular choice.

INGREDIENTS

2·5 litres (2 quarts) good beef or veal stock

PREPARATION

1 Simmer the stock over medium heat for 8-10 hours, skimming the surface of any froth or fat, until the stock has reduced to a thick syrup. As the stock reduces, change the size of the pan accordingly.
2 Remove from the heat and pass through a sieve.

Egg Techniques

It is hard to imagine a kitchen without eggs: they can be eaten on their own or used in combination with other ingredients in countless different dishes – the list is seemingly endless.

Separating an Egg

Eggs are easy to separate if you use the shell. Alternatively, you can filter the white through your fingers or use an egg separator. Many recipes call for separated egg whites or yolks, so this is an important technique to learn.

1 Crack the egg at the broadest point over a bowl. Break it open, and let the egg white slip out.

2 Repeatedly tip the yolk from one shell half to the other, to detach the remaining white.

To separate an egg with your fingers: *tip the egg into a bowl, catching the yolk with your fingers.*

Poaching Eggs

Eggs can be poached in water, stock, or wine. The secret to successful poaching is the addition of vinegar to the water. The vinegar seizes the egg white together, and helps the egg to retain its shape. Vinegar is unnecessary if poaching in stock or wine.

1 Bring a pan of water to a boil with 3 tbsp vinegar. Crack the egg into a bowl. Lower the heat, and carefully slide the egg into the simmering water.

2 Poach the egg for 3-4 minutes; the white should set and the yolk be soft to the touch. Remove the egg with a slotted spoon and drain on paper towels.

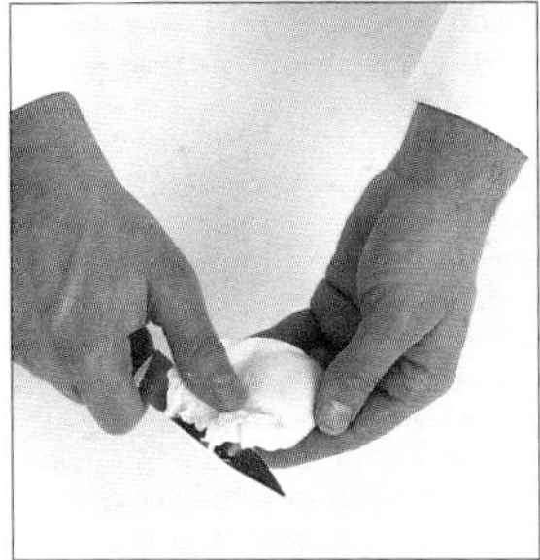

3 If not using straight away, keep the poached egg in a bowl of warm water until ready to use. Trim the ragged edges to make the egg look neat for serving.

Deep-Frying Eggs

Deep-fried eggs are a classic French garnish. It is essential that the oil is very hot when deep-fat frying, around 190°C (375°F). A piece of stale white bread added to the oil should turn brown within 1 minute when this temperature is reached.

1 Carefully slide the egg into the hot oil. Begin to fold the white over the yolk, using 2 wooden spoons.

2 When the yolk is covered, cook the egg for 1 minute, or until done to your liking.

3 Remove the deep-fried egg with a slotted spoon and drain on paper towels before serving.

Making a Crepe

The most celebrated of all crêpes must be *Crêpes Suzette* (see page 105), always an elegant dessert, especially when flamed at the table. The secret to perfect crêpe batter is to allow it to rest for at least 30 minutes before using. This allows the starch granules to expand and produces a lacy effect when the crêpes are cooked.

1 Heat some clarified butter in a crêpe pan. Pour off the excess butter and ladle in enough batter to cover the base. Immediately tilt the pan so the base is evenly covered.

2 Cook the crêpe until it begins to form bubbles on the surface and the edge turns light brown. Use a palette knife to carefully loosen the edges of the crêpe.

3 Turn the crêpe over with the palette knife (or try to flip it over with a flick of the wrist), and cook for a few seconds until the second side is lightly browned. Slide the crêpe out of the pan.

Making an Omelette

Omelette-making is a fundamental technique in the French kitchen. There are three different types: folded, flat, and soufflé. The folded omelette, as illustrated here, is by far the most common. The perfect folded omelette should be quite soft on the inside but firm and golden brown on the outside. Two to three eggs are usually sufficient for each omelette, to serve one person. Either butter or oil can be used to grease the pan.

1 With a fork, beat the eggs together with the seasoning (and herbs, if using) in a bowl.

2 Heat butter or oil in an omelette pan over a medium heat. Pour in the lightly beaten eggs.

3 Stir the eggs with a wooden spatula and pull them into the centre until they begin to set at the edge.

4 Once the eggs begin to set, stop stirring, and let them firm up. Cook until the bottom is brown and the top slightly runny.

5 Fold the omelette over, either with the wooden spatula or by tapping the pan so the top edge of the omelette flips over.

6 Tilt the pan away from you so that the omelette slides out, folded over, on to a plate. Make sure that the seam is underneath.

Desserts Techniques

Learning how to prepare fruit, toast nuts, make sponge fingers, and whisk Chantilly cream are among the first steps towards giving your desserts a professional finish.

Preparing a Pineapple

Pineapple can be prepared in a variety of ways. The first step is to remove the top plume and the base. The skin should then be sliced deep enough to remove the "eyes" from the pineapple flesh.

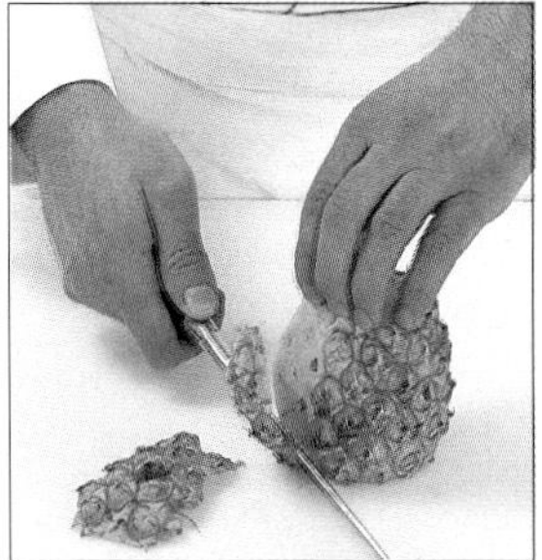

1 Slice the skin away from the pineapple, working from top to bottom against the curve.

2 Cut the pineapple lengthwise into quarters; remove the central core from each quarter.

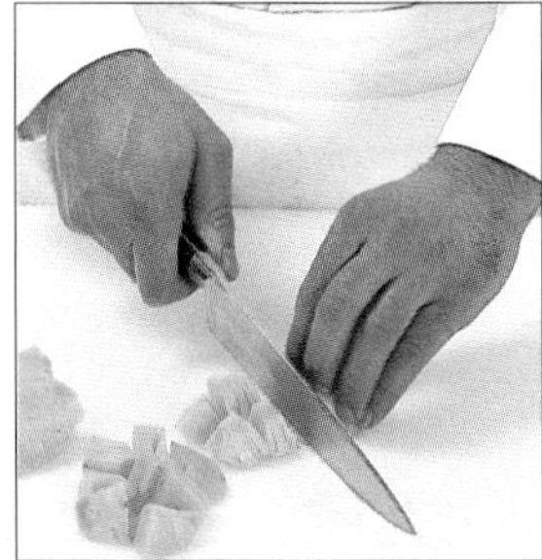

3 Cut across each quartered pineapple section to make even-sized pineapple chunks.

Peeling and Dicing Apples

Once the flesh of apples is exposed to the air, quickly sprinkle it with freshly squeezed lemon juice to prevent discoloration.

1 With an apple corer, core the apple, keeping it whole. Peel the apple with a vegetable peeler.

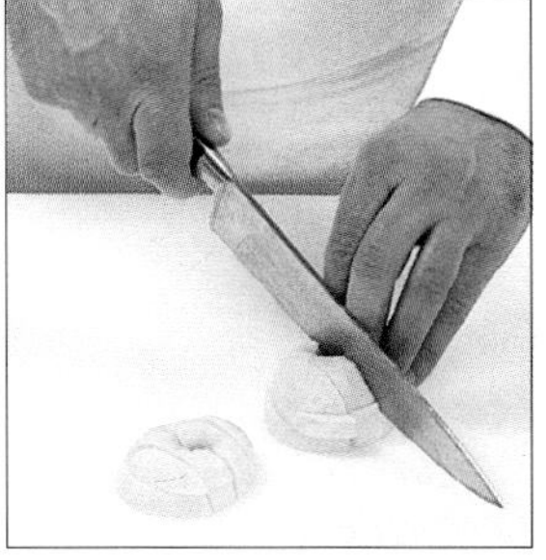

2 Halve apple crosswise, and cut horizontally into slices. Stack the slices and cut across into strips.

3 Cut across the apple strips to make dice of the desired size, guiding the knife with bent fingers.

Toasting Nuts

Toasting nuts brings out their full flavour, and it also loosens the skin from some types of nuts, such as hazelnuts. The high oil content of nuts causes them to scorch very easily, so turn them while toasting and watch closely.

1 Spread a layer of nuts on a baking tray and bake in a preheated oven at 180°C (350°F, Gas 4) for 5-10 minutes until golden.

2 To remove the skins: place the toasted nuts on a tea towel. Rub the nuts with the tea towel until the skins start peeling off.

Peeling, Stoning, and Slicing a Mango

A mango has a flat, central stone, which is quite difficult to locate and remove. By following the steps illustrated here, you will find the technique extremely easy.

1 Peel the mango, working from top to bottom with a vegetable peeler or small knife.

2 Slice the mango lengthwise, cutting on either side of the flat central stone. Discard the stone.

3 Thinly slice the two mango sections, carefully guiding the knife with bent fingers.

Zesting Citrus Fruit

The zest, or outer coloured part, of citrus fruit skin is the part that contains the essential oil and flavour. When removing it from the fruit, take care that none of the bitter white pith is included.

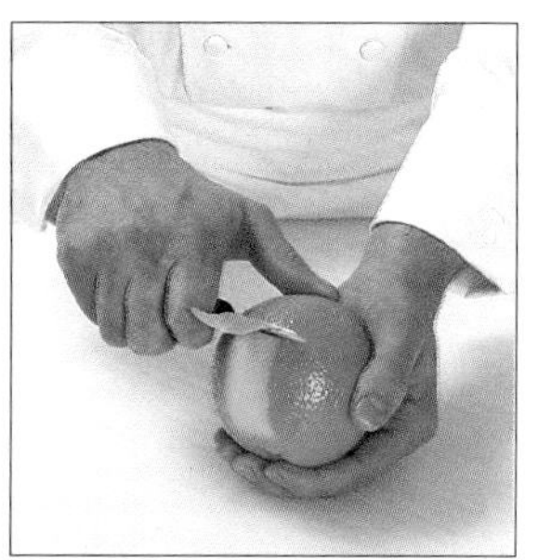

1 Using a vegetable peeler, cut away strips of zest from the fruit. Remove any white pith from inside the strips.

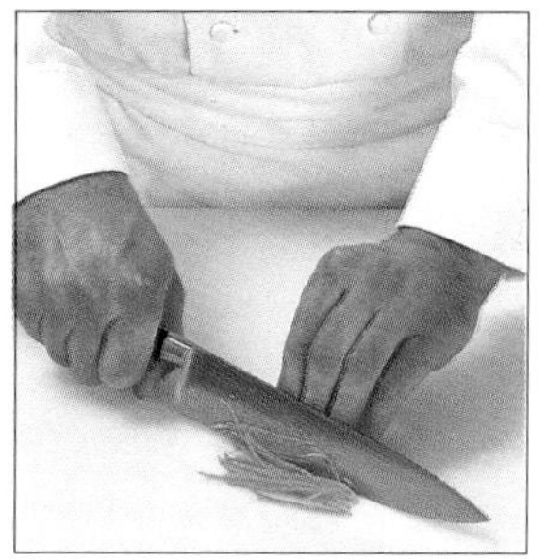

2 Lay the citrus zest strips flat on a chopping board and cut them into fine julienne strips, using a chef's knife.

Cutting Citrus Fruit into Segments

This method of cutting citrus fruit into segments ensures that none of the tough, unpalatable skin, pith, and membrane is included with the fruit.

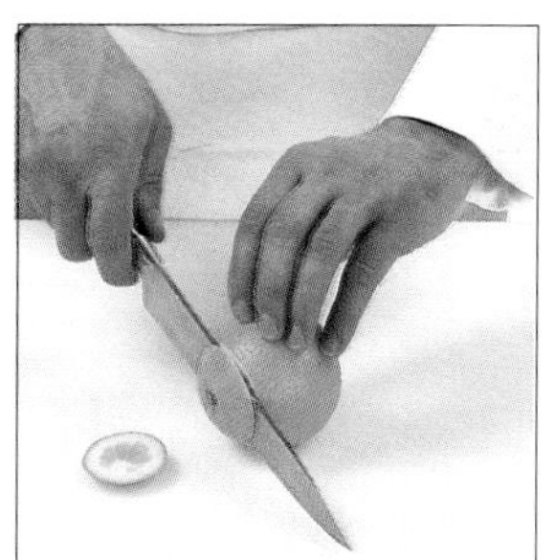

1 Cut off the top and bottom of the fruit. Stand the fruit upright on one of the cut surfaces.

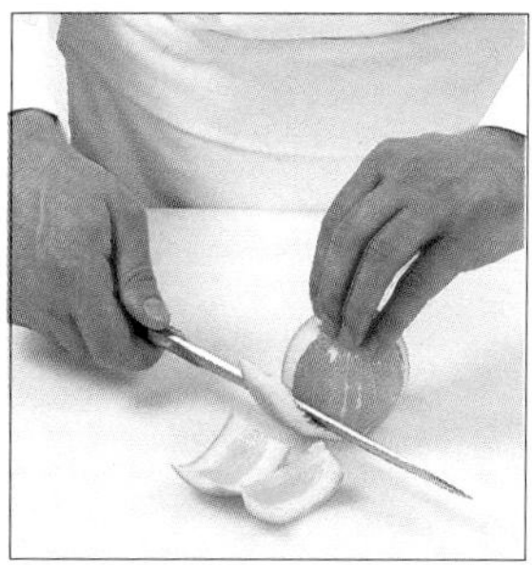

2 Following the curve of the fruit, cut away the zest, pith, and skin.

3 Over a bowl, cut down each side of a segment to remove it. Repeat with remaining segments.

Making Chantilly Cream

Chantilly cream is a whipped cream flavoured with a spoonful of icing sugar and a few drops of vanilla essence, or occasionally a liqueur. It is used in many French desserts, such as charlottes and Bavarian creams, and it is often used to decorate desserts.

1 Whisk the cream with a balloon whisk or an electric mixer in a bowl placed over an ice bath. (The ice bath speeds up the thickening process.)

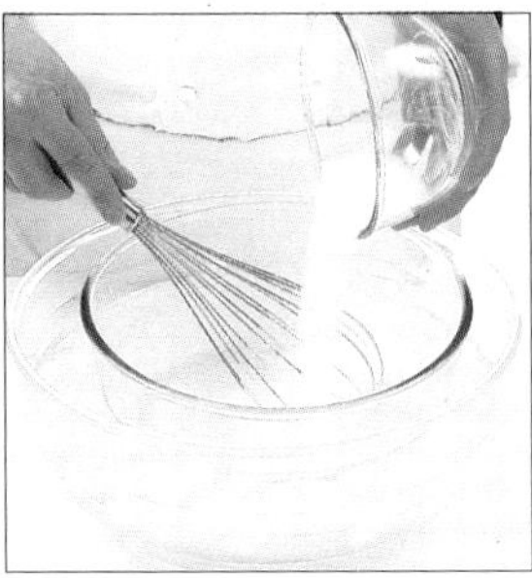

2 Once the cream begins to thicken, add the sugar, vanilla, or other flavourings. Continue whisking until the ingredients are well blended.

3 Continue whisking the cream until it forms stiff peaks; the whisk should leave clear marks when lifted. If overwhipped, the cream will separate.

Whisking Egg Whites

Egg whites are whisked until stiff but not dry. They add volume to numerous different mixtures, including soufflés, mousses, and cakes. Make sure that your bowl is completely free of water, grease, and egg yolk before you start whisking, or the whites will not whisk to full volume.

1 Slowly begin beating the whites with a balloon whisk, using a circular motion from the bottom of the bowl to the top to work in as much air as possible.

2 As the whites begin to increase in volume, make the circular motions larger with the whisk and increase the whisking speed. Adding a pinch of salt helps achieve maximum volume.

3 The whites are ready to use if stiff peaks form when the whisk is lifted. Sugar can be added and whisked into the egg whites if you wish to make a meringue.

Filling a Piping Bag

Piping bags and nozzles make light work of decorating with cream or meringue. They are also an alternative to spooning when filling small containers. When piping, make sure there are no air pockets in the bag.

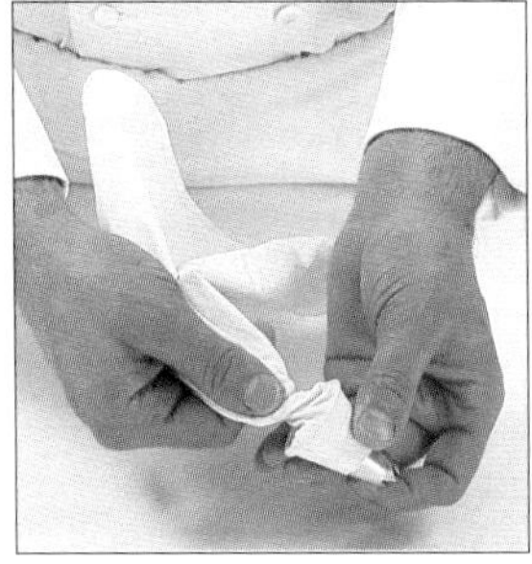

1 Drop the nozzle into the piping bag and twist, tucking the bag into the nozzle. This will prevent any mixture from leaking.

2 Fold the top of the bag over your hand to form a collar. Add the mixture, using a spatula and scraping it against the edge.

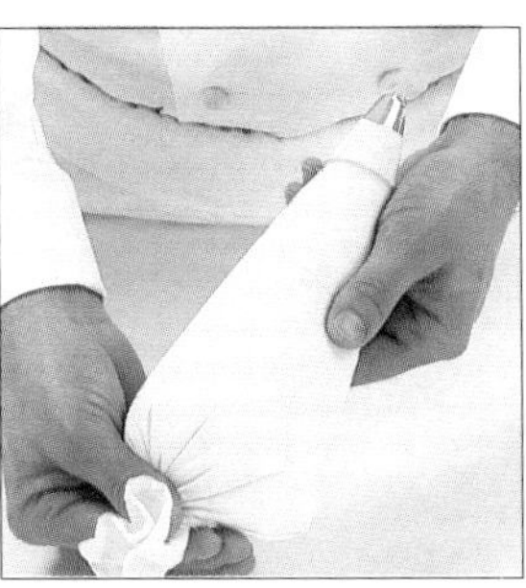

3 When the bag is full, twist the top so there is no air left in it; squeeze the bag lightly to start the mixture flowing.

Making Sponge Fingers

These shaped biscuits are traditionally used to line charlotte moulds, but they are also quite delicious to eat on their own. They can be made in a special sponge-finger mould, or they can be piped free-form on to a baking tray, as illustrated below.

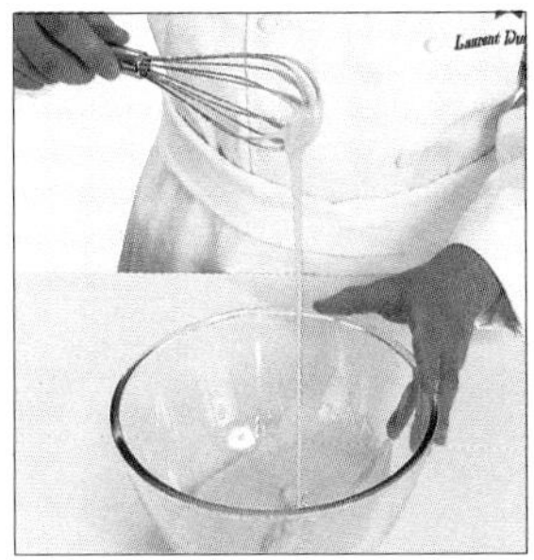

1 Beat egg yolks and half of the sugar until thick. A ribbon trail should form when the whisk is lifted.

2 Whisk the egg whites until soft peaks form. Add the sugar, and whisk again until the meringue becomes stiff.

3 Carefully fold the whisked meringue mixture into the beaten egg yolk and sugar mixture, using a rubber spatula.

4 Carefully incorporate the sifted flour and salt into the egg yolk and meringue mixture.

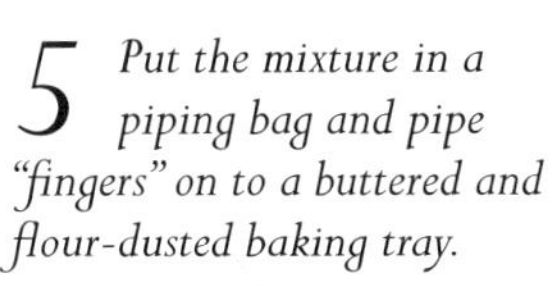

5 Put the mixture in a piping bag and pipe "fingers" on to a buttered and flour-dusted baking tray.

Pastry Techniques

Many cooks are afraid to attempt pastry making. Here, Le Cordon Bleu chef-instructors demonstrate the techniques for three different types of pastry. If the steps are followed correctly, successful pastry making will come easily.

Making Choux Pastry

Choux is used as both a savoury and sweet pastry. It is perhaps the easiest of all French pastries to master. Milk can be added with the water, for a rich, creamy pastry.

INGREDIENTS
250 ml (8 fl oz) water
100 g (3½ oz) butter
1 tsp salt
1 tsp sugar
150 g (5 oz) flour, sifted
4 eggs

1 Bring the water and the butter just to a boil. Do not boil for too long. Remove from the heat, add the flour, and beat with a wooden spoon.

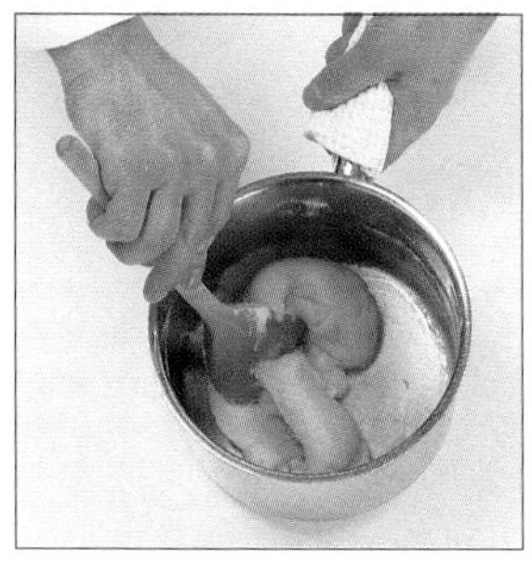

2 When the mixture is smooth, return the pan to the heat. Beat the mixture until it is dry and very smooth, and pulls away from the side of the pan.

3 Off the heat, add the eggs one at a time, stirring until the pastry appears shiny and drops from the wooden spoon when lifted out of the pan.

Making Pate Brisee and Pate Sucree

Pâte brisée is the French equivalent of shortcrust pastry. It is usually used for savoury tarts and quiches, whereas the sweetened version, pâte sucrée, is used solely for sweet pastries. Apart from the addition of sugar for pâte sucrée, the method for making these doughs is exactly the same. The blending technique in step 4 is called *fraisage*.

INGREDIENTS
Makes about 400 g (14 oz) pastry

200 g (7 oz) flour, sifted
100 g (3½ oz) butter
1 egg
1 tsp salt
2 tsp water
1 tbsp sugar (optional)

1 Make a well in the flour. In the centre of the well, put the butter, egg, salt, and water. If making pâte sucrée, add the sugar.

2 Using your fingertips, work the ingredients until they resemble crumbs. Use a pastry scraper to incorporate the flour.

3 With your fingertips, press the crumbs firmly together to form a ball of dough. Add a little more flour if the dough is sticky.

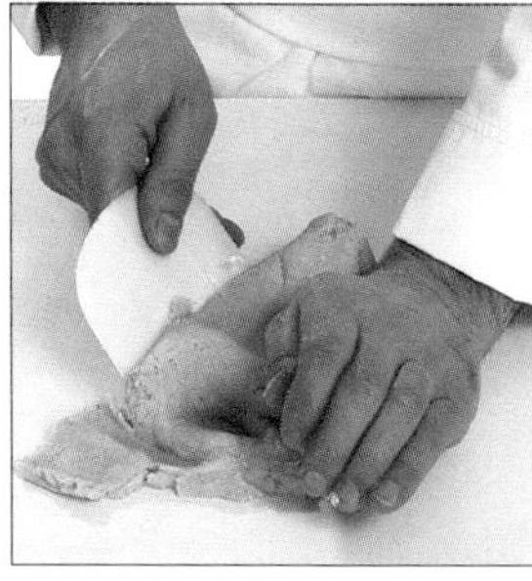

4 Blend the ingredients together until smooth, pushing with the heel of your hand. Wrap and chill for at least 30 minutes.

Lining a Flan Tin

Pie dishes and flan tins are both lined in the same way. It is important not to stretch the dough when lining, and to chill the pastry shell for about 30 minutes before baking, so that the pastry does not shrink when baked.

1 On a floured surface, roll out the dough into a large round. Wrap the dough around a rolling pin.

2 Lifting the dough on the rolling pin, carefully drape it over the tin. Press it into the bottom and edge of the tin.

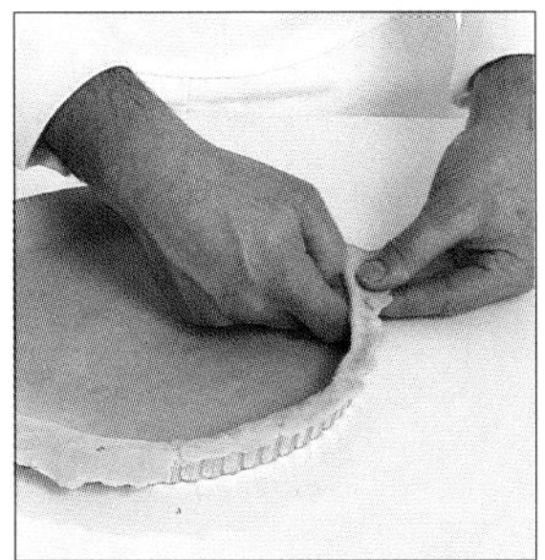

3 Use your fingertips and fingers to overlap the dough slightly inside the rim of the tin, so extra dough is left at the edge.

4 Roll the pin over the top of the tin, pressing to remove excess dough. Press the dough up the side to increase height of shell.

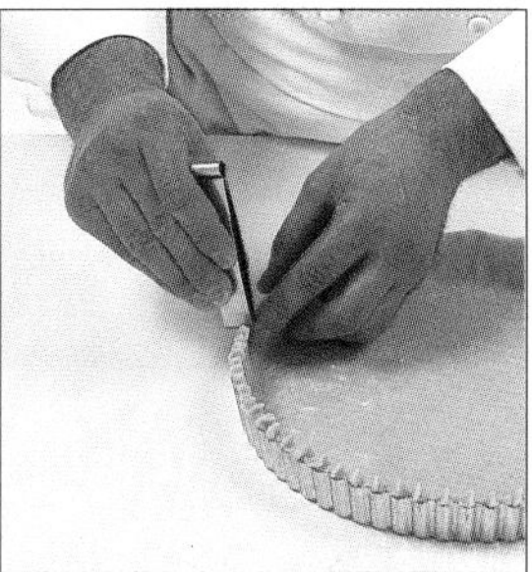

5 If you like, decorate the edge of the dough by scalloping it with pastry pinchers or shaping the edge with your fingertips.

Baking Blind

Baking blind is a technique used to bake a pastry shell when a filling that does not need cooking is to be added later, or when a moist filling is going to be added. Pâte brisée and pâte sucrée are usually baked blind on a heated baking tray in a preheated oven at 180°C (350°F, Gas 4) for 10-15 minutes.

1 Prick the bottom of the pastry shell all over with the tines of a fork. Line the shell with non-stick paper, pressing it well into the bottom edge.

2 Weight down the paper by filling it with dried beans or rice to ensure that the pastry shell does not rise and create bubbles during baking.

3 Bake the shell for about 10 minutes, until set and the shell rim is golden. Remove the beans and paper. Continue baking for 5 minutes. Let cool.

Making Pate Feuilletee (Puff Pastry)

There are three major steps when making puff pastry. The first step is to make the *détrempe,* which is the foundation of the dough. The second is to add the butter to the détrempe, and the third is to make the "turns" needed to give the pastry its layers.

Probably one of the most important elements in making successful puff pastry is the temperature of the dough. It should always be cold. If the butter begins to break through while making the turns, chill the dough until it is firm.

INGREDIENTS

Makes about 1·25 kg (2½ lb) pastry

500 g (1 lb) flour
250 ml (8 fl oz) water, more if needed
75 g (2½ oz) butter, melted
2 tsp salt
300 g (10 oz) butter

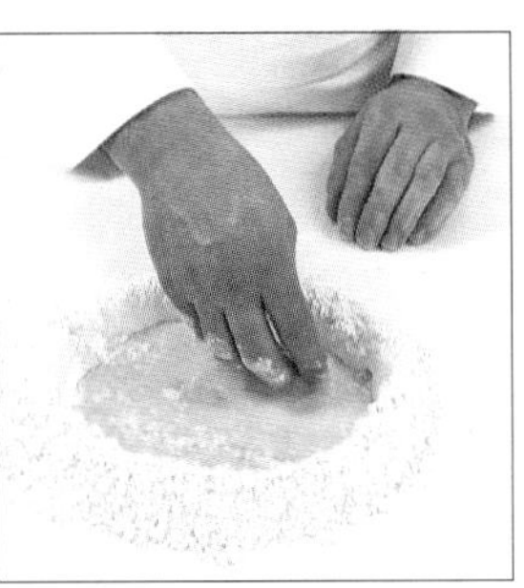

1 Make the détrempe: sift the flour on to a chilled surface. Make a well in the centre. Add the water, melted butter, and salt to the well. Mix the liquids together with your fingertips until the salt dissolves, and gradually incorporate the flour to the liquid, sweeping it into the centre with a pastry scraper.

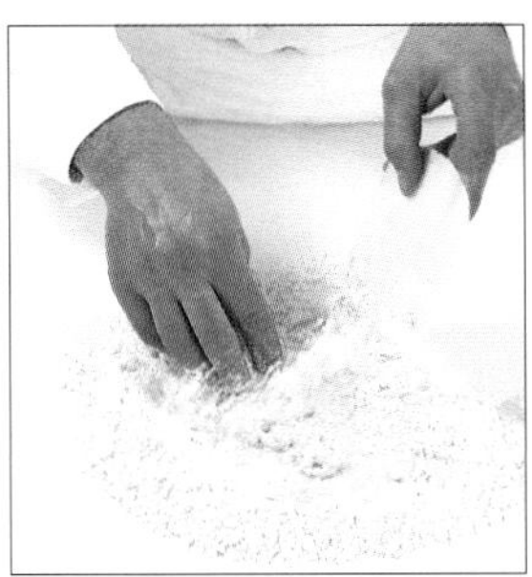

2 Work the ingredients together with the pastry scraper until loose crumbs form. Add a little more water if the crumbs seem dry. Work the dough into a slightly moist ball, and mark an "x" on top to prevent shrinkage. Wrap the dough in floured non-stick paper, and chill for 30 minutes.

3 While the détrempe is chilling, place the remaining butter between two pieces of non-stick paper. Use a rolling pin to pound out the butter until softened. Shape the butter into a square measuring approximately 2 cm (¾ inch) thick. Chill in the refrigerator if the butter has become too soft.

4 On the chilled surface, roll out the détrempe into a rough cross shape (as shown above), leaving the dough slightly thicker in the centre than at its four corners. Place the butter in the centre of the dough and fold in the four corners, stretching the dough slightly to completely seal the butter in a package.

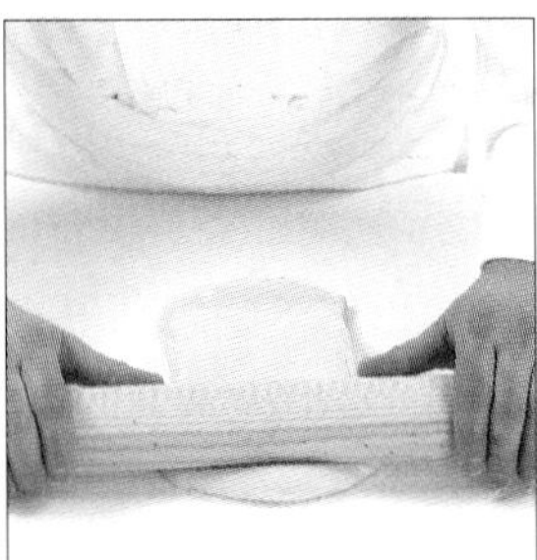

5 Lightly flour the work surface, and turn the dough and butter package on to it, with the seam side down. Gently tap the top of the dough with the rolling pin to seal all of the edges. Prepare the dough by rolling the pin over the surface of the package once or twice to get an even top so that it is ready for rolling out.

6 Roll out the dough into a long rectangle about 20 cm (8 inches) wide and 45 cm (18 inches) long, keeping the corners square. The edges should be even and straight, and the rectangle should be of uniform thickness. Roll the dough away from you, using firm even strokes with the pin.

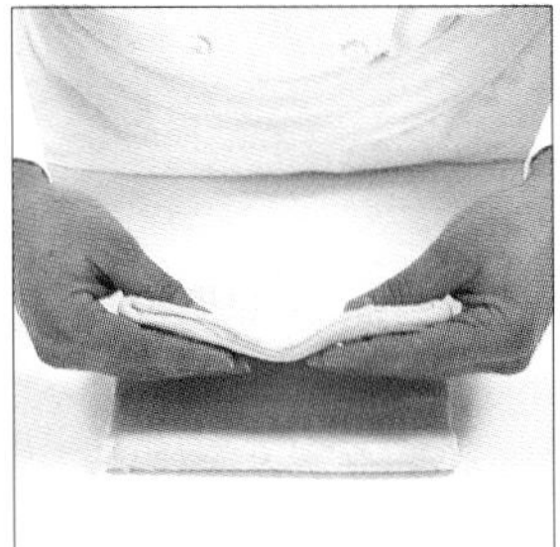

7 Fold the dough into three, bringing the top third down and the bottom third up. Turn the dough so the long edge is facing right. Gently press the edges to seal. This completes the first turn. Repeat steps 6 and 7 to complete a second turn. Chill for 30 minutes. Repeat 2 turns twice more, until 6 turns have been completed.

BUTTER TECHNIQUES

Butter is the basis of many classic sauces, such as béchamel and hollandaise. Unsalted butter is most commonly used in France, because it does not affect the seasoning of the food.

CLARIFYING BUTTER

Butter contains milk solids that will burn at high frying temperatures. This clarifying technique removes the milk solids from the butter, thus eliminating the risk of burning.

1 Gradually melt the butter over a low heat until a white foam of impurities appears on the surface. Skim and discard.

2 Slowly pour the clarified butter into a separate bowl, leaving the milky solids on the bottom of the pan.

3 Discard the milk solids on the bottom of the pan. Make sure the surface of the clarified butter in the bowl is clean.

USING BEURRE MANIE

Kneaded butter, or *beurre manié,* is used to thicken sauces and stews at the last moment before serving. A combination of equal amounts of flour and butter is worked into a paste.

1 On a plate, make paste from equal parts of flour and butter. Use a fork to make sure all the flour is mixed into the butter.

2 Drop a small amount of beurre manié into a hot sauce, whisking constantly. Add until the sauce begins to thicken.

3 Make sure all of the butter has melted and the flour has had time to cook. The sauce should be thick and smooth.

PREPARING A ROUX

A *roux* (the French for russet brown) is a mixture of equal volumes of flour and butter used at the beginning of cooking to thicken many classic French sauces. There are three types of roux classified by colour and flavour: white, blond, and brown.

1 Gently melt butter in a heavy-based saucepan until bubbling. Immediately add all of the flour.

2 Whisk the flour into the butter until the mixture is smooth. This forms a white roux.

3 Cook for 2-3 minutes for a blond roux, and a further 2-3 minutes for a brown roux.

INDEX

P

Q

R

S

Y

Techniques

Acknowledgments

Photographers David Murray and Jules Selmes
Photographers' Assistant Steven Head
Chef Eric Treuillé
Home Economist Sarah Lowman
Recipe Translation Norma MacMillan
Typesetting Kevin Barrett and Debbie Lelliott
Production Consultant Lorraine Baird
Text Film by Disc to Print (UK) Limited

Le Cordon Bleu owes special thanks to the twenty-six full-time chefs, operating in its four schools throughout the world, for this 1895-1995 centennial book, as well as to the whole team who made it possible.

Le Cordon Bleu, Paris: 8 rue Léon Delhomme, 75015 Paris, France. Tel: 33/1 48 56 06 06
Chefs Patrick Terrien, Christian Guillut, Didier Chantefort, Jean-Claude Boucheret, Patrick Lebouc, Alain Villiers, Michel Besnard, Laurent Duchène, with Benoit Blin, Christophe Bellet, Philippe Moreau, Jean-Luc Dreux.
For the administrative back-up: Pierre Camino, Sandrine Debeauvais, Isabelle Perrais, Denis Vignal, Patrice de Jeu, Catherine Baschet, Anne-Marie de Figueredo, Magali Claustre, Josephina Bosqued, Eva Walhstrom, Nathalie Hernandez, Andrea Werbel, Carole Jory, Jim Doyle, Marie-Christine Bourgeois, Slyvie Vansegbroek, Aliette Saman, Setsuko Shoai, Natasha Holland, Kimberely Guerrant, Nathalie Boris, Souad Kadi, Suzana Muhadzer, Carlos des Santos, Thierry Ricles, Sambou, Jorge Fernandez.

Le Cordon Bleu, London: 114 Marylebone Lane, London W1M 6HH, England. Tel: 44/71 935 3503
Chefs Michel Perraud, Jean-Claude Herchembert, Shaun Whatling, Matthew Hardy, Claire Clark, Mark Godly.
For the administrative back-up: Lesley Gray, Susan Eckstein, Ian Porteous, Carolyne Dahill, Deepika Sukhwani, Natasha Brooks-Baker, Hilary Dodd, Nathalie Guinet, Larry James, Nzunguta and Watanu Bungisa, Claude Mampuila, Noriko McTavish.

Le Cordon Bleu, Japan: ROOB-1, 28-13, Sarugaku-cho, Shibuya-ku, Tokyo 150, Japan. Tel: 81/3 5489 01 41
Chefs Daniel Martin, Kuzuhiro Onozaki, Jean-Paul Thiebaut, Raoul Billet, Thierry Duflos, Gregory Steneck, Thierry Dumouchel, Denis Chojnacki, with Yumino Horiuchi, Rie Tsujiuchi, Naotoshi Sugata, Kazuyo Goda, Satoru Umezawa, Atsuko Motegi, Yoshini Katagawa.
For the administrative back-up: Minori Kumazawa, François Lavergne, Noriaki Fujiwara, Akiko Koyama, Keiko Kanzaki, Reiko Noda, Maki Watanabe.

Le Cordon Bleu, North America: 404 Irvington Street, Pleasantville, New York, NY 10570 USA
Tel: 1/914 741 0606
Toll Free Number USA: 1-800-457 CHEF
Chefs Patrick Martin, Michel Denis, Philippe Guiet, Erick Le Pors.
For the administrative back-up: Steve Goldshlag, Gerard Breissan, Sandra MacInnis, Julie Clark, Sylvie Deraspe, Jacqueline Viau, Mohamud Eggeh, Chiara Interrante.

André J. Cointreau extends special thanks to Jeannette V Hasse Ewin for all her efforts at the birth of the book, to the Amy Carroll and Denise Brown team, and above all would like to offer special thanks to the leading force behind the book, Chef Didier Chantefort.

21